Presidential Institutions and Democractic Politics

Presidential Institutions and Democratic Politics

Comparing Regional and National Contexts

EDITED BY KURT VON METTENHEIM

The Johns Hopkins University Press
Baltimore and London

The Johns Hopkins University Press
2715 North Charles Street
Baltimore, Maryland 21218-4319
The Johns Hopkins Press Ltd., London

Library of Congress Cataloging-in-Publication Data will be found
at the end of this book.
A catalog record for this book is available from the British Library.

ISBN 0-8018-5313-3
ISBN 0-8018-5314-1 (pbk.)

Contents

PART IV   The Eastern European Context
Presidential Institutions and the Dual Transition to
Democratic Politics and Market Economies

Preface

This book was written by scholars deeply concerned about the theory, conceptualization, and empirical analysis of presidential institutions and democracy in the post–cold war world. This round of concern about presidentialism began in Latin America, after the dramatic transitions from military rule during the 1970s and 1980s provided a unique opportunity to reassess politics and institutional design in the region. And like theories of dependent development, bureaucratic authoritarianism, and civil society empowerment that emerged from Latin America to influence politics and perceptions in other areas, debate about presidential and parliamentary government became central to rethinking politics and democracy after transitions from military and Stalinist rule around the world.

In this respect, the work of Juan Linz and Arturo Valenzuela provided fresh air by framing the debate about institutional design in Latin America.[1] They criticized the excessive centralization of power in Latin American presidencies and helped to place constitutional and institutional reform on the agenda in Brazil, Chile, Argentina, and other Latin American countries. Venezuela and Colombia were also forced to consider reform after military coups and guerrilla insurgency brought long-standing democracy under fire. Indeed, debate about the relative merits of presidential and parliamentary government became an important part of the intellectual landscape in the region about the time reform in the Soviet Union and the transitions in Eastern Europe began.

Despite calls for reform of presidentialism, or indeed for the wholesale adoption of parliamentarism, empirical analysis of party-electoral development in contemporary Brazil reveals trajectories of change surprisingly similar to the U.S. experience in the late nineteenth century.[2] It is now clear that surprise, like beauty, is in the eye of the beholder. In retrospect, the rapid development of party-electoral politics in Brazil appears surprising only because it differs from accepted ideas about parties and party systems in Western Europe. A central goal of this volume is to encourage scholars to recognize mechanisms of change in presidential and federal systems. Eduardo Gamarra also confirms the importance of rethinking presidentialism in Latin America against the reformist, parliamentarist grain. For Gamarra, despite the imposing tasks related to debt, inflation, and democratic transition, the unique features of Bolivian presidential institutions allow political elites to deepen popular support in first-round voting, to negotiate durable party coalitions in second-round voting (held in the Congress), and to sustain viable policies of economic adjustment and modernization.

The October 1992 conference that commissioned the papers presented here was held under the auspices of the Department of Political Science at the University of Pittsburgh. The conference emerged from discussions among my colleagues at Pittsburgh which convinced me that debate about presidential institutions in comparative politics was far too Eurocentric. Open-ended analysis of national and regional experiences with presidential institutions was possible in the department because scholars tend to cross the disciplines of American politics and comparative politics and work in dynamic regional centers on Latin America, Western Europe, Eastern Europe, and Russia.

The papers were commissioned from leading scholars of four world regions, in an attempt to develop new perspectives on presidential institutions and democratic politics. The central goals were to bring the U.S. experience further into the field of comparative political analysis, to improve understanding of traditional presidencies in France and the United States, and to clarify the character of presidential institutions and democratic politics after transitions from authoritarian rule in Latin America, Eastern Europe, and the new republics of the former Soviet Union. The conference provided a context for observers of four world regions to work through similar concerns in different contexts. The opportunity to reach beyond specific regional and national experiences proved critical for developing new comparative perspectives on presidential institutions and democratic politics.

Special recognition is due Charles O. Jones for stressing that the American government is separationist more than presidentialist and that standard definitions in comparative politics tend to overlook this link between American presidentialism and the liberal, democratic, and pluralist tradition (chap. 1). It is ironic that, while comparative political analysts once again seem to reject the U.S. experience as exceptional, scholars of American politics are reassessing their government in terms at odds with the assumptions of comparativists. Major debates among Americanists emphasize legislative productivity rather than gridlock during periods of divided government, emphasize the ability of President Reagan and President Clinton to reverse declines in popularity, and debate the political opportunities provided by an increasingly volatile electorate.

The events of 1989 that shattered the Soviet Union and its dominance of Eastern Europe have increased the importance of understanding presidential institutions and democratic politics. Michael Bernhard, Valerie Bunce, and Jonathan Harris demonstrate considerable dexterity in analyzing presidencies during the dauntingly complex transitions of Eastern Europe and Russia after Stalinism (see chaps. 7, 8, and 9). The specific risks and opportunities of presidents and presidencies in Eastern Europe and Russia are quite different from those stressed in general debates about presidential and parliamentary government. These regional generalizations reinforce a central methodological principle that informs this volume: substantive conclusions emerge from careful analysis of national and regional experience. The dramatic transitions in Eastern Europe and the new nations of the former Soviet Union will undoubtedly continue to produce new concerns about—and new hopes for—presidential institutions.

Given the importance of France as a model for those building democratic institutions in Eastern Europe and Latin America, the analysis of John Keeler and Martin Schain provides a critical contribution, one that emphasizes context, political creativity, and the unusual centralization of power in the French presidency (see chap. 4). And far from providing a single model for institutional design, Keeler and Schain argue that the hyperpresidentialism of French institutions was forged in a sequence of political innovations during the Fifth Republic which often overstepped constitutional limits on executive authority.

B. Guy Peters and Bert Rockman also contribute new perspectives on institutional arrangements and democratic governance that surpass the forced dichotomy between presidential and parliamentary rule and draw attention to complexity, diversity, and context (chaps. 2 and 3). Peters clarifies the need to rethink formal conceptions of parliamentarism in Europe by emphasizing de facto practices and structures in European parliamentary institutions that tend to separate and diffuse power along lines normally associated with presidential government. Rockman's analysis of an immense

variety of institutional arrangements sharpens claims about how
presidential and parliamentary institutions shape democratic governance.

Generous support from institutions and individuals at the Uni-
versity of Pittsburgh made this volume possible. At the University
Center for International Studies, special thanks go to Professor
Burkhart Holzner, director, Professor Thomas McKechnie, assistant
director, and Linda Butero, assistant to the director. The Department of Political Science chair, B. Guy Peters, the Center for Latin
American Studies and its director, Mitchell Seligson, the Center for
Western European Studies and its director, Alberta Sbragia, and the
Center for Russian and Eastern European Studies and its director,
Ron Linden, all provided constructive criticism and financial support. Their help made it possible for scholars from outside Pittsburgh to participate in the October 1992 conference. Special thanks
also go to those who served as discussants at the research conference: Ron Linden, the late Douglas Ashford, Morris Ogul, Robert
Walters, and graduate students at the University of Pittsburgh. Finally, the executive editor of Johns Hopkins University Press, Henry
Tom, his staff, and two anonymous reviewers also provided insightful comments and editorial advice.

Presidential Institutions and Democractic Politics

Presidential Institutions and Democratic Politics

Kurt von Mettenheim

The late twentieth century will be remembered as an unprecedented period of constitution writing. Since the mid-1970s, military, authoritarian, and Stalinist regimes have been replaced by a stunning succession of largely nonviolent political transitions in Southern Europe, Latin America, Eastern Europe, and the former Soviet Union. The imposing tasks of recasting economies, opening societies, and building democratic political institutions have so far been met with equally impressive entrepreneurial, social, and political imagination. However, unlike the careful consideration of presidential institutions and the separation of powers in preceding periods of democratic transition, proponents of parliamentary government, which tends to fuse power, seem to have prevailed in current debates about institutional design and democratization.[1]

This volume argues that presidential institutions and the American experience can provide compelling institutional alternatives for emerging democracies. Presidential institutions satisfy democratic aspirations by directly electing both executives and legislatures, provide a series of safeguards against tyranny by separating and diffusing powers, and permit the articulation and institutionalization of universal tensions between notions of direct popular sovereignty and the requirements of representative government. Samuel Huntington's accusations to the contrary, presidential institutions and the doctrine of the separation of powers are not simply premodern relics of the Tudor period unsuitable for mass democracy.[2] This volume seeks to improve understanding of presidential institutions in widely different regional and national contexts by focusing on the long-extant presidential systems of the United States and France, the impact of presidencies during democratic transitions, and the prospects for deepening new democracies through presidential initiative.

Careful, open-ended analysis of presidential institutions and democratic politics in these different contexts is needed because re-

cent critics of presidentialism focus on vices but not virtues, emphasizing risks but not opportunities. Beginning with Juan Linz's
thought-provoking work in 1984, scholars such as Fred Riggs, Alfred Stepan, and Arturo Valenzuela have attempted to draw direct
causal links between presidentialism and problems of ungovern-
ability, instability, and democratic breakdown.[3] Presidential institutions may indeed retain a greater burden of proof because they are
fewer in number and can easily be confused with directly elected
authoritarian executives. But recent advocates of parliamentarism
misrepresent the American experience and its liberal-democratic
tradition, fail to provide a positive account of political development
within presidential institutions, and tend to overestimate the impact
of broad institutional designs on political life.

PRESIDENTIAL INSTITUTIONS AND THE
SEPARATION OF POWERS

The central characteristic of presidential government is the separate election of the executive and the legislature for fixed terms.[4]
This minimal definition of presidential government excludes all
other attributes of presidentialism so that they may be discussed in
terms of empirical evidence or evaluated on the basis of liberal and
democratic theory.[5] Although minimal, this definition of presidential government is not without content. The separate election of the
executive and the legislature has its origins in political theories from
antiquity through the eighteenth century which saw the separation
and diffusion of powers rather than their concentration as the key to
effective sovereignty. But presidential institutions not only embody
a recurring position in the history of political ideas. They also remain vital today for reconciling core conflicts between liberal conceptions of indirect representative government and the realities of
direct popular appeals in competitive mass politics.

In contrast to this minimal definition strategy, recent definitions
of presidential systems in comparative politics tend to emphasize
the direct election of executives and underestimate the separation of
powers.[6] This emphasis fails to distinguish between the direct election of authoritarian executives and the separate, competitive election of the legislature and the executive. While Lijphart recognizes,
for example, that presidential systems are based on Montesquieu's
principle of the separation of powers, he nonetheless classifies dem-

ocratic institutions according to whether executives are elected indirectly and remain dependent on the confidence of legislatures or
whether executives are elected directly.[7] This classification effectively distinguishes cases of parliamentary government from all
cases of directly elected executives. But it fails to differentiate between the direct election of authoritarian executives through
plebiscite and the diffusion of powers encouraged by separately
electing legislatures and executives in presidential government.

Linz also argues that a basic characteristic of presidentialism "is
the president's strong claim to democratic, even plebiscitarian, legitimacy."[8] For Linz, separate elections in presidential government
tend to produce a problematic "dual democratic legitimacy," while
fixed terms tend to create institutional rigidity. Among the many important and groundbreaking aspects of Linz's work is his clarifica-
tion of the real risks associated with presidential government, such
as inflammatory plebiscitarian appeals, unproductive conflict between legislature and executive, and policy gridlock. But by charac-
terizing these risks as vices inherent in presidentialism, Linz asserts
a causal hypothesis about the consequences of presidentialist
arrangements that is unrelievedly negative. This critical stance toward presidential institutions shifts attention away from viable
causal hypotheses about the political opportunities that may also be
generated by presidential institutions.[9]

While not blind to the risks of presidentialism identified by Linz
and other recent critics, this volume also focuses on political opportunities. The analyses presented herein suggest that separation of
powers theory and presidential government provide both moral
grounds and institutional settings for reconciling plebiscitarian,
populist, and nationalist appeals with the sober realities of governance by forcing separately elected and empowered executives and
legislatures to negotiate. The trajectories of America and France, as
well as recent experiences in Latin America and Eastern Europe
during transitions from authoritarian rule, suggest that, despite certain risks, the institutional arrangements of presidential government provide significant opportunities for the development of liberal and democratic politics. Both social scientists and writers of
constitutions have largely overlooked these opportunities.

Three types of argument provide informed grounds for this op-
timism. First, the core idea behind presidential government—that
liberty, the dispersion of powers, and effective government are mu-

tually reinforcing—pervades political theory from antiquity through contemporary liberalism and provides alternative solutions to the Hobbesian style of concentrating powers in parliament. Second, since the extension of suffrage and the development of mass politics, separate executive and legislative elections have taken on greater importance because of the need to reconcile traditional liberal theories of representative government with the direct popular appeals typical of mass politics. Third, Charles Jones, David Mayhew, and other analysts of American politics provide strong evidence that legislatures remain productive when U.S. presidents lack legislative majorities.[10] Contrary to recent critics of presidentialism, gridlock is far from necessary in situations where presidents lack legislative majorities. Although each of these responses merit careful analysis beyond the bounds of this volume, brief explanations are in order.

PRESIDENTIAL INSTITUTIONS AND POLITICAL THEORY

Presidential Institutions embody a position that appears throughout the history of political theory: that not only do mixing, separating, diffusing, and dividing powers tend to avert tyranny, they are also necessary to produce popular legitimacy and effective governance. Political theorists, from Plato, Aristotle, Polybius, Cicero, Saint Thomas, and Machiavelli (of the *Discourses*), through Locke, Montesquieu, the American Federalists, and contemporary liberals, all argue along these lines in strikingly similar terms. Although the legacy of political theory is no substitute for empirical evidence, this core position toward liberty and power first appeared in Greek conceptions of mixed constitutions, was reaffirmed by both medieval and Renaissance observers of politics, and has been restated by liberal and democratic thinkers since the Enlightenment.

Greek and Roman political theorists recognized the utility of dispersing powers through diverse mechanisms, but their arguments in favor of what they called mixed constitutions are most relevant. Mixed constitutions are those that distribute powers among institutions designed to represent monarchs, oligarchs, and citizens at large. Plato admired the mix of dual monarchs, elders, and ephors (elected representatives) in the Spartan constitution because he thought that dispersing powers among these groups increased the effectiveness of sovereignty.[11] Although subject to dispute, Polybius's comparative analysis of ancient Sparta and Rome also concluded that mixed constitutions are more likely to resist violent overthrow, facilitate imperial expansion, and protect the liberty of citizens.[12] Even Machiavelli argued that ancient Rome achieved imperial greatness and secured liberty for its citizens because the separation of institutional powers caused persistent and productive conflict between the Senate and the people.[13]

After the displacement of monarchs diminished the utility of mixed constitutions, eighteenth-century liberals modernized the idea that liberty, the dispersion of powers, and effective government reinforced new theories such as the separation of powers, checks and balances, and federalism. Indeed, the desirability of separating legislative and executive powers first became a central theme in liberal thought during this new era of revolutions and democratic constitutions.[14] From Locke and Montesquieu through the American Federalists, the separation of powers is defined primarily in terms of separating the executive and the legislature. Locke argued that the executive and legislature must be separate "because it may be too great a temptation to human frailty, apt to grasp for power, for the same persons who have the power of making laws to have also in their hands the power to execute them."[15] Montesquieu also argued that "if there were no monarch and the executive power were entrusted to a certain number of persons drawn from the legislative body, there would no longer be liberty, because the two powers would be united."[16] Madison and the American Federalists advocated not only separate elections and institutional prerogatives for legislature and executive but an additional dispersion of powers through institutional checks and balances.[17] While the historical context and institutional solutions of Locke, Montesquieu, and the American Federalists differ, they shared a concern about diffusing powers in a new era of revolutionary governments.

This new generation of liberal-democratic theorists also defended dispersing powers for a new reason—that of ensuring minority representation. American constitutional debates reveal not only a consistent fear of majority rule but also specific recommendations designed to ensure minority representation.[18] The need to effectively represent minorities to avert tyranny and ensure effective government continued to be of concern in nineteenth-century American political thought. For example, Calhoun argued that opposition was critical in American government and introduced the concept of concurrent majorities.[19] Indeed, contemporary American political theorists in the liberal tradition still argue that increasing opportunities for the representation of minorities through separating and dispersing powers is critical.

Hannah Arendt also argues that a lost legacy of the eighteenth-century revolutionary tradition (and specifically the American Revolution) was the insight that separating and diffusing powers throughout society, far from reducing the power of political institutions, is the key to constructing effective, efficient, and legitimate democratic governance.[20] Arendt focuses primarily on local councils as the preferred institutional site for liberal and revolutionary government. But her insistence that the assertion of differences, the dispersion of powers, the empowerment of citizens, and effective governance are all mutually reinforcing is another in a long line of arguments that seek to link humanistic ideals to viable theories of government.

PRESIDENTIAL INSTITUTIONS AND TENSIONS BETWEEN LIBERALISM AND DEMOCRACY

The second response about the continuing relevance of presidential institutions focuses on their ability to articulate and institutionalize core contradictions between liberalism and democracy in mass society. If eighteenth-century political theories of separation of powers attempted to reconcile conflicts between displaced monarchs and newly empowered parliaments, current debates about parliamentary and presidential systems can be said to tap core conflicts between traditional liberal notions of indirect representative government and new realities of direct popular appeals and democratic ideals in mass politics.

Ever since plebiscites were used by Napoleon to confer imperial and consulate powers upon himself (1799–1804), direct appeals by authoritarian leaders to popular acclaim have shaken liberalism by providing alternative visions and formulas for national representation.[21] Both Marx and Tocqueville were horrified by Louis Bonaparte because they recognized that the extension of universal male suffrage and direct elections for executive office during the Second French Republic had produced unexpected and imposing new forms of mass power.[22] For Tocqueville, strong presidents in nineteenth-century France would simply recreate a new type of absolute monarch.[23] For Marx, Louis Bonaparte asserted a new type of divine right to authoritarian rule by combining direct plebiscitarian acclaim and the militaristic mobilization of the lumpenproletariat.[24] This combination of plebiscitarianism and social leveling, which Marx and Tocqueville abhorred in 1851, reappeared during the twentieth century as fascism, whose direct popular appeals, mass mobilization, functional representation, terror, and genocide remain associated with strong executives.

However revolting these authoritarian abuses of direct popular appeals may be to liberals and democrats alike, the tensions between liberalism and democracy that gave rise to these political outcomes must be recognized as an integral part of modern politics. Contemporary ideas that fuse liberalism and democracy into a single liberal-democratic tradition often fail to recognize that democracy means the transparent, immediate, and direct rule of the people. Tyranny and despotism troubled political theorists from Aristotle through Tocqueville precisely because of the frightening combination of popular support, powerful government, and social leveling. Since the extension of suffrage and the development of mass politics, a core task of liberal-democratic politics is to provide an institutional setting capable of balancing this recurrent and essential tension between the democratic content of direct plebiscitarian appeals to social and economic justice (in the sense of social leveling) and traditional liberal models of representative government.

How can presidential systems provide opportunities and institutional settings for the coexistence of these somewhat contradictory principles of direct democratic and indirect representative government? Verney suggests that, "in countless ways almost incomprehensible to those accustomed to parliamentarism, the presidential system exhibits the mutual independence of the executive and legislative branches of government."[25] The importance of complex links between separately elected presidents and legislators was emphasized by nineteenth-century observers of American politics such as Max Weber and James Bryce, became a central concern once again in debate about party-electoral politics in nineteenth-century America, and continue to inform contemporary analyses of executive-legislative relations.[26]

A central argument of this volume is that presidential institutions provide significant opportunities for reconciling and institutionalizing tensions between direct popular appeals and responsible governance by combining the principles of direct democracy and indirect representative government. Linz and other advocates of parliamentarism do not fully incorporate into their analysis the urgency of bringing the irreversible realities of direct appeals in the age of mass politics into the institutional procedures of direct competitive elections for executives. To be fair, Linz recognizes that "presidential elections do offer the indisputable advantage of allowing the people to choose their chief executive openly, directly, and for a predictable span rather than leaving that decision to the backstage maneuvering of the politicians."[27] But because critics of presidentialism focus on the risks of inflammatory populist and nationalist appeals and the zero-sum character of direct executive elections, they fail to consider the opportunities for ameliorating these risks. Presidential institutions can counterbalance demagoguery and democratic excesses through separate elections for legislatures and other checks and balances.

Observers of American politics from Max Weber to Carl Friedrich saw this combination between direct plebiscitarian appeals and representative government as central to understanding presidential institutions and political development in the United States.[28] Their work suggests not only that the direct election of executives is more democratic but that it can also be functional for political development. Subsequent scholarship by V. O. Key, W. D. Burnham, William N. Chambers, Theodore Lowi, and others clearly demonstrates that precocious democratization occurred in the United States throughout the nineteenth and twentieth centuries largely because of critical elections and electoral realignments shaped by direct presidential elections (ameliorated by the electoral college).[29] America has been a model for newly democratizing states since its revolution.[30] A central goal of this volume is to use these social scientific accounts of American political development to provide new perspectives on presidential institutions and problems of democratization in Latin America and Eastern Europe.

PRESIDENTIAL INSTITUTIONS AND DIVIDED GOVERNMENT

A third response to the general question of whether separation of powers can produce effective government can be found in recent debates about divided government in the United States. Mayhew's pathbreaking book entitled *Divided We Govern* has provoked extensive reconsideration of American executive-legislative relations by suggesting that presidents facing congressional majorities of the other party performed at least as well as presidents with legislative majorities from their own party.

Unfortunately, debate about divided government in American politics has yet to gain widespread influence among comparative political analysts. Instead, critics of presidentialism (and proponents of constitutional reform in the United States) tend to rely on models of unified party government that are more atypical than characteristic.[31] A powerful strain in American political thought has insisted that the United States should emulate the Westminster model of parliamentary government. From Woodrow Wilson's criticism of American politics at the turn of the century and Progressive-era reformers, through calls for a more responsible two-party system in the 1950s, and including proposals for reform of American political institutions during bicentennial celebrations, the quest for a system of concentrated power has continued.[32] And despite considerable evidence to the contrary, advocates of parliamentarism in Latin America and Eastern Europe continue to cite divided government as a vice of presidentialism, ignoring the more complex picture revealed by analysis in the United States.

In his contribution to this volume, Charles Jones deepens the contemporary debate about divided government by linking the ability of American political institutions to perform while presidents lack majorities in Congress to classic assertions in liberal political thought about the functionality of competing legitimacies. While further empirical and conceptual work is required to clarify how divided government works, the analyses of Jones, Mayhew, and others clearly suggest that liberal political theories are still valid. The diffusion and separation of powers is still necessary for effective governance. In fact, concentration of powers may well fail to increase governability. The transparent nature of accountability in Westminster-style parliamentary systems can produce an unwillingness to undertake actions for which the government will be directly blamed.[33]

THE FUSION OF POWERS IN
PARLIAMENTARY GOVERNMENT

Placing presidential systems within the liberal tradition of the separation of powers suggests that the core difference between presidential systems and the traditional Westminster model of parliamentary government is their respective diffusion and concentration of powers. Although analysts often emphasize the importance of coalition government, recent arguments about the utility of parliamentary government for consolidating democracy in Latin America and Eastern Europe may be precariously close to the Hobbesian tradition of seeking to concentrate power in a single sovereign to avert possible conflicts. A corollary of separation of powers theory is that the fusion or centralization of powers does not necessarily generate effective and efficient governance. Although comparisons of parliamentary and presidential government suggest that differences are easily overstated, two comments are in order.[34]

First, the link between presidential government and a tradition in political theory that spans ancient political theory through contemporary liberal and democratic political philosophy stands in marked contrast to arguments for parliamentary institutions and unified government. This volume is grounded in the belief that effective government requires the separation and diffusion of powers to permit the expression of diversity, the organization of complexity, the assertion of opposition, and the negotiation of differences. The efficient, effective, and legitimate resolution of conflicts requires institutional procedures capable of representing the diversity and complexity of modern societies, not the centralization of powers in one chamber, which tends to exclude perspectives and impede communication.

Second, the conception of parliamentary systems as a type of unified government is overstated and has little relevance beyond the English experience. Instead, wide variation among parliamentary systems in Europe and beyond suggests that comparisons between the traditional Westminster model and presidential government are flawed. In addition, as both Rockman and Peters argue in this volume (chaps. 2 and 3), parliamentary systems vary in terms of their relative concentration or separation of powers. Indeed, parliamentary institutions modeled on the British experience appear to be going out of style. New Zealand is introducing a mixed electoral system that combines district and proportional representation voting. Canada altered the Westminster model by diffusing powers to the provinces through federalism and the direct election of governors. The reforms of 1982 also expanded its Senate powers. The Australian system retains a separate Senate chamber. In sum, the United Kingdom appears to be the only country to have retained the central features of the Westminster model, and even it may not be immune to efforts at institutional reform.

Presidentialism thus must be defined on the basis of the separate, direct election of the executive and the legislature for fixed terms. This definition implies a return to important legacies in political theory and to the liberal tradition that suggests that diffusing and separating powers, rather than concentrating them, increases both liberty and governability. This definition restates the separation of powers doctrine by providing an institutional setting capable of reconciling core tensions between liberalism and democracy in mass politics (that between direct plebiscitarian appeals and indirect representative government). Finally, this perspective suggests that both the American experience of precocious political development under presidential institutions and recent evidence that legislatures function quite well during periods of divided government require more open-ended inquiry into presidential institutions and democratic politics in other settings.

EMPHASIZING CONTEXTS: REGIONAL AND NATIONAL EXPERIENCES WITH PRESIDENTIAL INSTITUTIONS

Because presidential institutions and their contexts vary considerably, careful consideration of diverse regional and national experiences is critical before constructing broader cross-national theories. Understanding the impact of presidential institutions requires careful assessment of the links between presidentialism and the separation of powers in political theory, the historic evolution of presidencies in established democracies, the nature and extent of current problems with the American and French presidencies, and the impact of presidential institutions during and after the recent transitions from authoritarian rule outside of North America and Europe.

This strategy of analyzing national and regional experiences also builds on recent work in political science that emphasizes the importance of institutions. New institutionalists have taken a central place in postbehavioral political science by generating a variety of insights about national and comparative politics.[35] Comparative historical analysis has also focused on the place of institutions in the evolution of American and European politics.[36] And recent debate about presidential and parliamentary government has generated discussion of the relative impact of these types of political institutions.[37]

The emphasis on regional and national contexts in this volume develops the methodological and theoretical implications of recent comparative analysis that suggests that, while institutions matter, they must be placed in their complex contexts. The work of Kent Weaver and Bert Rockman provides clear ground for this volume by conceiving of the relative impact of presidential and parliamentary institutions in terms of the risks of—and the opportunities for—specific government capabilities.[38] These capabilities, however, are not singularly dependent on the choice of parliamentarism or presidentialism but instead are contingent on additional factors, such as other institutional rules and procedures, the particular constellation of sociodemographic cleavages, and the legacies of past policies. Weaver and Rockman conclude that "highlighting the consequences of parliamentary and presidential differences is . . . not the end point of analysis *but rather a place to begin what is inevitably a more complex and subtle analysis* of institutional influence on government effectiveness."[39] This volume seeks to accomplish two goals. First, it tries to clarify the opportunities and risks presented by presidential institutions for democratic politics in the diverse regional and national settings of the United States, France, Latin America, Eastern Europe, and Russia. Second, it attempts to clarify the causal relationships between presidential institutions and other factors in these different settings.

PRESIDENTIAL INSTITUTIONS AND DEMOCRATIC POLITICS: A LOOK AHEAD

The contributors to this volume pursue open-ended analyses of the content and context of presidential institutions and democratic politics in the United States, France, Latin America, and Eastern Europe. The volume consists of four parts. In part 1, Bert Rockman and Charles Jones address the theoretical-constitutional foundations, historical development, and contemporary problems associated with the American presidency. Essentially, their work suggests that definitions of presidential systems in comparative politics fail to adequately consider a core characteristic of American political and constitutional theory: the doctrine of separation of powers. According to Jones, recent analyses of the United States in comparative politics are flawed because the American system is more "separationist" than presidentialist. Rockman pursues the implications of this separationist perspective by arguing that, given the considerable variation among parliamentary systems, the relative concentration or diffusion of powers across both presidential and parliamentary systems is far more important than the simple distinction between two nominally polar types of presidentialism and parliamentarism.

In part 2, B. Guy Peters examines how European democracies separate and diffuse powers through formal and informal practices, while John Keeler and Martin Schain clarify the different models of presidentialism that have prevailed in France. Peters suggests that careful analysis of European political processes often reveals a functional, if not structural, separation and dispersion of powers as well as plebiscitarian impulses and other features that are associated in their purest form with presidential systems. Keeler and Schain argue that, despite widespread emulation, the French experience fails to provide a single model of mixed or hybrid presidentialism for new democracies in Latin America and Eastern Europe. Instead, they suggest that French presidential institutions evolved through five rather different phases, which reflected, not formal design or written constitutions, but political innovation by de Gaulle and others, which at times clearly exceeded constitutional limits.

In part 3, Eduardo Gamarra and Kurt von Mettenheim analyze the Bolivian and Brazilian experiences with presidential institutions during and after their transition from military rule. Gamarra argues that separate executive and legislative powers permitted Bolivian presidents to build popularity and form new party coalitions after redemocratization but that external constraints and domestic austerity programs consistently hampered the building of democratic politics during the 1980s. The Bolivian system, which requires that first-round elections producing no absolute majority be settled in the legislature, has forced presidential candidates to balance the plebiscitarian appeals needed to get votes in the first round with subsequent realities: first, forming party coalitions in the legislature and, then, renegotiating obligations with foreign creditors in order to avert capital flight.

In the following chapter, von Mettenheim argues that understanding presidential institutions in Brazil requires shifting comparative perspectives away from European experiences to the American trajectory of political development. The Westminster ideal of well-organized, ideological parties, disciplined political elites, and gradual evolution within parliamentary institutions is simply not relevant in Brazil. Instead, from 1945 to 1964 and again during the protracted transition from military rule (1974–85), party development occurred in Brazil because direct populist appeals mobilized voters during executive elections and because presidents, governors, and mayors were able to nominate professional politicians directly to thousands of administrative posts. Whereas European parties are now seen as forming exclusive political cartels, the Brazilian system is a more fluid one that tends to resonate closer with popular impulses and distribute state patronage.

In part 4, Valerie Bunce, Jonathan Harris, and Michael Bernhard assess the impact of presidential institutions after the collapse of state socialism. Bunce stresses, perhaps more than any author in this volume, that specific national contexts shape institutions; this was especially true of Eastern European transitions, which sought to simultaneously recast command economies, single-party politics, and highly controlled societies. Nonetheless, contrary to the arguments of Linz, Bunce suggests that presidential institutions may very well play important roles in these transitions by offsetting weak parliaments and providing new leaders able not only to speak for entire nations but also to negotiate in a rapidly changing context rife with domestic and international military, economic, and ethnic pressures.

Harris and Bernhard focus on presidential institutions in Russia and Poland. Harris traces the rapid pace of change in Russia to the plebiscitarian character of direct elections and the wide popular appeal of Russian executives. He also suggests that protracted conflict between Boris Yeltsin and the Russian parliament may provide institutional bases for resolving complex issues of political and economic transition. On the other hand, Bernhard emphasizes the dangers of direct popular appeals and charismatic leadership during the Polish transition. For Bernhard, the plebiscitarian character of the

Polish presidency contributed to Lech Walesa missing several critical opportunities to devolve state power and to deepen democracy in Poland.

The conclusion returns to the implications of presidential institutions and their separation of powers for both democratic politics and research in comparative and cross-national politics. The analyses presented in this volume suggest that the American experience of political development and the liberal tradition it embodies can indeed provide new perspectives for those building democratic institutions in Latin America and Eastern Europe. The purpose is not to replace the Eurocentric character of much comparative political analyis with an American model. Instead, a central conclusion of this volume is that wholesale institutional changes—for example, to or from parliamentary or presidential systems—are ill advised. The analyses suggest that constitution writers and scholars avoid extravagant claims and, instead, carefully consider the day-to-day realities of crafting complex political institutions in diverse national contexts.

PART I

The American Context
The Separation of Powers in the United States

CHAPTER 1

The American Presidency
A Separationist Perspective

Charles O. Jones

"Whoever said the U.S. President was powerful?" This provocative question was Anthony King's way to encourage a comparative analysis of the presidency. In addition to the familiar reason that "empirical theories are easiest to construct when the number of cases is large," King explained that comparative analysis facilitates understanding "why the institutions of one's own country work as they do."[1] This rationale is particularly important for the study of the American presidency. First, there is great resistance among scholars of that institution to view it comparatively. Second, a revised perspective of the American presidency is required if it is to be the model for other political systems. Therefore, whatever stimulates presidency scholars to study how the institution works within the national political system can only be good.

This chapter sets forth a separationist perspective to aid in comparing the American presidency with executives in other governments. In so doing, it challenges the common notion that the United States has a presidential system. It begins by considering the broad, less country-specific definition of presidentialism offered by G. Bingham Powell Jr. in his fine work, *Contemporary Democracies*. Powell explains that

> the major characteristic of the presidential system is the selection of a strong chief executive for a fixed term, usually in a direct election. . . .
>
> A second aspect of the presidential system, the separation of the legislative and executive bases of power, has mixed implications. It may well help prevent executive overthrow of democratic regimes when the executive does not control the legislature through a party majority. . . . However, the division of executive and legislative authority often makes it difficult to create and implement coherent, positive programs to deal with national problems.[2]

Powell finds that this combination of a fixed-term direct election and separate legislative and executive departments results in greater

durability than other constitutional arrangements. Yet the executive
may have to be hardened to the problems of working with an unac-
commodating, sometimes hostile, legislature.

This description certainly sounds familiar to scholars of the
U. S. experience. But I am hesitant to adopt it entirely. In keeping
with King's advisory, a review of how presidential systems are characterized outside the United States raises questions as to whether
that label, *presidential system*, is serviceable in reference to the American national government. Indeed, the Powell definition (which appears to be common among comparative government scholars) may
in fact contribute to, or at least be consonant with, an overemphasis
on the role of the president in the national policy process.[3] To begin
with, it contributes to a presidency-centered perspective that is of
doubtful applicability in the American setting and may even mislead
scholars. To accept this definition ultimately distorts analysis of the
role of the American president, often precluding treatment of the
cross-institutional policy work that takes place. It also encourages
criticism of individual presidents for not conforming to an inappo-
site model as well as the promotion of reform proposals of doubtful
validity.

Note that Powell speaks of "the selection of a *strong* chief executive" as characteristic of the presidential system. The fact is that
American elections guarantee no such thing. Certainly, the president
is not strong solely due to constitutional prerogatives: mere occu-
pancy of the White House does not ensure strength of position in
national decision making. Further, just as Richard E. Neustadt,
among others, has told us to expect, presidents diverge substantially
in their sources of power as perceived by those whom they desire to
influence.[4] Powell and others acknowledge that the political separation of the legislative and executive branches creates difficulties for
governing; it is this separation that often precludes the development
and implementation of "coherent, positive programs."

> Students of American politics are familiar with the frequent deadlocks
> of the presidential and legislative branches. Not only are such dead-
> locks common when the party controlling the presidency is in the leg-
> islative minority—a frequent occurrence in all the presidential sys-
> tems—but the differing constituency bases of president and legislators
> seem to hinder the development of coherent, disciplined national party
> systems and to create policymaking tensions even when the same party
> controls both.[5]

It is true, and not in the least surprising, that the White House and Congress as institutions often have very different outlooks on public problems. As discussed below, the writers of the Constitution fostered this variation by providing for different bases of representation. What then is the problem? It derives mostly from the expectation that a "strong" president will somehow overcome the legitimate separation of institutions and representational experience and will dominate. As Mark A. Peterson explains it, by this strong presidency view "the president *should* serve as the fundamental guiding spirit within the government, a clear first without equals or empowered skeptics."[6] If the president does not take charge and produce a "coherent, positive program," then the system has failed. Deadlock is predicted to be the result—and that is bad. Presidency-centered analysis of this type fails to prepare us for real political and policy outcomes in the American system. Peterson argues that "the presidency-centered perspective is incomplete and risks distorting our understanding of how the presidency and Congress function together as policy-making bodies."[7] He offers a "tandem institutions" approach, with the two institutions each participating in lawmaking. "In short, the two must act in tandem."[8]

And there is more. Deadlock is not a necessary consequence of the failure of the president either to produce a "coherent, positive program" or of Congress's failure to pass it, as such, if he does offer one. As is definitively demonstrated by David R. Mayhew, among others, major laws can be passed under the worst possible circumstances, at least as identified by presidency-centered analysts. He shows that production does not vary between unified and divided government—and that important work is done when one least expects it. For example, during the Nixon-Ford Congresses, the number of major laws passed exceeded that of the Kennedy-Johnson Congresses. Few, if any, analysts even noticed that the government continued to work during a time in which it was expected to cease functioning. Mayhew puzzles about this, concluding that "journalists, in effect, deprived of an opportunity for a carry-out-the-mandate script, tended to reach for a deadlock-between-institutions counterscript that probably underreported real legislative action."[9]

Of course, one consequence of reviewing various systems labeled *presidential* may simply be that of labeling some as weaker than others. In his review of the heads of nine governments, both presidential and parliamentary, King places the American president quite low in relative power within his system.

> Judgments on this matter will inevitably differ, but a reasonable approximation to the truth would be that, in terms of power within his own governmental system, the U.S. president probably belongs in the middle rank of heads of government, possibly toward the bottom of it. On the one hand, his control over the executive branch is probably somewhat greater than that of most heads of government (though not the French president's); on the other, his lack of control over the legislative branch puts him more on a par with the prime minister of Italy than with the prime minister of Canada or Great Britain. Most recent American presidents have often looked extremely Andreottilike.[10]

The implications of Powell's identification of the problems for the president in the American system and King's placement of the president in comparison to heads of government in both types of systems lead me to doubt the usefulness of the terms *presidential* or *presidentialist system* for the United States. Isn't it odd that King finds the heads of government in what are called *parliamentary* systems to be more powerful than the president in what is called a *presidential* system?

Is there a more suitable label for the American system? Absolutely. It is drawn directly from the constitutional structure. The United States has a *separated* system. That has meaning for me. In parliamentary systems the executive draws its legitimacy from the parliamentary selection of a government. That format was debated at the constitutional convention; indeed, it existed in the Articles of Confederation and was proposed in both the Virginia and New Jersey plans. Seemingly, the emergence of a party system under either the Virginia or New Jersey plan would have resulted in a parliamentary system. The final decision, however, was that the means of legitimation of the executive and legislature would *not* be unified and continuous—that is, of the legislature by election and then of the executive by party organization (as in a parliamentary system). By plan, legitimation would occur separately for each of the three major elective, policy-making institutions: the House, the Senate, and the presidency. This separation is the distinctive quality of the American system. Accepting it as such does not mislead one into expecting presidential command of policy making. Rather, the scholar is naturally curious to discover how it is that a separated system, with independent sources of legitimacy, functions to produce law.

PAYING ATTENTION TO THE ORIGINAL DESIGN

Richard E. Neustadt has enhanced his already considerable reputation by pointing out that "the constitutional convention of 1787 is supposed to have created a government of 'separated powers.' It did nothing of the sort. Rather, it created a government of separated institutions *sharing* powers. 'I am part of the legislative process,' Eisenhower often said in 1959 as a reminder of his veto. Congress, the dispenser of authority and funds, is no less part of the administrative process."[11] This interpretation is consistent with Peterson's. Institutions that share power will, perforce, have to work in tandem if laws are to be passed. And either explanation—that of Neustadt or that of Peterson—casts doubt on the reliability of a standard, presidency-centered model of national policy making.[12]

Based on my understanding of the constitutional structure and how it has evolved, I propose a substitute formulation. The United States has a government of separated institutions *competing for shared powers* (or shares of shared powers). Whether a consequence of ingenuity, heresthetics (as William Riker claims), or the practicality of satisfying multiple interests, the result in Philadelphia was to produce a mixed representational system.[13] Legitimacy is fundamental to political representation, and that legitimacy is typically bound up in the process of selecting those to serve as representatives. Few processes of legitimation for any government at any time can match the intricacy of that devised at the Constitutional Convention. How all that should happen for the executive and legislature was central to the deliberations in Philadelphia. The "separationists," as Riker refers to them, were determined that "the several parts should be independent from each other." Riker quotes James Wilson, who favored popular election of the executive. Wilson "wished to derive not only both branches of the Legislature from the people, without the intervention of State Legislatures, but the Executive also; in order to make them as independent as possible from each other, as well as of the States."[14]

Wilson's formula was not exactly followed, but his goal was achieved. The executive and the two branches of the legislature were independent from each other in method of election. That independence derived in substantial part from a legitimacy as representatives attributable to direct or indirect linkages to the people. Representatives were elected directly by the people, and often. Senators were selected by state legislators, who were, in turn, elected by the people. So they were endowed as well with a corporative legitimacy associated with the collectivity of state representatives. It was not simply the people electing senators but the representative-legislators of a sovereign state acting for the people.

The president was to be selected by the most elaborate and untested process of legitimation. The Electoral College was to be state based, allocated on the basis of the number of representatives and senators (but not permitting them to serve as electors), with selection of electors to be prescribed by state legislatures (thus allowing for popular election). Should no candidate receive a majority of electors, the president would be selected by the Senate in the original version of the plan, by the House in the final version. It was all put together at the last minute. And as Riker observes, "It is astonishing that a compromise put together over a weekend to satisfy diverse, parochial, and temporary interests has, with only slight modification by the Twelfth Amendment, served adequately for two centuries."[15]

On March 15, 1789, Thomas Jefferson wrote to James Madison, expressing concerns about the new government: "The executive, in our governments, is not the sole, it is scarcely the principal object of my jealousy. The tyranny of the legislatures is the most formidable dread at present, and will be for many years. That of the executive will come in its turn; but it will be at a remote period."[16] If Jefferson perceived alternative scenarios at that early time, surely it is within our power to do the same. The combination of mixed representation and legitimacy along with the allocation of shares of powers meant that the dominance of one institution over the other would vary through time and, with an expanded agenda, across issues.

Separation of powers never meant equality of institutional place in policy making. As a working concept derived from the deliberations in Philadelphia, it never even settled the matter of which institution was *most* legitimate. And so at the most elemental level of analysis, one might expect the branches to protect themselves from encroachment by the other and to expand their role in decision making in the face of perceived weakness elsewhere. The justification for this behavior is simple and basic: as an institution, each unit—the presidency, the House, and the Senate—has a legitimate claim to represent the nation. Participants in each place typically understand the legitimate role of the other (though not invariably, the Nixon years being one recent exception), yet each can fully justify taking charge should one unit falter (i.e., lose its claim to legitimacy). The danger in a legitimacy-derived justification for encroachment is precisely the tyranny that Jefferson feared. Ernest Barker believes that the tendency to encroach is endemic to institutions.

> Instead of seeing itself as a part, which must play its function as such, and claim no more than that, each institution is prone to see itself as a whole, to regard itself as a rounded O, and to claim a total sovereignty. That is an aberration. . . . No part is sovereign. The one thing sovereign is the whole—the whole system of representation—the whole system of reasoning debate, which runs through all the parts; which needs *each* part and *every* part; which needs, above all, the interadjustment and balance of all the parts. That, and that only, is the miracle of reasoning self-government, which is the highest reach of the practical reason of man.
>
> No nation has yet perfected this miracle of reason.[17]

Jefferson's and Barker's worries about excesses aside, a reasonable deduction from the legitimacy of claims to represent is that sometimes one institution may be preponderant and other times a different institution may be preponderant. And when that happens, one may expect analysts to be alarmed, even to the point of proposing reform. Thus, Woodrow Wilson's was concerned about "congressional government" (not unlike Jefferson), and this concern motivated him to recommend change; James MacGregor Burns found both good and bad in "presidential government."[18] Writing shortly after Lyndon Johnson's electoral triumph of 1964, Burns observed that "the Presidency today is at the peak of its prestige."[19] In the preface to the 1973 edition of his book, Burns is much less sanguine about the future of presidential government. Arthur Schlesinger's "imperial presidency" appeared to frighten both him and his readers.[20] The Johnson and Nixon presidencies (especially the latter) led to a concern that the balance of power had shifted dangerously toward the White House.

> The imperial Presidency, created by wars abroad, was making a bold bid for power at home. The belief of the Nixon administration in its own mandate and in its own virtue, compounded by its conviction that the republic was in mortal danger from internal enemies, had produced

an unprecedented concentration of power in the White House and an unprecedented attempt to transform the Presidency of the Constitution into a plebiscitary Presidency.[21]

James L. Sundquist records the "two centuries of ups and downs" in the institutional balance between the White House and Congress. As he views it, "the Constitution, in effect, put two combatants in the ring and sounded the bell that sent them into endless battle."[22] Sundquist quotes former Senator J. William Fulbright (Democrat from Arkansas) approvingly from his "vantage of retirement" as Fulbright expressed the need for "a shifting of the emphasis [between a dominant presidency and an aggressive Congress] according to the needs of the time and the requirements of public policy." Sundquist observes that

> regardless of whether he [Fulbright] or anyone else believed the emphasis should shift back and forth between the branches, it almost surely would. The balance between president and Congress had gone through nearly two centuries of ups and downs; in the third century the seesaw would continue. With each shift, the automatic stabilizer would be public opinion, as the politicians responded to what the people wanted—or lost their jobs to those who would.[23]

In summary, the Constitution fosters a separated system by which institutions legitimated by elections are encouraged to compete for their share of governing authority. However much a strong executive might be desired on grounds of efficiency or effectiveness, members of Congress could be expected to act on their claims to participate in policy making. This is not a fitting description of presidential government or presidentialism as that concept is used by scholars of comparative government.

PLAYING THE OPTIONS: VARIATIONS IN DIVIDED GOVERNMENT

One legitimate option for the public in controlling the excesses or encroachment tendencies of the two institutions is to place different groups or interests in charge of each.[24] The development of the modern two-party system made that simpler for the voter. Two parties, three elected institutions (House of Representatives, Senate, presidency), separated and interim elections—these are the ingredients for intriguing and wholly legitimate combinations of governance.

As it has happened, the voters have frequently exercised their option of returning a split government, most notably in the second half of each century. Tables 1.1 through 1.3 show when divided government has occurred since the founding of the modern two-party system and what the patterns have been. Note that, while a split-party result was frequent in the nineteenth century, it tended to occur as a result of midterm elections. In only three cases did a president begin his administration under these conditions, and in each instance his party failed to achieve a majority in just one house. These three instances did occur in sequence, however, producing the longest period of split-party government in history—fourteen years (table 1.2).

The three instances of split-party government in the first forty-six years of this century all came following midterm elections, each presaging a loss for the president's party in the subsequent presidential election. Seemingly, the presidency-centered perspective derives from analyses of this period, particularly given that it culminates in the presidency of Franklin D. Roosevelt, the quintessential strong president by which others are typically measured. Further, it may well be that it is analysis of this period that leads to the view that divided government is a corruption—one associated with peculiar circumstances (e.g., as in 1910, 1918, and 1930) and therefore a condition soon to be corrected.

The third period is one in which there was a split-party government a majority of the time. As shown in table 1.1, it has become common for the division to occur in presidential elections (Eisenhower once, Nixon twice, Reagan twice, and Bush once). And though the longest period of twelve years (1980–92) does not quite match that in the last century (1874–88), when combined with the eight-year span of the Nixon-Ford administrations, it represents an extraordinarily high percentage of divided government over a twenty-four-year period (83%).[25]

Is split control a corruption? Notice that in table 1.2 the middle period has the fewest years of split-party control. If we drop it out of the calculation, then the varying forms of divided government shown in table 1.3 occur over half the time (53%). Even if this period is included, however, the government has been divided 40 percent of the time. A phenomenon that occurs two-fifths or more of the time is not a corruption and indeed could be called common. As a concession to the presidency-centered, responsible-party devotees,

Table 1.1 Presidential Administrations and Instances of Opposition Party Control in Congress, 1856-1996

Presidency	Opposition Party Control		Election When Opposition Party Took Control	
	Both Houses	One House	Presidential Election	Midterm Election
First Period				
Buchanan, D, 1858		x (H)		x
Grant, R, 1874		x (H)		x
Hayes, R, 1876		x (H)	x	
Hayes, R, 1878	x			x
Garfield, R, 1880		x (S)[a]	x	
Arthur, R, 1882		x (H)		x
Cleveland, D, 1884		x (S)	x	
Cleveland, D, 1886		x (S)		x
Harrison, R, 1890		x (H)		x
Cleveland, D, 1894	x			x
Second Period				
Taft, R, 1910		x (H)		x
Wilson, D, 1918	x			x
Hoover, R, 1930		x (H)[b]		x
Third Period				
Truman, D, 1946	x			x
Eisenhower, R, 1954	x			x
Eisenhower, R, 1956	x		x	
Eisenhower, R, 1958	x			x
Nixon, R, 1968	x		x	
Nixon, R, 1970	x			x
Nixon, R, 1972	x		x	
Ford, R, 1974	x			x
Reagan, R, 1980		x (H)	x	
Reagan, R, 1982		x (H)		x
Reagan, R, 1984		x (H)	x	
Reagan, R, 1986	x			x
Bush, R, 1988	x		x	
Bush, R, 1990	x			x
Clinton, D, 1994	x			x

Source: Compiled by the author from data in Harold Stanley and Richard G. Niemi, *Vital Statistics on American Politics*, 3d ed. (Washington, D.C.: Congressional Quarterly Press, 1992).

a. The situation following the 1880 elections was extraordinary. The Senate was split evenly: thirty-seven Democrats, thirty-seven Republicans, two independents. After much maneuvering and two Republican resignations, the Democrats appointed the officers, the Republicans organized the committees.

b. Republicans, in fact, won a majority of House seats, but by the time the Congress first met, a sufficient number had died to permit the Democrats to organize the House.

Table 1.2 Opposition Party Control in Congress, 1856–1996

Period	Opposition Party Controls		Total Years (%)	Consecutive Years of Split Control
	Both Houses	One House		
First period:				
1856–1900 (44 yrs.)	2	8	20 (45%)	14 years (1874–88)
Second period:				2 years (1910–12;
1900–46 (46 yrs.)	1	2	6 (13%)	1918–20; 1930–32)
Third period:				
1946–96 (50 yrs.)	12	3	30 (60%)	12 years (1980–92)[a]
Total:				
1856–1996 (140 yrs.)	15	13	56 (40%)	

a. There were two other lengthy periods of split control: 1954–60 and 1968–76.

Table 1.3 Patterns of Split Party Control, 1856–1996

Presidential Party	Party Ruling House	Party Ruling Senate	Number
Democratic	Republican	Democratic	1
Democratic	Democratic	Republican	2
Democratic	Republican	Republican	4
Total			7
Republican	Democratic	Republican	9
Republican	Democratic	Democratic	11
Republican	Republican	Democratic[a]	1
Total			21
Total			28 (56 years)

a. This was the 1880 result in which the Senate was tied between Republicans and Democrats but was clearly not under the control of the president's party.

therefore, I accept that what we witness is a *common corruption*.

If scholars acknowledge that divided government is common *and* a wholly constitutional outcome, a corner will have been turned in analyzing the American political system. The task then is to explain how a separated system works, not how it operates when a president and Congress are controlled by the same party, but how it manages the rest of the time: the 40 percent of the time since 1856, the 53 percent of the time in the last half of the nineteenth century and most of the twentieth, the 79 percent of the time between 1968 and 1996. One starting point is to acknowledge that what we have before us awaiting analysis is not well served by the label *presidental system*.

THE ROLE OF THE PRESIDENT IN THE SEPARATED SYSTEM: AN INCORPORATIONIST APPROACH

I promote an incorporationist approach in analyzing the role of the president in the separated political system of the United States. *Incorporate:* "to cause to merge or combine together in a united whole; to become united or combined into an organized body." In order fully to comprehend presidential power in the American system, it is essential to determine how presidents fit themselves into an ongoing government. A prerequisite to accomplishing that end is the identification of the conditions under which presidents take office and serve. The incorporationist perspective, therefore, encourages the analyst to study the process or means by which the president seeks to merge or combine with an organized government (as well as the success he has in doing so). It fosters inquiry into the agenda, the continuity of institutions, and the electoral outcomes and how they are interpreted. By implication, this perspective raises serious doubts about whether one can analyze or predict presidential power and performance by studying the White House only. It overstates the capacity of a separated system to suggest that a newly elected president will merge with other institutions to form a "united whole." But an incorporationist perspective at least directs attention to that potential, which is realizable only through interaction among permanent, continuous institutions, each braced by a renewed legitimacy.

What, then, are some of the conditions facing presidents? What are the challenges for presidents in incorporating themselves into the ongoing government? I concentrate here on the nine presidents in that intriguing third period (those listed in table 1.1 plus Kennedy, Johnson, and Carter), a period when split-party government occurred a majority of the time. Several conditions are crucial for a president seeking to incorporate himself into the government: how he became president, what else happened in the election (notably in congressional elections), the changing role and functions of

Table 1.4 How Presidents Came to the White House, 1944–1992

	Percentage		
President and Term	Popular Vote	Two-Party Vote	Electoral Vote
Truman, 1 (not elected; assumed presidency due to death of Roosevelt)			
Truman, 2 (elected)	49.5	52.3	57
Eisenhower, 1 (elected)	55.1	55.4	83
Eisenhower, 2 (reelected)	57.4	57.8	86
Kennedy, 1 (elected)	49.7	50.1	56
Johnson, 1 (not elected; assumed presidency due to death of Kennedy)			
Johnson, 2 (elected)	61.1	61.3	90
Nixon, 1 (elected)	43.4	50.3	56
Nixon, 2 (reelected)	60.7	61.8	97
Ford, 1 (not elected; assumed presidency due to resignation of Nixon)			
Carter, 1 (elected)	50.1	51.1	55
Reagan, 1 (elected)	50.7	55.3	91
Reagan, 2 (reelected)	58.8	59.2	98
Bush, 1 (elected)	53.4	53.9	79
Clinton, 1 (elected)	43.3	53.5	69

Congress, and the nature of the ongoing agenda. I treat each briefly as prologue to judgments about the incorporationist behavior or strategies of post–World War II presidents, judgments that should contribute to an improved understanding of the separated political system.

How Presidents Came to Be There

The first and most obvious distinction among post–World War II presidents is whether they were elected, reelected, or not elected. Table 1.4 notes the patterns; the elections of Truman, Kennedy, Carter, and Clinton and Nixon's first election are remarkably alike in that the president's win was narrow—in four cases, a plurality only. The president's claim to leadership was muted by these returns. Truman, Kennedy, Carter, and Clinton had Democratic majorities in Congress. However, Nixon had to proceed even more cautiously as the first president since the founding of the modern two-party system to enter office without his party having majorities in either house.

The other four elected presidents—Eisenhower in his first election, Johnson, Reagan in his first election, and Bush—assumed office under similar circumstances. All achieved Electoral College wins of landslide proportions. The percentages of two-party popular vote for Eisenhower, Reagan, and Bush were similar (Reagan faced two opponents in 1980 and, therefore, had a lower total popular vote). Johnson exceeded even Roosevelt's 1936 reelection percentage. Likewise, the three reelected presidents—Eisenhower, Nixon, and Reagan—were remarkably alike in popular and Electoral College vote percentages in their second election. Interestingly, all three were Republican landslides combined with a return of a Democratic Congress. Two of the three (Eisenhower and Reagan) completed their terms, thus providing an interesting and useful comparison for a lame-duck, fourth-Congress administration.[26]

Then there are the special cases of the three presidents who were not elected, which differ in several respects. Truman and Johnson took over for fallen presidents—Truman very early in Roosevelt's fourth term, Johnson in the last year of Kennedy's first term. Given the circumstances of the takeover, neither could expect to be fully prepared to become president. Many of Roosevelt's cabinet members and White House staff were prepared to leave; most of Kennedy's cabinet members and White House staff were anxious to stay. Thus, Truman was in a substantially more advantageous position for creating his own administration than was Johnson. Ford could at least think ahead to the probability of taking over, given Nixon's problems with the Watergate scandal. But he was in an extremely weak position, not having been elected even as a vice president and having to take over for a disgraced president.

Legitimacy varies, based on how presidents enter the White House. All are sworn in, to be sure, but as shown in table 1.4, some presidents can point to substantial support among the voters, others are faced with having to reinforce their status through other means, and takeover, nonelected presidents have to establish their legitimacy from within the structure of the previous administration.

The Election Beyond

General elections produce a national government. There is a tendency to concentrate on the presidential result and to interpret congressional elections in the presidential orbit. Yet they were intended to be, and are in practice, separate events; even House and Senate elections are separate. So the government that results is not integrated by the electoral process. And in fact, split-ticket voting is common enough to produce frequent divided governments.

More than in most systems, therefore, the president is forced to incorporate the results of other elections into his personal calculations of power and strategic position. In so doing, the president may well rely on how others relate his election to congressional elections. The mandate concept is frequently relied on in this process. Under certain circumstances the presidential and congressional elections may be interpreted as conveying congruent results and messages. If so, then the president is said to have a mandate. Thus, for example, the 1964 and 1980 elections were widely interpreted as producing mandates for Lyndon Johnson and Ronald Reagan. All the conditions were seemingly met: an issue-oriented campaign, divergent issue and ideological positions by the candidates, a landslide win for the president, and a significant win for the president's party in Congress. There appeared to be similar policy messages deriving from all three elections—House, Senate, and presidential—thus encouraging analysts to declare a mandate for change.[27] Not surprisingly, the Eighty-ninth and Ninety-seventh Congresses were among the most legislatively active of modern times.

As it happens, however, the conditions for declaring a mandate to exist are seldom met. Therefore, interpreting the presidential result from an incorporationist perspective requires careful study of House and Senate elections and their meaning. How do the members themselves interpret the legitimacy of their election or reelection? Do they interpret their election in policy terms as related to the presidential outcome? If so, what are the issue bases for the connection? A related question—for which we have little or no evidence—is, Is the status of the presidency as an institution sufficiently high as to encourage congressional support of White House requests?

Given the rarity of conditions favoring the declaration of a mandate for change, I suggest other mandate-related concepts for probing the differences among presidential-congressional elections. The *status quo mandate* refers to the situation in which voters essentially approve the government then in place. Thus, for example, in 1956, 1972, and 1984, the policy message appeared to be "carry on." The president in each case won by a landslide, and there was a high return of House and Senate incumbents. Justified or not in strict policy terms, the president can logically view the returns as being congruent to supporting the status quo. The *mixed mandate* or *non-*

mandate is most perplexing from the point of view of the president. In this type of election, the president wins narrowly, and there is no obvious connection between his victory and the results in Congress. Examples include the 1960, 1968, 1976, and 1992 elections. In each of those elections, the president ran behind most of the successful members of Congress from his party; for example, in 1960 and 1976, Kennedy and Carter, respectively, ran behind 92 percent of the successful House Democrats; in 1992, Clinton ran behind nearly all winners due to a third candidate (Ross Perot). It is under these circumstances that the president must work hard at establishing policy connections between himself and Congress.

Finally, there is the problem of the *unmandate*, which can occur in a midterm election. However seemingly clear the relationship between the legitimacy of the president and Congress is in any one election, both institutions are just two years from possible change. Thus the congressional elections in 1966 (a net gain of forty-seven House Republicans and four Senate Republicans) were interpreted as flashing a "'Caution—Go Slow' signal to the Johnson Administration."[28] The 1980 Reagan mandate for change looked very different following the net loss of twenty-five House Republicans in 1982. And the status quo or approval elections of 1956, 1972, and 1984 were interpreted quite differently following the 1958, 1974, and 1986 elections.

Presidents face very different landscapes as they look out over the government they presumably lead. The challenge is to place himself realistically within that government, identifying and understanding his advantages sufficiently well as to make them work for him. A misreading of his position relative to the other elected officials in Washington can have seriously crippling effects on an administration, thus justifying the relevance of the incorporationist perspective in presidential politics.

The Changing Congress

One of the consequences of divided government over a period of time is that institutions adjust to changing circumstances. Congress enacted more reforms in the 1970s than in any period in its history. Many of these reforms were directed at providing members with greater resources for participating actively and more broadly in the policy process. Increased committee and personal staff, new and expanded policy analysis units, dispersal of leadership, a revised budget process, expanded oversight—these and other changes had a significant impact on the role of Congress. It can be argued that this added capacity was needed for Congress just to maintain its place. Perhaps so. But the result was to alter the look on Capitol Hill. Many more people work there now than thirty years ago. Members of Congress are better able to take policy initiatives and to critique proposals coming from the administration. Congress has become a policy machine capable of producing proposals on almost any subject; it is not as dependent as it once was on either the White House or the bureaucracy.

A collateral development is that of centralizing national Democratic Party policy making in Congress, notably in the House of Representatives. The Senate, for the most part, remains the Senate. Barbara Sinclair observes that, in contrast to the 1950s, "the Senate of the 1980s is superbly structured for the articulation of interests, agenda setting, and the promotion of policy." Yet this development has come at the cost of creating "problems of decision making." She concludes that "the Senate is never likely to become a truly efficient decision-making body, and if it were, something more valuable would be lost."[29] For the very reasons of preserving its advantage of expressiveness, it is unlikely that one party can ever fully control the lawmaking process in that institution.

The situation is very different in the House, where the Democrats have increasingly dominated lawmaking. Steven S. Smith explains that "Democratic leaders and Rules members began to design some special rules that virtually eliminated uncertainty about the amendments that would be offered in the Committee of the Whole."[30] With Republicans consistently winning the White House, the House Democrats came to be the not-so-loyal opposition. They redesigned the lawmaking process to virtually exclude the Republicans from meaningful participation. Presidents Reagan and Bush were forced to bargain with House Democrats and, in many cases, to respond to their policy initiatives. Ironically, when the Republicans won a majority in the House in 1994, they were able to use the rules contrived by the Democrats to *their* advantage.

No one who has studied national policy making and politics in the last dozen years can possibly be satisfied with concentrating solely on the White House. The separated system has taken forms that not one of the founders would have predicted and yet that several would doubtless have applauded. The work of the national gov-

ernment is done at both ends of Pennsylvania Avenue, with both institutions normally prepared to participate fully in the policy and
lawmaking process.

The Ongoing Agenda

It is common among presidential scholars to ascribe the agenda-
setting function to the White House. According to Neustadt, "Con-
gressmen need an agenda from outside, something with high status
to respond to or react against. What provides it better than the program of the President?"[31] John Kingdon agrees, noting that his interviews on agenda setting confirm "that the president can single-
handedly set the agendas, not only of people in the executive branch,
but also of people in Congress and outside of government."[32] Paul
Light explains that the president's agenda "determines the distribution of political benefits; it is a signal to the Congress and the public
of national needs."[33]

I don't disagree with these interpretations of the president's role
in agenda setting under certain conditions. I do, however, assert that
this role is variable—that sometimes it is critical but that many
times it is not. If we are to accept a common understanding of the
term agenda—say, that used by Kingdon: "the list of subjects that
are getting attention"—then much of the government's work is already in place when a president arrives, and that work continues
through his term.[34] As I stated elsewhere:

> Various studies emphasize that agenda setting at any level is a complex
> process involving events, organization, pressure, expertise, choices, and
> bargaining. The role of presidents in this process can not be under-
> stood merely by studying what *they* do but by clarifying what else is go-
> ing on that may have an impact on agenda formation. The trick then is
> to fit presidents into this complex set of activities, not to paste them in
> at the top of the organizational chart and conclude by that exercise that
> they are in charge.[35]

In a review of the work of the 102d Congress (1991–92), Janet Hook
and the *Congressional Quarterly* staff identify the following legislative priorities: "energy legislation; a tax bill to boost the economy
and aid cities in the wake of the Los Angeles riots; family leave legislation; and regulation of the cable television industry."[36] It would
be hard to establish that this was an agenda created by the president. It contains issues that are hardy perennials (energy and taxes),
those that are responsive to events (taxes), and carryover matters

from previous Congresses (family leave and the regulation of cable television). The newest issue, family and medical leave policy, derived not from the White House but from Congress.

The *Congressional Quarterly* total agenda for the 102d Congress contains eighty items. A rough categorization by source of each agenda item breaks out as follows:

— Inside Congress issues: 8
— Reauthorizations: 13
— Congressional initiatives: 22
— Presidential initiatives: 12
— Mixed (president and Congress): 25 (includes many budget, fiscal, and defense-related issues)

The bold fact is that the huge majority of items on this agenda were continuing issues, those already on the books. The conclusion is inescapable: presidents work within an active government that creates the policy for initiatives and priorities. Presidents set priorities and often establish a sequence of action, which decisions then serve as starting points for other policy actors. But settling on a priority among many potential agenda items clearly leaves out others. Experience shows that members of Congress often take up those other items.

This conclusion is supported by a detailed examination of twenty-eight major legislative enactments in the post–World War II period. I chose these laws from the list compiled by David Mayhew in his study *Divided We Govern* and traced the legislative heritage of these pieces of legislation. It became clear that most were part of a continuing agenda. Only three had little or no history in prior administrations: the Marshall Plan (1948), the War Powers Act (1973), and the Budget and Impoundment Control Act (1974). One of these was a presidential initiative, the other two were congressional initiatives.[37] There were five other cases of major legislation with relatively short histories, though all spanned more than one administration. The rest—twenty cases—had a substantial legislative heritage, one in which policy turf was well defined, leaving the president with the task of staking his claim to act.

The deficit is another important factor in constraining agenda options. Most policy solutions to public problems require money. If it is not available, or if a reallocation is required, policy makers lose flexibility in making choices. This constraint has dominated agenda setting since the dramatic rise in deficits in the early 1980s and was, in fact, an important factor before that time (in the Nixon, Ford, and Carter administrations). And when the deficit itself becomes a major agenda item, policy makers are encouraged to establish decision rules to prevent its becoming more serious or to abate present trends. These rules—the Gramm-Rudman-Hollings deficit reduction method, for example, or the stringent restrictions built into the deficit reduction package of 1990—create a revised policy process, one that tends to be dedistributive and therefore produces dyspeptic and peevish decision makers. Revoking entitlements is much less popular than granting them.

AN INCORPORATIONIST RATING OF POST–WORLD WAR II PRESIDENTS

There have been a number of efforts to classify presidents. That by James David Barber is well known: active/positive, active/negative, passive/positive, and passive/negative presidents. His principal interest is that of predicting performance from his understanding of the president's character, worldview, and style. Barber acknowledges the importance of the "power situation" and "climate of expectations," concepts encouraging an incorporationist perspective, but they are not central to his classification.[38]

Richard Rose provides a grouping based on "normative criteria for assessing modern presidents."[39] He relies on two dimensions: the "scope of the presidency," which has agenda implications; and the "assessor's view of actions," which can be likened to public support or approval. This produces four types of presidents—the leader, the imperial president, the guardian, and the imperiled president— and invites consideration of the context within which they work.

Erwin Hargrove and Michael Nelson offer a policy-oriented categorization, based primarily, it seems, on a review of the policy record of a presidency. "Presidents of preparation" offer new ideas and seek to build support for them. "Presidents of achievement" get legislation enacted, bolstered by "strong but temporary empowerment." And "presidents of consolidation" rationalize, alter, and build support for program implementation.[40] Although context is alluded to in forming these categories, the primary emphasis is on the president and his policy purposes.

I applaud these efforts to differentiate among presidents, since they promote study of the variable conditions under which presidents serve. As with the cycles of presidential leadership identified by Bert Rockman (chap. 2, this volume), one is persuaded to explore beyond the president's personal background and style for judging his place in national policy making. My principal conclusion is that presidential scholars have to take the implicit advice of these typologists and account for additional contextual features of individual presidencies. The goal is providing a comparative base for predicting the place and performance of presidents in a separated political and policy system.

This final exercise, then, is an early attempt to identify types of presidencies based on a composite of critical contextual variables. I acknowledge that what follows is a bulky endeavor, but it is difficult to refine that which has not yet surfaced. One useful deduction from a contextual or incorporationist approach is simply that a presidency is not necessarily, or even probably, coterminous with the years one person happens to occupy the White House. To insist on that definition limits the number of presidencies available for developing generalizations. However, by emphasizing variables that change throughout a president's term, that number is increased. For present purposes, I define a presidency as that period between congressional elections, counting as well each president who served in that interim.

This method produces twenty-six completed post–World War II presidencies, from Truman's takeover following Roosevelt's death to the second Bush presidency. These twenty-six presidencies are scored on the basis of several indicators of potential strength—percentage of Electoral College and popular vote, percentage of seats the president's party holds in the House and in the Senate, and the mean of his public approval rating and presidential support score (see table 1.5). The two election percentages are dropped following the midterm election, the assumption being that they are less relevant at that point—that the public approval ratings tend to take over as gauges of public support. These are inexact measures of power, to be sure, but they are often relied on as evidence, nonetheless. My purpose is simply to show the variation among presidents in the resources they have available for being integrated into—and leading—the national government. Clearly, the challenges are substantially different among these presidencies, even for the same president. The scoring range is from 43 for Gerald Ford following the 1974

Table 1.5 Ratings of Presidencies, 1945–1992

Presidency	Congress Divided or Unified	Electoral College Vote (%)	Popular Vote (%)	House Seats in President's Party (%)	Senate Seats in President's Party (%)	Public Approval Rate (%)	Mean Presidential Support Score	Mean of Public Approval Rate and Presidential Support Score
Truman, 1, 1945–46	U			56	59	62		59
Truman, 2, 1946–48	D			43	47	48		46
Truman, 3, 1948–50	U	57	50	60	56	47		54
Truman, 4, 1950–52	U			54	50	29		44
Eisenhower, 1, 1952–54	U	89	55	51	50	67	86	66
Eisenhower, 2, 1954–56	D			47	49	71	73	60
Eisenhower, 3, 1956–58	D	86	57	46	49	60	72	62
Eisenhower, 4, 1958–60	D			35	35	62	59	48
Kennedy, 1, 1960–62	U	56	50	60	64	74	83	65
Kennedy, 2, 1962–63	U			59	67	65	87	70
Johnson, 1, 1963–64	U			59	67	76	88	72
Johnson, 2, 1964–66	U	90	61	68	68	60	86	72
Johnson, 3, 1966–68	U			57	64	43	77	60
Nixon, 1, 1968–70	D	56	43	44	42	59	76	53
Nixon, 2, 1970–72	D			41	44	52	71	52
Nixon, 3, 1972–74	D	97	61	44	42	37	55	56
Ford, 1, 1974	D			44	42	59	58	51
Ford, 2, 1974–76	D			33	37	44	57	43
Carter, 1, 1976–78	U	55	50	67	61	54	77	61
Carter, 2, 1978–80	U			64	58	40	76	60
Reagan, 1, 1980–82	D	91	51	44	53	51	77	61
Reagan, 2, 1982–84	D			38	54	58	66	52
Reagan, 3, 1984–86	D	98	59	42	53	61	58	62
Reagan, 4, 1986–88	D			41	45	49	45	45
Bush, 1, 1988–90	D	79	53	40	45	67	55	57
Bush, 2, 1990–92	D			38	44	54	49	46

election to 72 for Lyndon Johnson following the assassination of President Kennedy and Johnson's landslide election in 1964.

As expected, a president's score typically falls following the midterm election. The only exception was President Kennedy, who gained 5 points due to the continuing strong position of the Democrats in Congress, the president's relatively high approval rating, and his impressive support scores. It is also the case that the two-term administrations show substantial deterioration from the first to the last score: 15 points for Truman (who came close to having two full terms), 18 points for Eisenhower, 10 points for Nixon-Ford, and 16 points for Reagan.

The source of strength and weakness does vary from one president to the next, even among those with high scores. It is this variation that leads one to propose various types of presidents from an incorporationist or contextual perspective. Table 1.6 ranks both governing presidencies (those with the highest scores) and participating presidencies (those with the lowest scores), notes whether the presidency was united or divided, identifies the principal sources of strength (electoral, congressional, senatorial, or personal), and notes the number of major pieces of legislation as classified by David Mayhew.[41]

Several comments are in order, as related to an incorporationist perspective. Not unexpectedly, those presidencies with the highest scores occurred during periods of unified control (nine of the thirteen highest), and those with the lowest scores occurred during periods of divided control (eleven of thirteen of the lowest). A majority of those with the highest scores had more than one source of strength (ten of thirteen), and conversely, a majority of those with the lowest scores had one source or no major sources of strength (twelve of thirteen). Further, there is but one presidency (Johnson, 2) that meets the standard criteria for a strong presidency—that is, substantial sources of strength across the categories: electoral, congressional, and personal. Of the rest, just two of the Reagan presidencies (1 and 3) drew substantially from all three (Republicans having had a majority in the Senate but not in the House during these presidencies).

One final observation relates to the production of major legislation during these twenty-six presidencies. There is no difference in output between presidencies with the highest scores and those with the lowest: 132 pieces of major legislation enacted for the top

Table 1.6 Ranking of Post World War II Presidencies

Presidency and Score	Party in Control of Congress	Source of Presidential Strength	Pieces of Significant Legislation[a]
Governing Presidencies			
Johnson, 1, 72	Same	Congressional and personal	7[b]
Johnson, 2, 72	Same	Electoral, cong., and personal	22
Kennedy, 2, 70	Same	Congressional and personal	6[b]
Eisenhower, 1, 66	Same	Electoral and personal	9
Kennedy, 1, 65	Same	Congressional and personal	15
Eisenhower, 3, 62	Other	Electoral and personal	11
Reagan, 3, 62	Other	Electoral, senatorial, personal	9
Carter, 1, 61	Same	Congressional and personal	12
Reagan, 1, 61	Other	Electoral, senatorial, personal	9
Johnson, 3, 60	Same	Congressional	16
Carter, 2, 60	Same	Congressional	10
Eisenhower, 2, 60	Other	Personal	6
Truman, 1, 59	Same	Congressional and personal	c
Participating Presidencies			
Bush, 1, 57	Other	Electoral and personal	10
Nixon, 3, 56	Other	Electoral	16
Truman, 3, 54	Same	Congressional	12
Nixon, 1, 53	Other	Personal	22
Nixon, 2, 52	Other	Personal	15
Reagan, 2, 52	Other	Senatorial	7
Ford, 1, 51	Other	Personal	6[b]
Eisenhower, 4, 48	Other	Personal	5
Truman, 2, 46	Other	No major source	10
Bush, 2, 46	Other	Personal	c
Reagan, 4, 45	Other	Personal	12
Truman, 4, 44	Same	No major source	6
Ford, 2, 43	Other	No major source	14

a. David R. Mayhew, *Divided We Govern: Party Control, Lawmaking, and Investigations, 1946-1990* (New Haven: Yale University Press, 1991), 90.

b. One year or less.

c. Unavailable.

twelve; 135 pieces enacted for the bottom twelve (no data are available for Truman, 1, and Bush, 2). Here is yet another version of Mayhew's theme of "divided we govern." Note, for example, that half again as many important pieces of legislation were enacted during the lowest-scoring as during the highest-scoring Republican presidencies (Ford, 2, compared to Eisenhower, 1); or that the lowest-scoring of the Reagan presidencies (4) was more productive than either of the two highest scoring (3 and 1); or that the relatively low-scoring Truman presidency (3) was nearly as productive as the combined, high-scoring Kennedy-Johnson presidency. It is true, as Mayhew points out, that these pieces of legislation are not all the same weight; assigning weights to pieces of legislation would alter the numbers somewhat. But such an exercise is unlikely to change the general point being made here: that major policy work is done by governments differently formulated, with the president necessarily playing a variable role. The separated system appears to provide compensatory advantages to weak presidencies (by standard measures).

The rankings, in juxtaposition to the production of major legislation, suggest two broad types of presidencies. Those with the higher scores (58–72) are *governing presidencies*. They are characterized by impressive resources in the competition for shared powers. They are not, however, equally active in agenda setting and policy development. Thus a distinction can be made between those who are more *active* and those who are more *passive*. Not surprisingly, the Democrats tend to be more active—to use their resources for policy-making purposes; the Republicans tend to be more passive—to bank their resources for use in resisting policy encroachments. Examples of governing/active presidencies are Johnson, 1, 2; Kennedy, 2, 1; Carter, 1; Reagan, 1; Johnson, 3; Carter, 2; and Truman, 1. Examples of governing/passive presidencies are Eisenhower, 1, 3; Reagan 3; and Eisenhower, 2.

Those with lower scores (43–57) are *participating presidencies*. Lacking resources, these presidents are less well positioned in the competition for shared powers. The active and passive subcategories are serviceable here as well, but they may be made somewhat more meaningful as a distinction between two approaches: *adversarial* and *bargaining*. Examples of participating/adversarial presidencies are Reagan, 2; Bush, 2; Ford, 1; Eisenhower, 4; Truman, 2; Reagan, 4; Truman, 4; and Ford, 2. Examples of participating/bargaining presidencies are Bush, 1; Nixon, 3; Truman, 3; and Nixon, 1 and 2.

I readily concede that these categories need considerably more refinement. Measures of presidential initiative in agenda setting and policy development are needed, as are gauges of confrontation and bargaining. An analysis of state of the union messages would be useful, as well as a careful study of the use of the veto as a strategy. Crude as it is, however, this exercise exhibits intriguing variations in the role played by the president in the separated system that characterizes the national policy process.

CONCLUSION

There appears to be substantial interest in the American national political and policy-making system at the very point in history when Americans themselves are displaying serious doubts about its viability. One should not be misled into believing that the system is in jeopardy. Even if a period of unified government were to occur, an understanding of the politics of such a period would be enhanced by adopting a separationist rather than a presidentialist perspective. A concentration on the White House as an object of study in a period of unified party government should consider the political, institutional, and policy context within which presidential decisions are made.

Therefore, the central message of this chapter is that in the comparative study of the American system with other systems it is well to avoid a dominant responsible party, strong presidency model in favor of a diffused responsibility, separated institutions model. The separation is rooted in independent legitimation processes, which permit, perhaps encourage, widespread and tenable participation in policy making. The president has an active role to play, should he be motivated to do so. Presidents vary significantly in the resources they have available in the competition for shared powers, just as Neustadt and others tell us. An early exercise in identifying these resources demonstrates these differences and directs attention to four types of presidencies.

The Performance of Presidents and Prime Ministers and of Presidential and Parliamentary Systems

Bert A. Rockman

In this chapter, I want to draw two levels of comparison. One is at the individual level, the other at the collective level, of the political system. The individual level comparison deals with the role of presidents and prime ministers as the executive heads of their systems, examining in particular the constraints under which they operate and the opportunities these leaders have to exercise discretion. The second comparison is no doubt the more important one: here, the relevant comparison is between presidential and parliamentary systems and their capacities for effective governance (a notoriously subjective concept).[1] It is often assumed that the more executive discretion available, the more effective the performance of government will be.

Effective governance, however, is a multidimensional phenomenon. As in any organization, there are two principal and potentially contradictory organizational needs: *goal attainment* and *political maintenance*.[2] By goal attainment, I mean the capacity of the system to make policy and to steer a new course; by political maintenance, I mean the ability of the system to represent interests and to ameliorate the possible estrangement of groups within the polity.

We are likely to be most sensitive to problems of goal attainment when we take maintenance (the legitimacy of the political order) for granted. This assumes that maintenance in the form of legitimation is the sine qua non of effectiveness. But the fact is that it is hard to know whether legitimacy is maintained best by weakening the goal attainment capabilities of government or, in the long run, by strengthening them. There are only tentative answers rather than definitive ones to the quite central issue of whether the divergent needs of goal attainment and political maintenance require divergent institutions. When viewed through Marxian or even interest group lenses, goal attainment is taken to mean, in reality, only the goals held by some dominant interests within the society or polity. Naturally, each segment of the polity is likely to rationalize its own preferences in the context of collective goals. In a pluralized society, direction is likely to draw resistance. When the resistance incurs sizable political costs, goal attainment is likely to become a less powerful ambition for political leaders than simply leaving well enough alone.

Cleavage structures certainly are likely to influence the balance of moving and resisting forces. Institutions are also crucial to this equilibrium. They are especially likely to influence the site and, therefore, the timing of movement and resistance to policy initiatives. Here, then, is one difference between parliamentary systems, however varied they may be, and the separation of powers system of the United States. Resistance in parliamentary systems tends to come early and to be most decisive at that stage and less decisive when a matter moves to public debate. In the United States, resistance tends to accumulate and, therefore, to develop later in the process and to become more decisive as matters move to public debate. These features affect the strategies of politicians and other policy actors.

Similarly, institutions can influence the ways in which policy ideas or even fads come to public attention. Parliamentary systems tend to have more limited channels for communicating such ideas because, in significant part, they are more organized. Organization tends to inhibit the flow of ideas. The less organized U.S. system, by contrast, provides numerous pathways for ideas to travel on and numerous authorities to be influenced. Such an environment also provides fertile ground for policy entrepreneurs to exist outside of official roles. As a consequence, when it comes to answering the question, Do institutions matter? the answer is that surely they do but that they are not all that matters.

MICROCOMPARISONS: PRESIDENTS AND PRIME MINISTERS

Inasmuch as this chapter explores the relative capabilities for action of presidents and prime ministers as well as of presidential and parliamentary systems, my first focus is on the relative power of presidents and prime ministers. Which system, if either, provides greater capability for these central leaders?

It is important to note that institutions are probabilistic and indirect rather than deterministic when it comes to predicting the behavior of leaders and the performance of systems. Other variables often intervene to influence these relationships. Thus, the opportunities provided by institutions for central leadership do not mean that these opportunities will be taken, nor do the constraints that institutions impose on central leadership ensure that all central leaders will be weak.

Institutions can locate power centrally even while they provide relatively little power to any single leader. Such a case is exemplified by the relatively weak political status of the Japanese prime minister. While the Japanese government is relatively centralized, the major sources of influence within it are the bureaucracy and party leaders, the latter of whom often hold cabinet positions. Although, in theory, the prime minister sits at the apex of a formally centralized governing system, its formal centralization is belied by an extraordinary web of political and social interdependencies.[3] If the role of the Japanese state is considerable, that of the Japanese prime minister, with extremely rare exceptions (such as Tanaka and Nakasone), is weak. For the most part, Japanese prime ministers are caught within this intricate web of constraints. The power of the state and that of the central executive within it, Anthony King reminds us, ought not to be confused with one another.[4]

Structures and Norms

It is, of course, reasonable to think that the same institutional structures that might serve to strengthen or weaken the directive leadership capabilities of the leader at the top would equally serve to strengthen or weaken the capabilities of government for collective action, and vice versa. The equation, however, is not so simple. To assume the existence of that simple identity constitutes a position of structural determinism. It implies that the capacity for collective action must necessarily emanate from highly centralized concentrations of power resources and the power of political command.[5] This cross-level equation further assumes a mode of governance based on adversarial politics, where majoritarianism prevails, rather than on a mode of governance based on accommodationist politics,

where negotiation prevails. Putatively, the vintage case of a powerful leader in structural terms is the British prime minister, whose
party normally commands a parliamentary majority, in itself a
rather rare case. The Westminster system is, in fact, uncommon and
has not been bred outside of the British Commonwealth.

Whereas presidents have to gain the support of their legislatures
in systems that provide formal checks and balances, prime ministers have to gain the support of their cabinets. A central distinction
between parliamentary and presidential systems is that a prime
minister is much more part of a collective executive than is a president. The cabinet is, in some sense, a collective decision-making
body or, at least, a collective sounding board and not merely a set of
presidential underlings who head departments. One thing that this
means is that prime ministers are hedged in by the expectation that
they must achieve some measure of consensus from their cabinets
for the government to go forward with a proposal.

In some instances, as in the German Federal Republic, the process of gaining approval is formally specified and gives each minister considerable autonomy. In other cases, as in Britain, norms take
the place of formal legal or rule-based specification.[6] However,
norms do change, and it may well be that leaders endowed with a
sense of boldness and perhaps a splash or two of self-righteousness
alter the norms. At the very least, they may successfully contravene
them. Note, for example, the redoubtable Margaret Thatcher, who
dumped overboard those of her colleagues about whom she felt un-
kindly. In the end, of course, she too was dumped overboard by
mutinous party members in Parliament when the moment seemed
propitious.

Norms are continuously being challenged when the prevalent
ones create disadvantages for some set of actors. The logic of this is
evident in E. E. Schattschneider's "socialization of conflict" theo-
rem, which notes the propensity of losers to appeal private losses in
the public arena.[7] If the loss is part of an accepted ebb and flow in a
repeated game, the norm of reciprocity is likely to be sustained and
actors are unlikely to seek appeal. But the less the game is seen as
repetitive and the more one of the actors thinks they can gain an advantage, the more likely one of the actors will be tempted to seek advantages beyond previous boundaries of acceptance.[8]

In this context, the condition of divided government in the
United States and the weak political leverage of presidents has led to

a growing dependence on presidential use of administrative regulations and executive orders to take the place of, and indeed sometimes to seemingly override, statutory mandates. Charles Tiefer observes these tendencies and notes that the weaker the presidential sources of legitimacy, the greater the reliance on the use of such unilateral instruments.[9] In this sense, presidents in the separation of powers system have a degree of potential control over the bureaucracy as a direct policy-making instrument, control that prime ministers in parliamentary cabinet systems lack. A strategy organized around governing through executive means alone, Terry Moe argues, is an inevitable outcome of the structural situation of separated and often divided powers that U.S. presidents find themselves in.[10] From this perspective, accordingly, the U.S. presidential office institutionalizes itself so as to dominate the executive branch and also to lessen the influence of Congress over it.[11] Successful strategies, should they become that, help to create new norms.

Leaders and Situations

It is also true that leaders to some extent make their office. After all, they vary considerably in their propensity for taking risks and in their commitment to achieving policy objectives. Compare Ronald Reagan and George Bush, or Margaret Thatcher and John Major, or Willy Brandt and Helmut Kohl. Different leaders acting differently within the same institutional framework suggest the limits of that framework as an explanation. It also suggests the extent to which institutional frameworks are pliable. Reagan, Thatcher, and Brandt were all high-risk politicians, a relatively rare breed. Despite the opportunities and constraints provided by their own systems, each maximized the chances they were given within the constraints of their systems.

Situations, nonetheless, dictate a lot of what can be done. Reagan, Thatcher, and Brandt also represented the politics of change. The political signals accompanying each into office were interpreted as a green light for change—until the energy these signals had summoned was exhausted. Major, with his narrowed parliamentary majorities, could not do what Thatcher did, even if he wished to. Nor could George Bush have done what Reagan did, since he came to office amid utterly (but typically) confusing political signals. The conditions under which leaders come to power and the political majorities with which they have to work certainly shape the political latitude these leaders will have, within the possibilities defined by the institutional framework. There are, in other words, surely differences across systems in the latitude provided for top political leadership, but such systemic differences are variable, not constant. Consequently, system differences can be sufficiently overshadowed by variation in internal political conditions, so that the latitude available to leaders within the same system might vary more than that available to leaders across systems.[12] One might ask, for example, whether it would be better to have stepped into Lyndon Johnson's U.S. presidential boots in 1964 (and especially 1965) than to have been in Alec Douglas-Home's prime ministerial shoes in nearly the same time period?

Despite the fact that plenty of room exists for situational and personal variability within any given system's institutional framework, systems do provide different central tendencies in regard to the discretion available to their executive leadership. Anthony King examines several contemporary democratic systems and concludes that the French president and the British prime minister (in that order) rank at the top of discretionary latitude, whereas the U.S. president ranks toward the bottom.[13] To be sure, the French president may have to "cohabit" with the prime minister (a form of divided government), though this, of course, serves to increase the latitude of the French prime minister by making him a kind of second president. Equally, the British prime minister may be held hostage by his or her party or be required to govern with narrowed or inconclusive mandates. All things being equal, however, the French president and the British prime minister operate under circumstances more favorable to the exercise of discretion than does the American president. A relationship that does not hold all of the time may, nonetheless, hold most of the time.

The Collective and the Individual Executive

In the *Federalist Papers*, the documents that illuminate the founding of American governmental institutions, Alexander Hamilton, the proponent of a strong central executive, argues (*Federalist* 70) that "energy in the executive" is most suitably engendered through a presidency occupied by a single officeholder rather than through a collective executive. Hamilton's writings preceded the development of mass-based party organization that could infuse energy into the collective executive—which is, after all, more characteristic of parliamentary systems. For, other things being equal, parliamentary systems tend much more than presidential ones to have the characteristics of a collective executive. Of course, this too varies. Cabinet government may be no match for a prime minister of relentless purpose, energy, and combativeness. Margaret Thatcher, for example, liked to point out that she was a conviction politician and not a consensus monger. Her leadership was colorful precisely because it was so exceptional. Exceptions, however, do not prove rules. In the more frequent cases of multiparty coalitions, the collective executive can be quite constraining for a prime minister who must seek consensus among ministers whose preferences, depending upon how the governing coalition was constructed, may be quite diverse. In any event, in such a setting with a minimum-sized coalition, the prime minister can ill afford to upset any of the parties crucial to the survival of his or her government.

By contrast, the U.S. president is under no such constraint. He does not have to seek anybody's agreement before doing what he pleases. Of course, discretion often dictates that he do so. But strictly as an executive leader, the president can be as much of a unilateralist as he pleases or as much of a consensus seeker as he deems appropriate. A president serving a fixed term is not brought down by political defeat. He may be bloodied when he ventures into the legislative arena, but he is able to carry on even after legislative defeat, regardless of whether that is a good or bad feature of the system. A wise president, if he chooses to try the legislative presidency route, will seek to discover the parameters around which congressional agreement can be built, but that is not necessarily the only route a president can take. A president, after all, might seek to mobilize political support by vigorously challenging or contesting Congress. And, as earlier noted, a president might seek to find other channels of governance, leading to what Richard Nathan and Terry Moe call, respectively, the administrative presidency and the politicized presidency.[14]

In sum, to the extent that the presidency is a singular executive, this executive can reflect the direction and energy of a single mind—but that is in fact astonishingly rare. Presidents are rarely of an unequivocal mind; cabinet officers weigh in; White House staff members weigh in; and congressional leaders weigh in. But rarely do any of these speak with a single mind. Presidents can override them (at least cabinet officers and staff members) when they are so disposed.

They also can provide clear guidelines when they know their minds. But most of the time, on most matters, they rarely do. Under these circumstances, differences within the executive appear, both substantive and tactical. If presidents are wise, they use procedural mechanisms to work out agreements to lessen the flow of material reaching the president's desk.[15] For the most part, a serious effort to master executive politics requires intrabranch discussion and bargaining, if for no other reason than that a president cannot know his mind about—nor care equally about—everything. There is, of course, the rare case when certainty and persistence combine in the presidency to produce remarkable clarity throughout the executive branch, but that clarity may not make it from one branch (the executive) to another (the legislature or even the judiciary).

Which, then, is stronger? Is it the single executive that Hamilton struggled for or the collective executive that more reflects the cabinet decision making of parliamentary systems? Clearly, the answer is that it depends upon governing style. Consensus is normally a prerequisite to the development of a government position in a parliamentary system, and the more fragile the coalition the more necessary consensual processes will be. The U.S. president need not develop consensus from the executive. Nominally, he is the boss. But if he chooses to pursue public policy goals that require cooperation both within the executive and with the legislative branch, he will be dependent upon reaching agreements. Within the executive branch, the president has the last word, should he care to have any. In engaging the legislative branch, unlike prime ministers on votes of confidence, he will frequently fail. But presidential failure in dealing with the legislature carries with it a resiliency lacking in parliamentary systems. The failure of a legislative proposal does not also endanger the incumbent's presidency, at least in the short run. The accumulation of wounds over time on the legislative front, however, will tend to sap executive energy. A weakened leader whose fixed term prevents his replacement is the basis of criticism of presidential systems. Will the weakened leader produce ineffective government and generate the potential for political crisis?[16]

Certainly, in one sense, the power of any leader is a function of his interdependencies. Some of these are structural: whether he shares power with an autonomous legislature, and whether the system is unitary or federal. Some are political: the extent to which governing political coalitions are fragmented, and the extent to which governing parties are factionalized. Some are social, demographic, and even geographic, recapitulating cleavages in society. Some are normative: the extent to which majoritarianism or consensualism prevails. Complexity along all of these dimensions increases interdependency and thus is likely to inhibit unilateral exercises of power on behalf of the top executive, though that need not mean a diminution in the capacity to generate collective goods. Simplicity along these same dimensions tends to infuse greater discretionary capacity into the top leadership, but this need not expand the capacity of the system to generate collective goods. In brief, the discretionary capacity of top executive leadership is not by itself tantamount to system capability.

MACROCOMPARISONS: PRESIDENTIAL AND PARLIAMENTARY SYSTEMS

Comparisons involving the collective performance of political systems are best restricted to those in similar economic and political circumstances, such as democracies that have equivalent levels of wealth and development. In the methodological jargon of political science, this is known as a "most similar systems" design, the purpose of which is to find variation and its causality in otherwise similar systems.[17] The need to constrain potentially confounding variance is particularly powerful in this context, because institutions pale in predicting performance when set against stark variation in economic capacity. This fact does not denigrate the influence of institutions so much as it places institutions in their proper perspective. Institutions can influence political performance, but they do so mainly when the political constraints, the problems faced by governments, and especially the resources available to them vary only moderately. Even among democratic systems, those that only recently have achieved a democratic political order or whose democratic institutions have been reborn tend to face problems that are more forbidding than those faced by more mature democratic regimes. The more fragile the experience with democratic rule, usually the more taxing the problems a government has to confront, especially with respect to creating a durable basis for democratic institutions.

The paradox, of course, is that, while the choice of institutions is relatively more open for recent democratic systems, the more stable democracies have the greatest experience with how these institutions actually function. My examples, therefore, are drawn from the small universe of countries that are both democratic and affluent. My base is the U.S. system, which is most commonly catalogued as presidential but which Charles Jones in his chapter more aptly describes as a separated system.[18] I use the U.S. system as my base point because I am most familiar with it but also because it is often criticized as being overly congenial to the creation of political and policy deadlock.[19]

Limits to Institutional Explanations

Even when wide differences in affluence and other conditions are controlled, however, the performance of institutions cannot simply be deduced from their structural properties. Why do institutional arrangements not always perform as expected? Broadly speaking, the reasons have to do with changes in political coalitions and circumstances, including the role of political leadership, the nature of political norms, and the openness of national systems to transnational forces.

Political Coalitions. First, political coalitions and circumstances may vary even though institutional arrangements remain stable. Stephen Skowronek argues, for example, that it is best to think of the leadership potential of American presidents as running in cycles, depending upon whether a president is at the beginning phase, the maintenance phase, or the dissolution phase of an existing coalition.[20] The reason for this is not simply that presidents are granted more power or less power but rather that there are moments in the American system when political forces seem to be running in one direction and thus provide strong impetus for a particular agenda. At other times—apparently, most of the time—political energies are less clearly aligned. A similar logic of energy, equilibrium, and exhaustion may apply to parliamentary systems as well, even in systems designed to produce majority governments. The James Callaghan government of the late 1970s in Britain, for example, had to plod along as a minority government when the Labor mandate seemingly had been exhausted. Such has been the case from time to time in other Westminster-style systems, though the existence of minority governments is not by itself an impossible condition for systemic effectiveness. Sometimes, as Feigenbaum,

Samuels, and Weaver show, even a minority government can be capable of producing policy innovation.[21]

Drawing inferences about performance based purely upon the structure of institutions and the behavioral logic extracted therefrom can lead to significant miscalculation. For example, the classic contrast between a parliamentary and presidential system is frequently made between the British parliamentary system with its unadorned majoritarianism and lack of competing institutions (parliamentary sovereignty and a unitary state) and the U.S. separation of powers system. The British system, by concentrating power, should make it easy for governments to reach decisions and thus to ensure their passage into law and their implementation. There is an expectation that what the elected government says it wants it will get. Veto points are not evident in the arrangements of the system. In stark contrast, the U.S. political system diffuses power both horizontally (through the separation of powers) and vertically (through federalism). Moreover, it frequently offers the prospect of divided government. Presumably, the U.S. system should be more or less in constant deadlock. Yet recent studies by both David Mayhew and Charles Jones note otherwise, even under conditions of divided government—conditions that should defy the possibility of policy accomplishment.[22]

What all of this suggests is that, by themselves, institutions shape much but, in the end, determine little. Rather, institutional arrangements have a degree of elasticity through which political actors work. The same institutions may operate differently in different circumstances: in the presence of a perceived crisis and with a galvanizing set of ideas, similar reactions may be produced across institutionally divergent political systems. Mayhew, for example, attributes "waves of lawmaking" in the United States to a context in which similar waves are occurring elsewhere, suggesting cross-national political conditions and a contagion of ideas across national borders.[23] In view of the ease with which policy ideas are now communicated, the international forums in which they are discussed, and the transnational regimes that limit national sovereignty (such as the European Union, the General Agreement on Tariffs and Trade, the NAFTA, and so on), Mayhew's hypothesis may be particularly pertinent. In any event, his hypothesis poses an interesting tension between the international sources of policy and the national institutional means through which policy initiatives are processed.

When contrasts are drawn between the two most divergent institutional patterns among the affluent democracies—the U.S. separation of powers system and the U.K. Westminster majority government model—there is no doubt that with persistent leadership and parliamentary majorities in place there are far fewer obstacles in the Westminster model to radical change, including changes that could evoke the displeasure of a significant bloc of voters. Pierson and Weaver, in this regard, note that the British government under Margaret Thatcher's enthusiastic direction had more success in cutting back pension benefits than the U.S. government had under President Reagan. But they also observe that both systems had more success in pension retrenchment than had the Canadian Westminster-style parliamentary system.[24]

In sum, with substantial parliamentary majorities, a strong leader (Thatcher), who was willing to take risks and to be persistent in her vision, managed risk-bearing change. With more veto points on the horizon and majorities in only one chamber of Congress, another strong-willed and risk-taking but less persistent leader (Reagan) had at least moderate success in stimulating risk-bearing change. The Canadian government under Brian Mulroney was relatively less successful. Clearly, factors other than institutions were at work to account for these outcomes. Institutional arrangements, however, did help Thatcher push changes farther than Reagan could. Institutions are neither unimportant to generating system capability nor determinative. It is best to think of them as providing a range of normal behavior.

Political Norms. In some views, norms are tantamount to institutions.[25] Whether they are or not depends upon how tightly or flexibly one defines institutions. Inasmuch, however, as this chapter deals with institutional structure (presidential vs. parliamentary arrangements), norms are treated exogenously rather than as an indigenous feature of institutions themselves. Consensual norms can cut through structures that might otherwise divide. Richard Fenno, for example, observed decades ago that members of the U.S. House Appropriations Committee operated within a common framework and language despite differences of party.[26] Johan Olsen also notes that the oil that greases the wheels of Norwegian democracy is likely to be found in norms of cooperation and reciprocity rather than in the institutional structures of the Norwegian polity.[27]

The origins of norms and the processes through which they change are obviously terribly important if, in fact, they influence positively or negatively the likelihood of collective action. The Appropriations Committee that Fenno discussed a few decades ago no longer operates under such unifying norms, nor is it even as important as it was then. The extent to which we understand the etiology of norms may allow us to see whether norms have an independent reality or are epiphenomenal—that is, whether they independently affect behavior or are themselves a reflection of more "objective" conditions or payoffs. To the extent that norms are independent, their power and durability are greater—but so, too, is their ineffability. What, after all, can cause them to change? To the extent, alternatively, that norms are merely epiphenomena, the product of other independent conditions, we are able to understand how they change. Yet when viewed as epiphenomena, norms appear to be mere rationalizations of or accommodations to more fundamental and causally determinative objective changes. In the nineteenth century these alternative perspectives on the role of norms were cast in the epistemologies of idealism and materialism. In contemporary social science, we are likely to see these conflicting interpretations in the form of cultural versus rational choice explanations. While the staying power of norms and their ultimate causality remains a matter of continuing debate and research, there is little doubt that norms can influence the possibilities for (or against) collective action above and beyond the structural character of political institutions. Indeed, norms may change even within the same set of political arrangements, thus also changing the culture.[28]

Global Influences. Richard Rose writes of a phenomenon he calls "the post-modern presidency" that circumscribes the latitude of contemporary U.S. presidents.[29] In a context of globalized influences, national sovereignty is inherently limited. And if it is so limited, then the autonomous power of national leaders to control national destinies is brought into question. If these conditions hold, then national institutions cannot fully determine responses.

It is certainly the case that global impacts on policy making are far more immediate than they once were, owing largely to incredible advances in communications technologies. However, it is probably exaggerated to claim that these influences are new. They are just more sudden. International finance and bond markets always have demarcated the role that governments could play, but instant reactions in markets of various sorts profoundly influence the political and economic policy strategies of government and limit the parameters within which those strategies can operate. International interdependencies based on dimly understood and even less controllable forces (currency markets, capital flows, and the like) weaken the power of governments and their leaders even as they magnify the vulnerability of each to their electorates.

Assessing Performance

Evaluating the performance of a political system requires specifying the dimensions of its performance. Much of the prevailing literature focusing on the performance of parliamentary and presidential systems tends to target two related dimensions: governing stability and political violence. Maintaining political stability and social peace are, of course, first-order functions of any polity. On the other hand, important as these functions are, they are not everything. Political violence, in particular, is less related to institutions than to historical animosities and political culture, features that admittedly are hard to measure independent of results. Nevertheless, power-sharing arrangements seem especially appropriate for the alleviation of conflict when majorities and minorities are concrete and identifiable: fixed groups of a racial, ethnic, religious, or linguistic nature rather than partially overlapping and fluid groups that may shift from one coalition to another. When disadvantages accumulate or when fears of being in a powerless minority mount, representation becomes especially important.[30]

Among the affluent democracies, however, political violence is a relatively minor phenomenon and, therefore, relatively less important than it might be for newer democracies coping with intense cleavages in multi-ethnic or multi-national settings, where the transaction rules of liberal democracy have yet to jell. Of course, it is precisely under such formative conditions that institutional architecture might have its deepest effects. The lack of power-sharing arrangements in Croatia and Bosnia, each with significant Serbian minorities, helped provoke the Serbian alliance and the civil wars that have accompanied their independence. By contrast, the power-sharing arrangements of the newly democratized Republic of South Africa seem to have deterred, at least for now, a potentially worse explosion of violence.

Weaver and Rockman identify three generic forms of governing capability.[31] One of these is the *steering* capacity of government; those aspects of government that involve active policy making and new direction, including those that impose political costs for future or broader benefit. These aspects are connected to the goal attainment functions earlier alluded to. Another form of governing capability is the *maintenance* capacity of government: those aspects of government that require standing behind previously generated commitments, even when these are unpopular. A third form of governing capability is the *political* capacity of government: those aspects of government designed to ensure social peace and the representation of a wide variety of interests, including those without voice. The political capacity of government is closely linked to the political maintenance functions described earlier.

Weakness in steering capacity means that governments will have difficulty in, among other things, imposing losses on segments of the politically aware populace, producing innovative policies, and targeting and setting priorities. A government deficient in maintenance capacity will have little stability and predictability, since its word cannot be trusted. A government deficient in political capacity will be unable to represent the variety of interests (tangibly expressed or otherwise) that exists in society and, indeed, may even have difficulty maintaining the always fragile bonds of the social order.

One thing is abundantly clear: no political system optimizes all of these values. Indeed, at least in logic and frequently in reality, there are serious trade-offs. For example, proportional representation systems, especially those with low threshholds for representation, optimize representativeness at the stage of government formation but often raise the cost of policy making. Alternatively, first-past-the-post and even majority systems, by excluding large percentages of votes, are likely to lower the cost of policy making, other things being equal, but do so by raising the price of representation.

Political theorists divide over whether these several governing capabilities are in some sense ordinal—that is, some being more critical than others—or whether they are sufficiently interactive that it is futile to try to order them based on importance. No doubt, theorists would agree that civil order and peace are fundamental to the survival of any governing system. But how can that condition be brought about? Broadly stated, one view, represented by Arend Lijphart, emphasizes procedures of representation and power sharing.[32] Such a view places considerable emphasis upon the political capabilities of governmental institutions and the representation of diversity. A different view suggests that institutional capacities for steering generate effectiveness and social well-being, thus enhancing the political legitimacy of the governing system.[33] This second view can be interpreted as claiming that representational excesses jam up the ability of government to make decisions (assuming, of course, that those decisions are for the better!) and thus create crises of governance.

Ironically, each side of this debate seems to emphasize the virtues of parliamentary forms of government over presidential ones. The proponents of power sharing believe that such arrangements take place mainly under parliamentary systems, whose governments are formed from the results of proportional voting. Equally, the proponents of forceful governmental decision-making capabilities also believe that this is possible only under a parliamentary regime. Each, however, has in mind different types of parliamentary systems. Power-sharing proponents are likely to see such arrangements as being possible mainly under coalition governments, particularly those of oversized coalitions. By the same token, the proponents of governmental decision-making capabilities have in mind majoritarian governments of the Westminster variety. The obvious fact is that, if parliamentary regimes are capable of this level of diversity, they are themselves not a single type of government but represent a wide variety of governing forms. This being the case, it seems likely that the distinction between parliamentary and presidential systems needs to be reformulated. Put in statistical terms, if intraclass variance is greater than interclass variance, the categories in use to differentiate systems are probably inappropriate.

The reality is that the distinction between parliamentary and presidential systems masks a far more vital distinction, namely the capacity to concentrate or diffuse power. The American system is a presidential one that, for the most part, vastly diffuses power but on occasion can amass power when electoral forces and political signals produce a sweeping concordance. The French system, partly by design and partly by precedent, concentrates immense power in the president. Nevertheless, the French Fifth Republic now has had two experiences with cohabitation (divided government), and these experiences certainly limit presidential political authority—mostly by limiting the president's role to foreign affairs. Among the more numerous parliamentary systems, variability is quite wide. Much of this variability stems from electoral rules and systems of representation and the rules and norms affecting the formation of governments.

Broadly speaking, the great divide is between the very few majoritarian-based systems and the occasional outcomes of one-party dominance, on the one hand, and the much more numerous multiparty coalition systems, on the other. Majority governments can result from first-past-the-post or majority electoral rules and tend to concentrate power and simplify accountability while wasting votes, that is, by ignoring the preferences of those who failed to vote for the winning party. Under the leadership of Margaret Thatcher, the Conservative Party in Britain never won more than 43 percent of the electorate's votes even as it constructed huge majorities in Parliament from that plurality. Moreover, Mrs. Thatcher's large parliamentary majorities gave her confidence that she need brook little dissent either from the opposition or from her own cabinet or party.

Coalition structures also vary enormously depending in part upon the particular nature of the electoral and representation systems in place. While coalitions necessarily formalize power sharing, agreements may be more or less fragile depending to some extent on the political distance between the partners or on the crosscutting nature of the political cleavages that the coalition partners represent. Pivotal minorities can play extraordinarily outsized roles. Consider, for example, the role played by the religious parties within a variety of Israeli governments, whose two principal parties divide along secular issues, or consider that of the Free Democrats (FDP) within a variety of German governments. In some instances, oversized coalitions are constructed to lend legitimacy to the government. In others, a dominant party, such as the Liberal Democratic Party (LDP) in Japan was itself so factionalized that it essentially diffused power within the government and required bargaining between the faction leaders.

In sum, we cannot know a great deal about the capacities of governments simply by knowing whether a system is parliamentary or presidential.[34] This, finally, also begs the question of whether we regard such things as the power of central banks as a part of the government or not. Certainly, to the extent that there are powerful and relatively autonomous state institutions designed to be impermeable to the entreaties of elected political leaders (the Bundesbank and the Federal Reserve Board, for example), these institutions pro-

vide potentially competing sources of power to the elected governors while they add consistency and stability to policy—which is, of
course, the explanation for their relative autonomy.

For the most part, coalition governments and separation of
powers systems tend to diffuse power and multiply veto points. Alternatively, majority party systems and single-party dominant systems (the latter being more the product of a favorable political coalition in the electorate than of a specific electoral design) tend to
concentrate power. All of this, needless to say, depends upon a lot of
ceterus being paribus. Granted this condition, systems that concentrate power tend to perform better than systems that diffuse power
at the steering functions of government—and less well than systems
that diffuse power at the political (or representational) functions of
government.[35] These results seem to be basically intuitive.

The effects of concentrating or diffusing governing authority are
subject to a number of caveats. Political conditions enhance or
weaken the capabilities of governments. The temperaments and
convictions of political leaders, similarly, have some influence on
how far the policy envelope can be pushed. And obviously the distribution of preferences in society influences what can be chosen
and how long it can be sustained. This said, however, institutions do
influence possibilities and probabilities. The need, however, is to
look beneath the nominalism that is at the core of the parliamentary-presidential distinction and focus on the connection between
elections and systems of representation and the procedures through
which governments are formed. These, after all, are likely to determine how many hands will be on the government tiller.

It is well, therefore, to remember the following principles: (1) a
change in institutions from presidential to parliamentary or vice
versa does not preordain a resulting concentration or diffusion of
power; (2) institutional structures are important only because of the
decisional characteristics that may accompany them (the multiplication of veto points, for example); (3) institutions determine nothing, but they do raise or lower the probabilities of successful policy
exertions; (4) political conditions everywhere are vital and give
meaning to how wide or how narrow the confidence bands around
the probabilities of successful policy steering will be; and (5) leadership counts. Compare Margaret Thatcher to John Major, for example, or Ronald Reagan to George Bush. Systems count, too: compare
Thatcher to Reagan. But leadership comes in a variety of forms. The

American system begs for cooperative leadership and the arts of bargaining and compromise. Without it, gridlock typically follows except in the aftermath of unusually conclusive elections.

CONCLUSION

Institutions and leadership are both important. One is a given, the other a variable. Institutional transformations, even if they work out as anticipated, will not by themselves solve the most dire problems facing a polity. Institutional change does allow for a shift in incentives. That is, of course, precisely the point. Institutions stretch or shrink the latitude for concerted action by increasing or decreasing the obstacles in its path. Conversely, they also may allow greater or lesser opportunities for the coexistence of different groups within the political community by seeking to prevent exclusive control by any one of them. But institutions do not dictate any given outcome. Moreover, institutions, as we have noticed, are differentially better (and worse) at distinctive sets of problems.

Undoubtedly, though, institutions do tend to affect the prospects of effective leadership. In his classic book, *Presidential Power*, Richard Neustadt concludes that, since Americans are not about to change their system of government, they had better search for savvy politicians who know how to make the separation of powers system work.[36] Unfortunately, it would be wildly optimistic to conclude that we have any truly serviceable criteria to figure out how that leadership could be provided. *Das Führerprinzip*, while a German expression, is ironically, an American obsession. Since we can neither predict leaders who can make the system move (arguably the best at this was a former movie actor) nor will political situations that facilitate steering and goal attainment, we look to institutions. But institutions, structurally defined, are less likely to provide the philosopher's stone to governability than are the norms that compose a political community. In this regard, Johan Olsen notes that in Norway "consultation and anticipated reactions are more important forms of coordination than command."[37] But such a situation, Olsen further speculates, may be dependent upon both slack resources and homogeneity.[38]

This chapter begins with a discussion of two functions of a polity: goal attainment and system maintenance. As a general matter, systems whose institutions diffuse power seem to be more adept at the latter function than those that concentrate power. Likewise, systems whose institutions concentrate power tend to perform better at steering and, thus, goal attainment. But these broad generalizations are remarkably contingent. And in this regard, neither type of system seems to affect the willingness of nations to honor their international commitments.[39] Finally, neither the concentration nor the diffusion of power through structural means necessarily has much to do with the nominal division of governing institutions into parliamentary and presidential systems.

The chapter also distinguishes between the discretionary power of top executive leaders and the governing capability of the political system, particularly in regard to steering. It is easy to equate one phenomenon with the other, but it is not necessarily accurate to do so. It is possible for collective leadership to limit the power of any one leader and to simultaneously generate more collective power. That is, after all, the modern concept of party government with its locus in the cabinet. It is possible also for norms of reciprocity, of give and take, and of problem solving to cut through structural impediments.

While institutions may be the least of the factors that contribute to a well-performing polity, when concerns about performance run deepest, institutional transformations are most likely to be seized upon to solve the problems. But the effects of such transformations are rarely optimal with respect to enhancing the various dimensions of effective governance. They are certainly never direct, only facilitative at best, and interactive with other conditions. Institutions are, however, the manipulable feature in a sea of largely nonmanipulable ones. That being the case, it is essential to make distinctions that have real discriminating power. In spite, therefore, of the sizable investments made in the parliamentary-presidential dichotomy, this distinction ultimately fails to provide much analytic leverage in thinking about the capabilities and performance of governments.

PART II

The Western European Context
Parliamentarism, the Separation of Powers, and French Presidentialism

CHAPTER 3

The Separation of Powers in Parliamentary Systems

B. Guy Peters

The debate over the relative virtues of presidential and parliamentary forms of government has concentrated on the political stability of the form of government, with a presumed higher probability of coups in presidential regimes. This debate has concentrated on the countries of the Third World, with the United States being (to that group of scholars) an anomalous case of a stable presidential system. The evidence about instability of presidential systems is not as clear as some enthusiasts would like us to believe, but even then that may not be the most important question about the impact of the structure of government on the process of governing.[1] This chapter is more concerned with the impact of institutional structure on the governing capacity of any political system than with the effects of those structural variables on political stability. Those two questions are, of course, closely interconnected in reality, but we should not focus our concern with institutional factors entirely on the apocalyptic events that may or may not be related to one institutional format.

Another aspect of the debate about form of government that bears closer examination is the implicit assumption that there is a clear differentiation between these two forms of government and that they are a simple dichotomy. As I point out below, it appears that the distinction is by no means so simple but rather that there is an underlying continuum of structural formats, with variants such as "semipresidentialist" regimes.[2] Even beyond that continuum, systems that may be clearly more presidential or parliamentary in formal, structural terms may in fact behave in somewhat different ways. The structural, constitutional format of the regime may simply be the place to begin to understand the impact of form of government rather than an answer to such a question.

If we are interested in the impacts of institutional structure on governing capacity, then the extent to which the wide variety of extant parliamentary systems diffuse rather than concentrate powers appears much more important than the theoretical differences between two polarized ideal types of presidential and parliamentary systems. This chapter examines the extent to which powers are diffused and separated in parliamentary regimes by focusing on recent trends in European politics, such as coalition governments, greater bureaucratic autonomy, increasingly regular terms of office and predictable election times, the modernizing of electioneering, and other institutional changes.

WHAT IS A PRESIDENTIAL GOVERNMENT?

The fundamental feature of a presidential government is, I argue, some marked division between the branches of government. This is especially important for the division between the legislative and executive branches. If we accept the definition of presidential systems in terms of separation of powers, then some of the literature that argues that parliamentary systems are becoming increasingly presidential may be misguided. One theme in this literature on presidential and parliamentary government is that if the prime minister becomes a strong, personal leader then there is a prima facie case of increasing presidentialism.[3] I argue, however, that a prime minister who is able to aggrandize his or her power at the expense of the cabinet or the parliament may make the system less of a cabinet government but not necessarily more presidential.[4] Thus, Margaret Thatcher's domination of her cabinet did not mean necessarily that she was becoming a president, only that she was becoming less of a traditional primus inter pares within the cabinet.[5] In this case, however, her failure to dominate Parliament and the increasing use of parliamentary devices such as select committees do appear to have separated executive and legislative powers, thereby making the system more presidential in the sense emphasized in this book.[6]

The nature of increased separation of powers in a parliamentary system, therefore, may be that both the executive and the legislature must have countervailing powers. Thus, in many formally parliamentary systems, the executive may have to become relatively *less* powerful in relation to the legislature. The recent history of most parliamentary regimes has been that of domination by the political executive, especially the prime minister, with both their own cabinet and the parliament suffering some diminution in power over public policy. This may be prime ministerial government, but it is not, in the sense of separation of powers, presidential government. There may be a continuing conflict over powers between the two institutions within a presidential system, as there certainly has been in American government, but both must have some basis of power.

Given that there is but a single clear example of a (constitutionally) presidential system among the industrialized democracies, there is no variance, except across time, in the degree of divided government within the United States. On the other hand, there are marked differences among parliamentary systems in the extent to which they conform to the textbook model of fusing executive and legislative powers in a parliamentary democracy. Germany, for example, has tended toward *Kanzlerdemokratie* and has accorded the chancellor somewhat greater powers than would be expected in most parliamentary regimes.[7] Also, one of the presumed features (and advantages) of a parliamentary system is the ability to sweep the rascals out at almost any time and to go to the public with new elections. The Scandinavian countries, however, have a tradition of regular elections, rather like a presidential system, and have chosen to live with whatever problems an election may produce until the next election. This practice often results in minority governments, often composed of only one or a few parties with a very small percentage of the total number of seats.[8] This pattern of governing may diffuse powers considerably and may result in divided government in the extreme, but it still works, given the history and political norms of these systems.

Although minority coalitions are the limiting case, all forms of coalition government tend to diffuse powers within parliamentary systems. Much of the conventional thinking of Americans about parliamentary governments is derived from the experience of the United Kingdom, which is actually one of the few parliamentary systems that has a functioning two-party system.[9] We therefore must be more cognizant of the importance of coalition dynamics in the governing of most Continental European countries.[10] Much as the president and the Congress in the United States must bargain and compromise to make policy, so too must a prime minister bargain to form a coalition and to keep it together.[11]

The need to bargain to form and maintain a coalition means that, in essence, the coalition is a form of divided government. The leader of the coalition is often in the same position as a president attempting to cajole—or to provide side payments for—legislators he or she needs in the coalition to pass legislation. This may not work, and coalitions formed for some purposes may not legislate effectively in other policy areas.[12] Likewise, just as legislators in a presidential system may look to the executive to initiate legislation, so too may parliamentarians look to their prime minister to set the policy agenda. This may be true even if the legislators are not of the same party and not necessarily in agreement with the prime minister. The role may simply require that degree of policy leadership.

All coalition governments are by no means the same, so we need to look at the extent to which there is division among the coalition members, politically and ideologically. This division will provide a rough estimate of the extent to which side payments must be made to assemble the coalition and keep it together. Some coalition governments are themselves deeply divided and must find means of reconciling the multiple and competing demands that exist within the government. One important element of the dynamics of this management of division is the desire of most political groups to participate: losing a policy battle in the short term is better than being excluded from involvement in future decisions. This is the political logic of the inclusion of interest groups in the policy process and also may be applicable to party involvement in forming governing coalitions.[13]

Parliamentary systems also separate and diffuse powers to the extent they have political control over the public bureaucracy and, therefore, to the extent they really have a unified government.[14] As Rose points out in his exposition of the concept of party government, even if the party or parties in office do have a majority within the legislature, they still must govern with and through their public bureaucracy.[15] That institution may well have ideas of its own about what constitutes the correct public policy, and its powers over both advice and implementation may enable it to shape policy. Political leaders therefore have employed a variety of means to gain control over the bureaucracy and make it conform to the political executive's desires, with consequent frequent complaints about the degree of politicization of the bureaucracy.[16] Without such control of the bureaucracy, however, the government in any country will be deeply divided, whether that government is presidential or parliamentary.

It also appears that there is some convergence, or at least attempted convergence, of the two types of government. The United

States, as the only clear example of a presidential regime among the industrialized democracies, appears to recognize some of the difficulties imposed upon it by its divided government and to be searching for some means of moving closer to a parliamentary system of government.[17] Woodrow Wilson often referred to his presidency as being prime ministerial, given that he had a Democratic majority in Congress and that he to some extent operated much as a prime minister. More recently, presidents have sought to operate with something resembling a parliamentary party government model.[18] They have sought to seize control of as many reins of office as they could and to extend their political control throughout the government. Recent experience in institutional politics in the United States, however, has been much more divided and presidential, with presidents (and state governors) often facing legislatures from the other party and with governments having more difficulty reaching decisions.

On the other hand, parliamentary regimes appear to be evolving in some instances toward increased separation and diffusion of powers, perhaps searching for some portion of the central leadership and the apparent stability that such a form of government can provide. Further, the nature of contemporary mass politics, with the enhanced role of the electronic media in campaigns and the associated tendency to focus on the personality and leadership capacity of prospective presidents or prime ministers, may contribute to the further separation of powers in presidential systems. In addition, parliaments have been attempting to recapture what they consider their rightful institutional role in the policy-making process and have been adding staff and other analytic and organizational resources in an attempt to serve as more effective checks on executives.

MEASURING THE DIFFUSION OF POWERS IN PARLIAMENTARY SYSTEMS

The several possible empirical indicators of the growing diffusion of powers in parliamentary systems (if it exists in reality) are premised largely on the above-stated notion that a presidential government will almost inherently be a divided government. Separation of powers is, of course, deemed characteristic of government in the United States, but in practice it is not confined to the United States.[19] In addition, a presidential parliamentary regime should not be taken to mean that governing will be dominated by the prime minister.[20]

A powerful prime minister is important to any growth of presidentialism, but what is needed is a powerful legislature *and* a powerful executive that are, to some degree, in conflict over policy. Governments other than the United States may not have the constitutional structure of a divided government, but they may develop the characteristics of such governments in practice. Any simple, formal distinction between the types of political systems inevitably misses the point of how governmental institutions react and adapt to changing demands and changing circumstances. What we are concerned with here is the extent to which division has been increasing in parliamentary regimes.

Electoral Politics

One dimension in the presidentialization of parliamentary regimes is the conduct of elections and the voting behavior of citizens. It is difficult to isolate presidentialization in electoral politics, but several factors do appear relevant. One is the manner in which campaigns are conducted and covered by the electronic media, and another is the capacity of voters to clearly choose their potential prime minister and, with that, the potential personalization of politics. In these, the question of division is not as relevant as the role of the prime ministerial candidates in the election campaign.

Campaigns and the Media. The tradition in parliamentary regimes has been to focus electoral media attention upon the programs of political parties as a whole, with the prime ministerial candidates being primi inter pares. This characteristic can be examined empirically by looking at the relative degree of such media attention as well as at the campaign strategies of the parties themselves.

The only readily available evidence on electronic media exposure in campaigns in parliamentary regimes is from the United Kingdom and does not appear to support the idea that there has been an increased focus during campaigns on party leaders. Studies of elections from 1970 to 1987 (table 3.1) show that the proportional coverage of party leaders has remained relatively constant or has even declined. In fact, coverage by the electronic media has become more open, with more politicians in both major parties appearing on the air and with the leaders receiving relatively less air time. Even a dominant political figure such as Mrs. Thatcher experienced a decline in the amount of air time she received. It is especially interesting that television coverage in Britain is slightly less focused

Table 3.1 Electronic Media Quotations of Prime Ministerial
Candidates, 1970–1987 Elections, United Kingdom (percent)

Year	Conservative	Labour
1970	58.7	56.7
1974 (February)	70.0	64.2
1974 (October)	48.9	52.3
1979	55.7	63.0
1983	46.2	34.2
1987	44.4	54.1

Source: David Butler and Dennis Kavanagh, eds., The British General Election Series (London: Macmillan, 1971, 1974, 1975, 1980, 1984, 1988).

on the prime ministerial candidates than is radio coverage.

This absence of increased concentration by the electronic media on the prime ministerial candidates is very interesting, especially in light of the American experience. One argument is that the tradition of responsible parties and of a focus on party manifestos may have persisted even in the face of changing campaign opportunities. Further, the earliest observations in these data were done in (for Britain) the early days of television involvement in campaigns, so there was a marked focus on the leaders, with that focus declining to a more "normal" level toward the end of the time period. As electronic media have become more common, they have spread their attention more broadly, with no real shift toward the coverage of the prime ministerial candidates but a vast increase in total coverage. Miller comments that the proportional media attention given to prime ministerial candidates is greater when there is not a campaign than when there is one in progress.[21] Finally, some of the observed absence of shifts in electronic media coverage may be a function of the individuals in such a small "sample," so that the presence of interesting politicians other than the leaders may shift some focus away from potential prime ministers.[22] Likewise, a relatively weak candidate, such as Michael Foot in 1983, may receive substantially less coverage.

Choosing a Prime Minister. Another electoral aspect of the increasingly presidential nature of politics in parliamentary regimes is the ability of voters to choose their executive leader in the election. This means that the coalitions that would produce a prime minister should be identifiable during the electoral campaign. In the few two-party, or quasi two-party, systems in parliamentary regimes, this is not a problem. The voters know who they are voting for as prime minister when they cast their ballots. Even in the "moderate multi-party systems" described by Sartori, these coalitions are readily identifiable, although it is not always clear who the prime minister emerging from each coalition will be.[23] The more interesting changes are expected in the more extreme multiparty systems, in which coalitions are more fragile and less predictable. If these potential coalitions do become more stable, and if they have clearly identified leaders during campaigns, then voters would have an opportunity to select their "president."

Finally, and somewhat in contradiction to the above statement, the often discussed dealignment of party systems in Western Europe may be seen as increasing the possibility of a more presidential form of government.[24] If there is such dealignment, then it may generate a rather negative form of presidentialism and conform perhaps too well to the dire statements about the presidential form of government made by its critics. The logic here is that dealignment and the volatility of voters will free voters for mobilization by new parties and, perhaps especially, by attractive individual candidates. I do not expect European politics to take on the personalistic nature of Latin American presidential systems, or even that of primaries in the United States, but the declining importance of the party may make politics more open to the appeals of "presidentialist" politicians. For example, the leader of New Democracy in Sweden (Ian Wachtmeister) is often cited as utilizing many of these personal appeals and, indeed, as acting as a presidential candidate might be expected to act.[25] The same might be said of Jean-Marie Le Pen in France.

Even without the presence of the new political parties and more personalistic leaders, partisan dealignment and an increase in electoral volatility make a contribution to a presidential style of electoral politics in European democracies. We might not expect a member of the militant Left to become a conservative voter overnight, but there would be room for more mixing in the center of the political spectrum and perhaps the enhanced importance of personal appeals—on the basis of substantive as well as personality, or character, issues—from the candidates.

Institutional Changes

Several other important dimensions of behavioral and institutional change may be associated with increasing separation of powers in parliamentary regimes. To what extent do the political dynamics of parliamentary regimes correspond to those of presidential regimes? For example, do prime ministers tend to survive an entire parliament, and hence are there fewer dissolutions of parliaments? Further, are there changes in the norms by which prime ministers and ministers resign from office, and do those norms point toward executives behaving in a more presidential manner?[26] Similarly, do the same coalitions tend to remain together across several governments so that voters know that they are indeed voting for a clearly defined bloc when they go to the polls? The option that would be more compatible with a notion of parliamentary government might be voting for one party, which then must bargain after the election to form a coalition government.

Governmental Stability. The first factor to consider is the stability of governments, and especially of prime ministers, in the face of their presumed vulnerability to removal. Some argue that one of the principal characteristics of presidents is their invulnerability to removal except at regularly scheduled elections, but parliamentary executives sometimes enjoy increasing protection of the same sort.[27] Such increased longevity may be a function of the electoral factors mentioned above, with more stable relationships among the parties in the governing coalition. Some portion of the change also appears to be a function of changed behavior in parliament as well as changed norms concerning the responsibility of executives to parliaments. Prime ministers, and other ministers, may simply be less willing to resign in the face of policy or political failures but, rather, may choose to hang onto office until a more fortuitous political time for the election.

In European parliamentary systems from the 1960s through the 1980s, there was a declining number of changes in ministers in the top three positions (prime minister, minister of finance, and foreign minister; see table 3.2). This tendency is especially notable given that the 1980s were a period of economic uncertainty in many countries. Also, the 1980s were a period of great electoral volatility.[28] The number of parties represented in parliament tended to increase during the 1970s, and most continued to gain representation into the

Table 3.2 Number of Prime Ministers and Three Principal Ministers, Thirteen European Countries, 1960s–1980s

Country and Decade	Number of Prime Ministers	Number of Top Three Ministers[a]	Country and Decade	Number of Prime Ministers	Number of Top Three Ministers[a]
Austria			Italy		
1960s	3	11	1960s	7	23
1970s	1	12	1970s	7	24
1980s	3	12	1980s	9	23
Belgium			Luxembourg		
1960s	5	14	1960s	1	5
1970s	4	14	1970s	2	9
1980s	3	13	1980s	2	7
Denmark			Netherlands		
1960s	3	14	1960s	5	11
1970s	5	18	1970s	4	12
1980s	2	9	1980s	2	10
Finland			Norway		
1960s	7	18	1960s	4	13
1970s	9	32	1970s	5	15
1980s	4	16	1980s	5	9
France			Sweden		
1960s	4	12	1960s	2	5
1970s	4	15	1970s	3	14
1980s	5	15	1980s	3	10
Germany			United Kingdom		
1960s	4	13	1960s	3	15
1970s	2	9	1970s	5	16
1980s	2	7	1980s	2	10
Ireland					
1960s	2	7			
1970s	4	13			
1980s	5	19			

Source: Chris Cook and John Paxton, *European Political Facts, 1918–1990* (New York: Facts on File, 1992).

a. Prime minister, minister of finance or equivalent, and foreign minister or equivalent.

1980s (table 3.3). Many of these parties represented either new interests or ideologies that were difficult to assimilate into conventional politics.

Executive Advisory Capacity. Another institutional indicator of separation of powers in European systems is the development of strong personal advisory and policy capacities for prime ministers,

Table 3.3 Parties Represented in Parliament, Thirteen European Countries, 1950s–1980s

Country	1950s	1960s	1970s	1980s
Austria	4	4	3	3.67
Belgium	5.33	5.67	9.25	10
Denmark	5.25	6	9.2	8.4
Finland	6	7.5	7.75	8
France	8	6.67	6	5.33
Germany	3	3	3	3.67
Ireland	5	3.67	3	4.4
Italy	7.5	6	6.67	8.5
Netherlands	7	9	8	5
Norway	6.5	7	8	7.33
Sweden	5	5	4.75	6.5
Switzerland	8	7	9	9.5
United Kingdom (excluding Northern Ireland)	3	3[a]	4.75	6

Source. Cook 1992.

a. The Scottish National Party did win one by-election in 1967, but it is not included in these data.

somewhat like the Executive Office of the President in the United States. Some prime ministers have had such staffs for some time, for example the Bundeskanzlersamt in Germany, while for others such staffing is a more recent development.[29] The supporting apparatus for the Italian prime minister, for example, dates only from the mid-1980s but has since developed into a sizable staff.[30]

While professional staffs and personal offices are important for a prime minister, the ability to recruit a variety of ministers is also important. Advocates of presidential government argue that bringing in cabinet ministers from outside government threatens the legitimacy and even the quality of decision making.[31] I argue quite the contrary, expecting governments that recruit experts from outside parliament to govern better, everything else being equal. J. Blondel, for example, points to the differences between Austrian and Belgian economic management, arguing that Austria's use of outside experts has improved its decisions.[32] Further, the French practice of making ministers be outsiders, regardless of whether they started in parliament, is thought to have enhanced political stability.

Evidence on recruitment of ministers from outside parliament is spotty, but the practice appears to have increased. The evidence is

Table 3.4 Staff Support for Parliaments, Seventeen European Countries

Country	Personal Staff[a]	Committee Staff	Legislative Reference and Research
Austria	From party	No	Very limited
Belgium	No	Yes	Yes
Denmark	From party	Yes	Yes
Finland	Yes, also from party	Limited	Very limited
France	Yes	Yes	Yes
West Germany	Yes	Yes	Yes
Greece	Limited	Limited	No
Ireland	Limited	Limited	Very limited
Italy	From party	Yes	Yes
Luxembourg	Yes	Very limited	No
Netherlands	Limited; also from party	Yes	Very limited
Norway	From party	Yes	Limited
Portugal	No	Very limited	Very limited
Spain	From party	Yes	Very limited
Sweden	Limited	Yes	Yes
Switzerland	Limited	Yes	Limited
United Kingdom	Limited	Very limited	Limited

Source: Inter-Parliamentary Union, *Parliaments of the World* (New York: Facts on File, 1986).
　a. Paid for by government.

difficult to assess, given that an expert from the civil service may be moved into a safe electoral district or onto a safe place on an electoral list in order to secure his or her expertise for government. The career pattern is really that of a specialist, but the route of entry into government appears to be the party and the parliament.[33]

Parliamentary Staffs and Structures. Parliaments, like prime ministers, may also attempt to become more capable actors in policy making.[34] If indeed these legislative bodies are to become more presidential, then they must be able to act in a more autonomous manner. There are substantial variations among countries in the staff and analytic capacities of their legislatures and in the structures of these bodies that may contribute to being an effective counter to executive domination (table 3.4). Some parliaments, such as the Riksdag in Sweden, have functional committees with sufficient staffs to monitor executive performance and to develop some of its own legislation.[35] Others, such as the British Parliament,

Table 3.5 Legislative Activity, Thirteen European Countries, 1975 and 1985

Country	Government Bills as Percent of Totals		Government Success Rate	
	1975	1985	1975	1985
Austria	78	65	87	96
Belgium	63	23	96	137[a]
Denmark	88	69	89	84
Finland	7	48	93	102[a]
France	11	22	68	82
Germany	72	74	69	101[a]
Ireland	98	90	9	9
Italy	NA	29		51
Netherlands	98	98	89	85
Norway	98	90	98	99
Spain	92	58	91	81
Sweden	15	99		
United Kingdom	45	92	93	92

Source: Inter-Parliamentary Union, *Parliaments of the World* (New York: Facts on File, (1976, 1985).

a. Percentages total over 100 because of additional bills submitted by House of Lords.

provide their members with little or no staff and have a relatively weak system of committees to monitor executive performance.[36] Of course, the important question is perhaps not so much whether one legislature is more effective than another as it is whether there have been shifts in all of their capacities relative to the executive and (somewhat ironically) whether the parliament really can be an effective policy-making body in a nominal parliamentary government.

Legislative Activity. Following from the above, we can also inquire whether parliaments are active in introducing their own legislation or whether they depend upon the executive for the initiation of new policies. The involvement of executives in proposing legislation varies rather significantly across countries (table 3.5), with the parliaments of the United Kingdom and the Netherlands depending almost entirely upon the executive for legislation, while the Bundestag in Germany and the parliament in Belgium initiate a large proportion of the legislation.[37] This is potentially a deceptive measure, given that some of the legislation initiated by members of parliament or by parliamentary committees may be of relatively minor consequence, dealing with the affairs of individual constituents—the *leggine* passed by the Italian parliament—but these data do provide some measure of the activity of a legislative body.

On average, European legislatures have become more active in introducing legislation, and the success rate of such legislation being accepted by the prime minister increased significantly by the 1980s. Such success may be a function of governments choosing their legislative battles more carefully or of the increased power of stable governments such as those of Thatcher in Britain, Lubbers in the Netherlands, and Kohl in Germany. Or it may be that prime ministers want to assert their power vis-à-vis their colleagues in the cabinet. Parliamentary autonomy may mean that the parliament perceives a need to provide an alternative policy voice and to make the political system truly parliamentary. Ironically, of course, in so doing it may actually make the system appear more presidential, according to the criteria established above: that is, divided government.

The Prime Minister in Parliament

The degree of involvement of the prime minister in the business of the parliament is another measure of presidentialism. To the extent that the prime minister is the dominant actor, then the system may be said to be prime ministerial, if not presidential. While such a measure may not indicate divided government per se, it may indicate such a tendency. This is especially true if the centrality of the prime minister is symmetrical—for example, if the prime minister dominates debate at the same time that the legislative body attempts to control that executive.

Again, the evidence is easiest to come by for the United Kingdom and again indicates that there is not much movement in that direction. Jones's and others' work on the role of the prime minister demonstrates a strong secular decline in the role of the prime minister in Commons.[38] Not only has the relative amount of time spent by the prime minister in making parliamentary speeches declined, but the relative amount of time the prime minister spends answering parliamentary questions has also declined—although the latter measure has declined less. At least in the United Kingdom, the parliamentary role of the prime minister has diminished. If the prime minister is less central in parliament, then he or she may be more of an executive, and therefore, some separation of powers may actually have developed.

PRESIDENTIAL AND PARLIAMENTARY SYSTEMS: MAKING THE CHOICE

The discussion concerning presidential and parliamentary systems contains a strong element of institutional design, largely oriented toward questions of political stability in the Third World. Although the evidence of the relationship of form of government to stability is not as clear as some scholars would have us believe, there are a number of political and policy questions that also should be considered when choosing among alternative forms of government. The Swiss government, for example, is considering a wide range of alternative forms of government, including a presidential system, and has developed criteria that could be used to judge those alternatives.[39] There as yet has been no choice to move from the status quo, but Switzerland's possible membership in the European Community and, even without membership, its having to cope with an increasingly integrated EC as a neighbor, generated interest in structural change. The continued instability of Italian governments is also forcing a reconsideration of its constitution, with a national commission charged to investigate all possibilities, not the least of which is adopting a presidential form of government. This official consideration is paralleled by a political movement for a referendum on form of government, again with a strong advocacy of a presidential system.

Why should a government select one form of government rather than another? There does not appear to be much to choose among them in matters of political stability, with exogenous factors appearing more important than structural factors in predicting the survival of a regime. Further, form of government may say more about the manner in which democratic governments fail than about whether they fail. In one, leaders may be more tempted to extend their powers, while in the other there may be more intrusion by external institutional forces.[40]

Another reason for the selection of one or the other system is the manner in which policy is made within each model. In this case, everything else being equal, separation of powers in a presidential government has an advantage at the agenda-setting and policy formulation stages of the policy process but perhaps some deficiencies at the legitimation and implementation stages. At the front end of the policy process, the virtue of the presidential system is that it is a redundant system, with multiple points of access for affected interests in the society and multiple sources of expert information that can guide in the formulation of policy.[41] It has become a truism by now that agenda setting is the crucial stage of policy making and that multiple actors, each with a (potential) political interest in raising new issues, tend to broaden the agenda.[42]

In addition to the posited advantages at the agenda-setting stage, the separation of powers in a presidential system is likely to enjoy some advantages at the policy formulation stage as well. A policy-making system that forecloses its programmatic options too readily and that restricts the type of information it uses to sources compatible with the views of the central executive risks errors in decision making greater than the inevitable ones that any government will make. Of course, even within a parliamentary system there will be some countervailing sources of information and power, usually within the public bureaucracy.[43] Those information sources, however, may not have the external support and public exposure they may need to be effective in the struggle over policy. A presidential system is unlikely to be a perfect information-processing system or a truly "discursive democracy," but it is perhaps better than the average parliamentary system in those regards.

Although a presidential system may have some advantages at the initial stages of policy making and some disadvantages at later stages, the divided government argument (and its associated phrases such as *gridlock* and *deadlock*) is explicit in assuming that a presidential system will have difficulty making policy choices and legitimating the decisions of government. Likewise, it is likely that the presence of two masters will divide the loyalties of the civil service and make policy implementation more problematic. The "micromanagement" of policy by congressional committees in the United States is a clear example of the difficulties of presidential government.[44]

CONCLUSION

This essay presents evidence concerning the possible increasing presidential nature of politics in European parliamentary democracies. As is often the case in political science, the evidence marshaled by these indicators is mixed. Some of this may be a function of the ambiguity of the concept of presidentialism, while some of it may be a function of the ambiguous changes occurring in the real world. Some changes have been in the direction of presidentialism, defined here as an increasingly meaningful separation of powers, other changes have not. Further, European governments are not moving together along the continuum of government type, so one might be able to make a case for either increasing or decreasing presidentialism if the right cases were selected.

The most important point to emerge from this analysis may be that, no matter where you are, the alternative political system may appear superior. To the United States, with a divided government, the (presumed) decisiveness of a parliamentary system and its seemingly greater control may be attractive. On the other hand, citizens of parliamentary systems may idealize the central focus and leadership apparently characteristic of the presidential form of government. Both sides appear to be searching for enhancing the capacity of democratic systems to provide that scarce commodity, governance.[45] The way governance can best be created is seen as varying and as absent from the government of the status quo.

It may also be that form of government is largely epiphenomenal, with the real success of governments being more a function of wealth and other exogenous factors rather than form. Poorer countries may have unstable governments whether presidential or parliamentary, and most countries appear to accumulate substantial budget deficits no matter what form of government they choose.

CHAPTER 4

Institutions, Political Poker, and Regime Evolution in France

John T. S. Keeler and Martin A. Schain

In recent years, experts on the French Fifth Republic have been flown to capitals around the globe to advise the constitutional draftsmen of fledgling democracies on the nuances of France's democratic institutions. From a comparative and historical perspective, this emergence of the French constitution as a model deemed worthy of emulation abroad is truly remarkable. After all, the French have been fighting constitutional battles for more than two centuries and have experienced so many regime changes that, in the words of an old joke, they have long tended to assume that the constitution of the day could be found only in shops featuring periodical literature. The introduction to a collection of the French constitutions produced from 1789 to 1969 proclaims that "France is without doubt the country which has known the greatest number of constitutions: fifteen constitutions in 180 years, or on average one every twelve years!"[1]

In line with tradition, the French continue to debate the merits of the Fifth Republic regime, but this original "hybrid" system has now endured for nearly four decades and has indisputably become one of France's leading cultural exports. "French semi-presidentialism," as Arend Lijphart notes, "has become an important model not only in formerly French-ruled countries or for a close neighbor like Portugal, but also for distant countries like Sri Lanka and Argentina."[2] Moreover, France's distinctive mixed presidential-parliamentary system has become the most influential Western model guiding the crafting of new democracies in Eastern Europe, from Poland to Ukraine (see Bunce, chap. 7, this volume). As an *Economist* article of June 1993 notes, the Russians are also now "following the French," in that Yeltsin's draft constitution is largely modeled on that of the Fifth Republic.[3]

How can one explain the current widespread appeal of the Fifth Republic's democratic model? This system was originally viewed as highly problematic by political observers within France, and political scientists such as Juan Linz argue that it is a risk-prone model poorly suited to many countries.[4] Linz's analysis stresses that the semipresidential model combines the most prominent "perils of presidentialism" with an additional unique drawback. The perils include the extremely high stakes and polarizing effects of zero-sum presidential elections, the danger that a president endowed with a direct mandate from the people might be inclined to interpret his powers in an expansive or even authoritarian manner (what the French would call the Bonapartist temptation), and the potential for conflict flowing from dual democratic legitimacy in a system with separate elections for the presidency and the legislature. The drawback is the very real possibility for conflict between the president and prime minister in a dual executive system that accords substantial and somewhat overlapping powers to each office.

Valid though such concerns may be, there clearly is another, more attractive, side to the Fifth Republic's institutional coin. As Linz himself notes, following Bartolini, the French model seems to appeal to newly independent countries in large part because they view a president elected by universal suffrage as providing an effective unifying "symbol of the new nation."[5] The American-style "pure" presidential system could fill this need too, of course, but it seems to be almost universally rejected because of the rigidity and potential for executive-legislative deadlock inherent in its extreme separation of powers. In contrast, the French model offers greater flexibility and executive authority, for it features a president empowered to appoint a prime minister capable of directing legislative affairs and to resolve executive-legislative conflicts by dissolving parliament or calling a referendum. For countries facing the extraordinary challenges of regime transition and economic restructuring, these aspects of the French system are especially compelling.[6]

As Linz, Stepan, and Suleiman stress, however, it is possible to argue that the image of efficacy currently enjoyed by the Fifth Republic constitution is rather spurious. Prospective importers should be warned, critics claim, that the Fifth Republic model's enticing aura derives less from the constitution per se than from the impressive record of stability and governability that France has enjoyed since that constitution was introduced through the initiative of Charles de Gaulle.[7]

While it is true that the Fifth Republic system entails some potential dangers and that its adoption hardly guarantees results similar to those achieved in France, these caveats require substantial elaboration if they are to provide effective guidance for institutional importers. The central purpose of this chapter, therefore, is to explain how the Fifth Republic system has evolved since 1958 and to clarify how institutional and noninstitutional factors combined to shape that process.

Our central arguments are the following. First, there is no single "semipresidential model" of the Fifth Republic. It is also misleading, albeit closer to the truth, to represent the Fifth Republic's regime as a single structure able to accommodate merely two phases, that is "parliamentary and presidential phases depending on whether or not the president's party has a majority in the legislature."[8] The regime has evolved substantially over time, with changes in both its formal institutions and its political dynamics (including but not restricted to the nature of the legislative majority), producing a minimum of five distinctive models of government through the early 1990s. Importers of the French constitution should carefully consider which model they prefer and how they might secure it rather than one of its alternatives.

Second, the Fifth Republic case illustrates vividly not only the extent of, but also the limits to, the importance of formal institutions. All reputable comparativists note such limits, of course, but it seems particularly important to stress this point in the case of a regime whose institutions are now being widely copied abroad in part because they are viewed as having made an unusually profound and positive impact at home. In an essay that generally attributes far greater force to "cultural factors" than to institutional variables, for example, Seymour Martin Lipset cites the Fifth Republic as the only case that provides clear evidence of political institutions "enhancing the possibilities for stable democratic government."[9] We agree with this assessment in general terms.[10] However, we argue that the case needs to be nuanced by acknowledging that some of the most prominent Fifth Republic institutions, especially the presidency, acquired their transformative capacity largely through the manner in which they were shaped by what can loosely be termed cultural factors. An examination of the evolving models of French government shows the significance of key institutions, to be sure, but it also underscores the extraordinary importance of factors such as individuals (especially Charles de Gaulle), unwritten rules, and political dynamics in determining the meaning of French institutions.

Third, even specialists on countries that have not attempted to emulate the French system should find illuminating the ways in which Fifth Republic actors have shaped the development of the regime by playing what might be termed recurrent games of political poker.[11] The history of the Fifth Republic is rich with textbook examples of how institutionally defined rules can be bent, broken, or ignored (or of course, formally amended) to the advantage of particular political actors. Far from fully determining the behavior of those playing the game, constitutional rules have sometimes constrained them little more than the way that holding a particular hand of cards may be viewed as shaping the behavior of poker players. Understanding the Fifth Republic's development thus requires knowing not only what constitutional hand has been dealt to each player but also what strategies the players have used in playing their cards—and whether certain players benefited from the willingness of others to aid them by misplaying their own cards (or agreeing to change the formal rules in the midst of the game). Those concerned with the fate of the emerging democracies in Eastern Europe may find it reassuring, if also rather sobering, to learn that some of the more controversial poker plays in the development of the Fifth Republic are viewed in retrospect to have produced essentially positive institutional effects.

Our analysis of the Fifth Republic's evolution is organized in terms of the five governmental models that have appeared since 1958: (1) the rationalized parliamentary model (1958); (2) the liberal dictatorship model (1958–62); (3) the hyperpresidential, or normal, model (1962–74, 1981–86); (4) the tempered presidential, or seminormal, model (1974–81, 1988–93); and (5) the premier-presidential, or cohabitation, model (1986–88, 1993–). In the conclusion we draw some of the major lessons of the Fifth Republic experience for comparative institutionalists and for importers of a French model.

THE RATIONALIZED PARLIAMENTARY MODEL, 1958

Comparativists assessing the new constitutions emerging across the former Soviet bloc would be well advised to reflect on the fate of the constitution of 1958 and the original Fifth Republic model that it embodied.[12] This document never really had a chance to operate in the fashion most observers anticipated at the time it was written. It seemed clearly to call for a new type of parliamentary model rather than the semipresidentialism with which it has become associated.[13] Ephemeral though the importance of this original model was, it must be examined if the regime's later development is to be fully understood.

The process of drafting the Fifth Republic's constitution began in May 1958, when the Algerian crisis compelled the leaders of the Fourth Republic to negotiate the terms of a return to power by Charles de Gaulle, and ended with the formal presentation of the text on September 4 and its approval in a referendum on September 28. Michel Debré, appointed by de Gaulle to supervise the drafting process, categorized the purpose of the constitutional reform venture as being not to create a "presidential system" but rather to "renovate the parliamentary regime."[14]

This was to be a "rationalized parliamentary system" in the sense that the balance of power between the parliament and the government (the cabinet), weighted heavily in favor of the former in the Fourth Republic, would be restructured to strengthen the latter. For example, it was made more difficult for parliament to oust a government with a censure vote, the powers of parliamentary committees were curtailed, and the government was granted more control over the parliamentary agenda and greater power to legislate through decree. In addition, the government was granted a variety of "constitutional weapons" that could be selectively employed to limit parliament's ability to shape legislation or delay the legislative process: Article 44.3 enabled the government to reduce parliament's ability to amend a particular bill; Article 45.4 allowed the government to circumvent the senate when that body proved uncooperative; and Article 49.3 allowed the government to declare a bill an issue of confidence and thus secure its passage if the National Assembly proved incapable of passing a motion of censure.[15]

Under normal conditions, it appeared, most of the executive powers in the new regime would be exercised by the government under the direction of a prime minister appointed by the president but responsible only to parliament. According to Article 20, the government "shall determine and direct the policy of the nation," and Article 21 stated that "the prime minister shall direct the operation of the government. He shall be responsible for national defense. He shall ensure the execution of the laws. . . . He shall have regulatory powers and shall make appointments to civil and military posts."[16] Moreover, the text clearly stipulated that the government (or prime minister) would directly wield, without the necessity of presidential approval, the "constitutional weapons" designed to ensure executive primacy over the "rationalized" parliament in the policy-making process.

The president was granted certain powers not provided to the chief of state under the Fourth Republic, for example, the right to dissolve the National Assembly ("after consultation with the prime minister"), the right to call a referendum (but only "on the proposal of the government"), and the right to invoke emergency powers ("after consultation with the prime minister" and others; Article 16) under rare conditions.[17] In general, however, the role of the president was seemingly to be that of the guardian of the constitution, "who by his arbitration" in exceptional circumstances was to "ensure the regular functioning of the public authorities" (Article 5).[18] An important implicit limit on presidential authority was the stipulation that the chief of state was to be elected by a large college of local notables (there were 81,764 electors in the indirect election of December 21, 1958).[19] As Debré noted, this mechanism would likely produce a political outcome very different from that related to direct election, for a "president who is elected by universal suffrage is a political leader bound by the daily work of government and command."[20]

Given the prospect that de Gaulle would serve as the regime's first president, and the concern on the part of the many proparliamentary members of the Consultative Constitutional Commission (CCC) that the general might seek to interpret expansively the powers of the chief of state, the CCC compelled de Gaulle to address publicly what everyone saw as a crucial issue: relations between the president and the prime minister. When asked directly whether he thought the president could dismiss, as well as appoint, the prime minister, de Gaulle responded: "No! For, if it were like that, he could not govern effectively. The prime minister is responsible to parliament and not to the chief of state in what concerns policy matters. . . . The president of the Republic, I insist on this, is essentially an arbiter who has the mission of ensuring, no matter what happens, the functioning of the branches of government." This statement and similar ones by other Gaullists largely "appeased the fears" of those who feared "the spirit of the presidential regime"

lurked in what looked like an essentially parliamentary text.[21] The final version of the crucial article (Article 8) on president-premier relations was worded as follows: "The president of the Republic shall
appoint the prime minister. He shall terminate the functions of the
prime minister when the latter presents the resignation of the government." Despite persistent concerns that de Gaulle as president
might well extract resignations from prime ministers, most CCC
members were convinced that the Fifth Republic was "parliamentary in text" and would certainly be so in practice after de Gaulle
had passed from the scene.[22]

As William Andrews sums up his review of the deliberations of
the CCC: "The original 1958 constitution established a parliamentary regime. This was the result of the drafting process, the intent of
the framers, and the clear meaning of the key provisions of its
text."[23] Right though Andrews is in most respects, a more precise
wording would have been "the *publicly proclaimed* intent of the
framers," for as he notes, de Gaulle would later acknowledge that he
was less than entirely honest in his exchanges with the CCC. In his
memoirs, he notes that he had envisioned the president's role as "all-
powerful," in contrast to the wishes of "the adherents of the outgo-
ing regime." And as he stated in a 1966 interview, he had long
thought "that the president of the Republic must govern, but no one
wanted that!" in 1958. In the political climate of the CCC deliberations, he continued, "I could not say so. Then, gradually, we got
there, with precautions, with detours, but, in the end, without much
difficulty."[24]

THE LIBERAL DICTATORSHIP MODEL, 1958–1962

Getting there, as de Gaulle put it, was greatly facilitated by two
factors. First, the context of crisis over Algeria provided de Gaulle
with many opportunities to wield extraordinary presidential power
and thus, to the extent his actions proved successful, to manifest the
potential utility of institutionalizing a stronger presidency than envisioned in the constitution of 1958. Second, many of de Gaulle's institutional maneuvers were possible only because of his unique
charismatic authority. His heroism and prescience as leader of the
Resistance during World War II and his restoration of the Republic
in 1944–46, followed by twelve years in retirement that allowed his
legend to grow, had given him a "miracle man" image in the eyes of

most French citizens.[25] A poll showed that 80 percent of the public supported his return to power in June 1958 and that most of these supporters expected him to resolve not only the Algerian crisis but also the country's other pressing problems.[26] Almost 77 percent of the more than eighty thousand electors voting for president in December 1958 supported him.[27] Looking back from the perspective of 1990, an opinion poll showed that most French considered him (mainly because of his Resistance role) the greatest Frenchman in history, ahead of Charlemagne and Napoleon I.[28]

The combination of extreme crisis and faith in (or resignation to the indispensability of) de Gaulle produced an era of "liberal dictatorship" that stretched from the end of the Fourth Republic through the first months of the Fifth Republic.[29] When de Gaulle was invested as the last premier of the old regime, an enabling act accorded him "full powers" for six months to take "the legislative measures necessary for the recovery of the nation." The powers thus conferred were essentially extended through February 4, 1959, by Article 92 of the new Fifth Republic constitution. While the rationale for granting such powers was the need for executive discretion to cope with Algeria, the powers were used so extensively that they "touched virtually every area of public policy." Scores of important "bills"—which would have been passed only in slow and diluted fashion, if at all, under the old regime—were pushed through rapidly as ordinances.[30] It has been argued that "no legislative program has ever transformed French life so much so fast" as the 378 ordinances issued by de Gaulle's government between June 1958 and February 1959.[31]

While the formal period of liberal dictatorship ended in early 1959, for the next few years de Gaulle continued to define his presidential role in expansive terms and to wield power in a fashion that generated constitutional controversy. At the Gaullist party conference in November 1959 an associate of the president elevated into doctrine de Gaulle's apparent assumption that foreign policy, defense, and Algerian affairs constituted a "reserved domain" of exclusive presidential power.[32] An outraged opposition spokesman, François Mitterrand, condemned this assertion as "the first legal coup d'etat of the general" and also criticized the many political officials who seemed content to accept such audacity as long as de Gaulle was moving toward a resolution of the Algerian problem.[33]

Two more "legal coups" followed in 1960. In March, de Gaulle triggered a heated legal confrontation with parliament when he refused to convene a special legislative session despite the fact that a majority in the National Assembly, in line with Article 29 of the constitution, voted for one. Not only opposition leaders but many jurists questioned de Gaulle's claim that Article 30 (requiring a presidential decree to open special sessions) genuinely conferred discretionary power on the chief of state in the wake of an Assembly vote.[34] The next alleged "legal coup" took place in June when de Gaulle engineered a constitutional amendment allowing member states of the French Community to become independent while retaining their Community membership. While many opposition leaders supported the political thrust of the move, the amendment procedure employed was contested even by the Conseil d'Etat and was deemed unconstitutional by most legal specialists.[35]

De Gaulle tested the limits of his constitutional powers again in 1961 when, in response to an attempt by four generals to seize power in Algeria, he invoked the emergency powers of Article 16. While some commentators contested the need for reliance on Article 16 in this instance, many more questioned the legitimacy of de Gaulle's retention of full powers under the emergency clause for five months after the immediate threat to the regime had ceased.[36] It was only after the opposition threatened a censure motion, and stormed out of parliament in protest when their motion was ruled out of order, that de Gaulle "quickly decided to appease parliamentary frustrations by abandoning his emergency powers."[37]

For the future of the regime, de Gaulle's most significant moves as constitutional poker player were those of 1962. In April, just after the referendum confirming the Evian Accords on Algeria, de Gaulle ignored the letter of Article 8 and dismissed—or forced the resignation of—his prime minister, Michel Debré. There was no doubt about Debré's desire to retain the office, but he had manifested "abnegation without limits" in twenty years of service to de Gaulle, so there was also no doubt about his complying if asked to "resign."[38] This step, along with the nature of the new premier (Georges Pompidou, a close associate of de Gaulle who was not a member of parliament and had never held any elective office), signaled that de Gaulle intended in the post-Algerian era not to loosen, but rather to consolidate, presidential dominance. Although prominent opposition leaders condemned de Gaulle for forgetting the pledge he had given when Article 8 was being debated in 1958, they were unable to stop a power play that became an important precedent in later years.[39]

The single most important and controversial step taken by de Gaulle in reshaping the original 1958 constitution was announced in September 1962. In the wake of an assassination attempt that nearly succeeded, de Gaulle seized the moment to propose a constitutional amendment to institute the direct election of the president; only such a reform, he argued, would give future presidents lacking his unique personal prestige the means to govern effectively. Such a change would clearly dash the hopes of most party leaders for a reversion to a "proper" parliamentary regime in the post–de Gaulle era, and that was reason enough for them to oppose it. But de Gaulle made his proposal doubly objectionable by asserting that he intended to use what was almost universally viewed as an unconstitutional amendment procedure: a simple referendum under Article 11 (which clearly seemed intended only for more modest changes) rather than a referendum following approval by both houses of parliament, as required by the article (89) entitled "Amendment."

The greatest constitutional crisis of the Fifth Republic ensued. One member of de Gaulle's cabinet resigned in protest, others objected privately, both the Conseil d'Etat and the Constitutional Council advised against the move, and the National Assembly censured the government. De Gaulle, far from being swayed by such opposition, claimed that "to deny the people a right which belonged to them, seemed to me . . . high-handed in that I myself was the principal inspirer of the new institutions, and it really was the height of effrontery to challenge me on what they meant."[40] The referendum went ahead, and with de Gaulle pledging to resign if the outcome proved negative or merely weakly positive, 62 percent of the voters approved the amendment. Before the reform was promulgated, the president of the Senate used his power to send it back on appeal to the Constitutional Council. In one of the most hotly debated rulings that body has ever delivered, the council simply stated that on technical grounds it was not empowered to overturn the law. "The Constitutional Council has just committed suicide," charged Senate President Gaston Monnerville, while Mitterrand opined that the council had proven itself "the derisory cap of a derisory democracy."[41]

In all of these steps from 1959 to 1962, the key to de Gaulle's success was his recognition that other relevant institutional actors in the regime would allow him, reluctantly or gladly, to overplay his hand. The opposition in the Assembly may have condemned him for abuse of power, but until the end of the Algerian War in 1962 they grudgingly tolerated his moves largely because they supported the general direction of his colonial policy. As Oliver Duhamel notes, for example, whereas 295 opposition deputies voted for the special session in the March 1960 confrontation with the general, only 122 of them were willing to go so far as to censure his prime minister in retaliation.[42] Another factor that led opposition deputies to underplay their hands was their (mistaken) belief that de Gaulle's regime would represent "just a parenthesis in French history," as the Fifth Republic would revert to its "proper" institutional balance (or even be formally changed) once the crisis had ended and de Gaulle was gone from the scene.[43]

De Gaulle's prime minister accepted the general's (mis)reading of Article 8 out of political loyalty. It is intriguing to speculate on what might have happened if de Gaulle's status had been a bit less exalted and Debré's proclivity to self-abnegation a bit less firm. Clearly, the result could have been a crisis similar to that recently triggered in Russia by Boris Yeltsin's difficult dealings with once-loyal backers in competing positions of power. De Gaulle's extraordinary authority seems all the more remarkable when one considers the experience of Poland's charismatic Lech Walesa, who "made" Tadeusz Mazowiecki prime minister and then could only "watch as a person he had treated as a tool started to outgrow him politically."[44]

The general public ignored de Gaulle's violation of the constitutional amendment procedure in 1962, despite the strong objections of most of their putative representatives in parliament, because they supported the institution of direct election to the presidency and were reluctant to jettison the general.[45] The Constitutional Council, faced with what seemed to be a clear violation of the constitution, refused to overturn de Gaulle's amendment on procedural grounds, seemingly out of deference to both de Gaulle (who had appointed three of its nine members and heavily influenced the appointment of three others formally chosen by the Assembly president) and the "sovereign" citizenry. Had any of these actors been more inclined to confront the Fifth Republic's first president, the institutions of the new regime would have been infused with a very different meaning.

THE HYPERPRESIDENTIAL MODEL, 1962–1974, 1981–1986

Even though the Fifth Republic's institutional die had been largely cast by October 1962, its developmental process was far from complete. The key actors mentioned above continued to shape the regime to such an extent that its institutions still needed to be understood (like those of Eastern Europe, described by Valerie Bunce, chap. 7, this volume) not only as independent variables but also as dependent variables. Let us briefly examine how various actors helped to define the meaning of the Fifth Republic's institutions.

In November the general public facilitated the consolidation of presidential power by giving de Gaulle, for the first time, a solid majority in the National Assembly. The Gaullist Union for the New Republic (UNR) and its allies received nearly twice as many votes on the first ballot as in 1958. Voters "massively turned away from deputies who had voted censure in favor of new Gaullist candidates"; the UNR-led coalition gained almost sixty seats and now held more than 55 percent of total seats.[46]

The behavior of the majority coalition in the National Assembly contributed to regime development as well, for an ethos pervaded the Gaullist alliance, according the executive an unusual degree of deference and autonomy.[47] The "timidity" of the majority in the Assembly was such that, during the entire decade of de Gaulle's presidency, parliament failed to set up even a single committee of inquiry to investigate the facts concerning some executive action.[48] Moreover, majority discipline was such that only a handful of Gaullist or allied Giscardian deputies ever supported a censure vote, and few deputies of either group even diverged from the government's line on roll call votes.[49]

With assured support in the Assembly, the president was able to reappoint loyal lieutenant Pompidou as prime minister, and over the next six years (with de Gaulle reelected in 1965 and Pompidou retaining his office until 1968) they firmly entrenched as the normal mode of regime operation the strictly hierarchical relationship between the two "heads" of the executive that conformed to Gaullist preferences. Despite the 1962 amendment, the powers of the chief of state remained quite limited in purely formal terms. In fact, as comparative institutional studies by Duverger and by Schugart and Carey note, the French president's formal powers in the Fifth Republic's "semipresidential" system rank among the most meager accorded anywhere to a popularly elected president.[50]

What the French gradually began to view as the norm, however, was a far different reality, which can best be described as hyper-presidentialism.[51] As Duverger describes the practice, presidents "exercised directly" the powers conferred on them by the constitution and "exercised indirectly the prerogatives of their prime ministers and governments, by reducing the latter to obedience."[52]

Despite their protests against the direction the regime was taking under the Gaullists, the opposition parties also contributed significantly to the consolidation of hyperpresidentialism. With great irony, given his status as the most formidable early critic of the Gaullist Republic, Mitterrand and his reformed Socialist Party played the most prominent role of this sort. From 1965, when he first ran for president, to the elections of 1974 and 1981, Mitterrand increasingly emulated de Gaulle's style as a presidential candidate and used the institution of direct presidential elections as a means of rebuilding and uniting the Left around himself and his party.[53] The Communists and centrists also gradually adjusted to, and grudgingly accepted various aspects of, the new regime.[54] Moreover, leaders of all major parties (in contrast to those of some other "semipresidential" systems such as that of Austria) helped to consolidate the primacy of the presidency by seeking that office rather than aiming merely for the premier's role.[55]

Georges Pompidou played an important role in regime development not only as the second premier but also as the second president (1969–74). Those who had hoped hyperpresidentialism would disappear with de Gaulle were quickly disabused of this notion. Different though his style was in certain respects, Pompidou's view of the Presidency scarcely differed from de Gaulle's."[56] Backed by a large majority in the National Assembly, Pompidou had the power to perpetuate the general's vision of the president's role, including what was now viewed as the traditional relationship between the chief of state and the premier. Indeed, Pompidou emphatically affirmed de Gaulle's interpretation of Article 8 (and apparent disdain for parliament) by firing his first prime minister, Jacques Chaban-Delmas, just after the premier had received a massive vote of confidence from the National Assembly.[57]

While the regime's "normal" hyperpresidential model gave way to another during the Giscard years (discussed below), it would be restored seven years later with the conquest of power by Mitterrand and the Left. Mitterrand narrowly won the presidential election in May 1981, dissolved parliament, and then led the Socialist Party to a smashing landslide victory in the legislative elections. Far from using the vast power at his disposal to "reinvent" the regime in line with the parliamentary vision of his early critiques, Mitterrand in essence chose to emulate (and legitimate) the hyperpresidential model developed under Presidents de Gaulle and Pompidou. "France's institutions were not made for me," commented Mitterrand, "but they suit me well enough."[58] From the dawn of his tenure until 1986, when he lost majority support in the National Assembly, Mitterrand made clear that it was he who would provide the basic orientations of the government and that the premiers drawn from his own party (Pierre Mauroy until 1984, then Laurent Fabius until 1986) would be expected to play the loyal lieutenant role perfected by Debré and Pompidou.

In general, Mitterrand also expected and received Gaullist-style deference to the executive from his party's National Assembly delegation. While he took fewer liberties with the constitution than de Gaulle had, he made full use of his presidential powers and even proved reluctant, despite an official plank of the Socialist Party platform, to call for a reduction of the president's term from seven years to five.[59]

The only major way in which hyperpresidentialism under Mitterrand differed from the earlier post-1962 versions was that, due to developments in the Giscard era, the government was now somewhat constrained in its policy-making capacity by the "counterpower" of an activist Constitutional Council.[60] The council, to which the opposition appealed with alacrity, struck down as unconstitutional at least some key articles of a good number of Socialist reform bills and deterred other policy steps by its mere presence. Despite this constraint, the experience of "Mitterrand I" was far closer to the Gaullist regime model than the more tempered presidential periods discussed below.[61]

THE TEMPERED PRESIDENTIAL MODEL, 1974–1981, 1988–1993

In a number of respects, 1974 marked a turning point in the development of the Fifth Republic. First, a non-Gaullist was elected president. Valéry Giscard d'Estaing, the leader of the "minority" of the traditional majority coalition who had served as a minister under both de Gaulle and Pompidou, narrowly won the special election to replace the deceased Pompidou. Second, Giscard became the first president who was not the leader of the largest party in the National Assembly; Giscard's authority was limited by the fact that, from 1974 to 1977, his own loosely organized party held only 55 seats, versus 183 for the neo-Gaullist UDR (renamed the RPR in 1976); from 1978 to 1981 it held 119 seats, versus 155 for the RPR.[62] Third, given that political situation, Giscard became the first president who felt compelled to appoint, at least initially, someone other than a loyal lieutenant as premier; for his first two years in office he was forced to work with the leader of the neo-Gaullists, Jacques Chirac, in Matignon. Finally, Giscard became the first president to institute an institutional reform that would at least modestly empower the opposition and thus check governmental power; he sponsored an amendment that, in effect, granted the parliamentary opposition the right to appeal bills to the Constitutional Council for judicial review. All together, the three political changes would temper the traditional hyperpresidentialism of the Fifth Republic for the short run, and the institutional change would do so, to some extent, in perpetuity.

What the new political landscape of the Giscard era underscored was the extent to which effective presidential power in the Fifth Republic, which de Gaulle had envisioned as a regime allowing the chief of state to govern "above" the parties, very much depended on the balance of party power in the National Assembly. This had been true before 1974, of course, but the reality was now more visible. From 1974 to 1976, Giscard attempted to govern essentially in the traditional hyperpresidential fashion, counting on Chirac to replicate the traditional Gaullist role of obedient premier and to deliver the support of the Gaullists in the Assembly. Even during the new president's honeymoon period, however, his lack of control over the "majority of the majority" forced him to abandon or water down a host of policy initiatives in the face of Gaullist opposition. Moreover, Chirac soon made it clear that he felt his status as leader of the Assembly's largest party entitled him to more autonomy vis-à-vis the president than any premier of the Fifth Republic had previously been allowed to wield.[63] When it became clear in 1976 that he would be granted neither "the means nor the liberty" that he expected, Chirac resigned, thus becoming the first premier in the regime's history to resign of his own volition.[64]

With Chirac back in the Assembly working to establish his status as the genuine leader of the majority (in part to position himself to defeat Giscard at the next presidential election), and with the Gaullists increasingly asserting "their autonomy, their identity, their independence and their disobedience," Giscard "reigned more than he ruled" for the remainder of his term.[65] The president's limited authority meant that his second premier, Raymond Barre, would come to appear as much a rival (also with an eye toward the presidency) as an assistant—to the extent that he was successful. The institutions of the regime still allowed for governmental stability (for example, Barre would continue as prime minister until the 1981 elections). Moreover, the constitutional weapons it made available to the executive (now used with unprecedented frequency), reinforced by majority solidarity in the face of increasing competition from the Left, still allowed for a good measure of governmental effectiveness. This was no longer the normal model of hyperpresidential government, however; it was at best a tempered, or rationalized, presidentialism.[66]

In the context of a different balance of party power, therefore, the key traditional players (from the president and premier to the electorate and the Assembly delegations) in the governmental game gave new meaning to the regime's institutions. In addition, during this period a formal change in institutions combined with unprecedented assertiveness to make the Constitutional Council a player of importance, a player that would henceforth serve to temper governmental power in a fashion de Gaulle had never envisioned. Not until 1971 (two years after de Gaulle's departure from the scene) had the council overturned a government-sponsored bill on constitutional grounds. Before Giscard's 1974 amendment empowering sixty senators or sixty deputies (i.e., the opposition) to appeal a bill to the council, however, the judicial body had received few cases to review.[67] In the wake of the 1974 amendment, appeals increased, and more significant government bills than ever before were overturned, on the basis of norms of reference that the council expanded with every ruling. The council would play a far more important role during the later reform governments of the Socialists (1981–86) and the Right (1986–88), when vast policy agendas led to proliferating appeals and waves of negative rulings.[68]

The second instance of tempered presidentialism emerged following the 1988 elections, when François Mitterrand won reelection to the presidency but was supported by a mere "relative" majority in the National Assembly. The logic of the Giscard model applied once again from 1988 to 1993 in several major respects: the policy-making capacity of the president, and the executive generally, was constrained by the absence of a stable and disciplined majority; the prime ministers of the era (Michel Rocard, Edith Cresson, and Pierre Bérégovoy) were able to obtain their central policy goals only by resorting frequently to the executive's "constitutional weapons," with Rocard especially breaking records for his use of Article 49.3; the need for premiers to use such weapons and arrange evanescent majorities in parliament accorded them a degree of power and autonomy unknown in hyperpresidential eras; and the president felt compelled to work with at least one premier (Rocard) who was a major political rival with an eye on a future presidency.[69]

Despite these similarities, Mitterrand enjoyed more power in this period than Giscard had earlier, given both his personal stature in the Socialist Party and his greater partisan assets in the National Assembly.[70] The Gulf War also provided the president with numerous opportunities to demonstrate his "absolute preeminence" in the "reserved domain" of defense.[71]

THE PREMIER-PRESIDENTIAL MODEL, 1986–1988, 1993–

Even more than 1974, the year 1986 marked a leap into uncharted political territory for the Fifth Republic. The legislative elections of that year produced, for the first time, a National Assembly majority hostile to the president; the two major parties of the Right held only a fragile edge, with the neo-Gaullists again the leading component, but their position was strong enough to present Mitterrand with the necessity of appointing one of their leaders as premier.[72] Mitterrand's choice of neo-Gaullist chief Jacques Chirac launched the first experiment with what the French termed cohabitation, that is, the awkward sharing of the Fifth Republic's dual executive by the Left and the Right.

The president—without a supportive majority in the Assembly and thus unable to wield ("indirectly") powers granted to the premier—experienced as never before limits on his formal powers. For the most part, Prime Minister Chirac was able to function as the acknowledged head of government and to manage parliament through manipulation of the executive's constitutional weapons. In the French case, however, what Lijphart terms "parliamentary-phase semi-presidentialism" was hardly reducible to an analogue of British parliamentarism.[73] "Premier-presidentialism" is a useful description for the model that emerged, for though the premier was predominant in most respects, both the president and aspirations to the presidency continued to play major roles in the political game.[74]

As for the president, Mitterrand continued to exercise considerable, if selective, power. At the outset, Mitterrand announced that he would be guided by "the constitution, nothing but the constitution. But all of the constitution."[75] In line with both the constitution and tradition, he was especially insistent on retaining a major say in the "reserved domain" of foreign policy and defense. His rival, Chirac, was especially poorly positioned (as leader of a movement that traced it origins to de Gaulle) to contest an expansive reading of presidential power in this area. Mitterrand was thus able to use his appointment power (Article 8) to veto Chirac's original nominees for foreign minister and defense minister and obtain acceptable (politically neutral) replacements. He also managed to maintain a high profile in diplomacy (though Chirac insisted on accompanying him to international summits) and to assert his authority on a variety of important matters related to defense.

On domestic matters, Mitterrand deferred for the most part to Chirac and his government. However, he did intervene in this sphere when he thought it was justified and when he could find suitable institutional levers to push. For example, just as de Gaulle had read presidential discretion into Article 30 in the March 1960 controversy, Mitterrand invoked Article 13 (requiring the president's signature on ordinances and decrees) to veto ordinances on matters such as privatization and the redrawing of electoral districts. Such moves could not stop the Chirac government from achieving its goals, but they did cause delay and allowed for parliamentary debate. Mitterrand also used his access to the media to speak out against government policy on certain issues.[76]

Throughout the first cohabitation era, the games played by Chirac and Mitterrand were affected by their calculations regarding the looming presidential election of 1988. Both the premier and the president seemed constrained in their assertions of power by the fact that the public was watching, would probably respond negatively to power plays that provoked constitutional crises, and would soon be judging them at the polls. Chirac was doubtless prevented from attempting to "radically undermine the office of the presidency" by the fact that his sights were set on that prize.[77] In the end, Mitterrand's restrained and statesmanlike behavior, combined with the public's tendency to blame the more powerful premier for economic and other problems, enabled the president to achieve reelection in 1988.

At the time this chapter was completed, the Fifth Republic's second experiment in Left-Right cohabitation was in its fourth month. The 1993 parliamentary elections triggered "cohabitation II," as Mitterrand's Socialists were routed in an unprecedented landslide that gave the two major parties of the Right roughly 80 percent of the seats in the National Assembly. It was too early for definitive assessments of this case, but some things were already clear. On the one hand, cohabitation II should produce a mode of governance somewhat closer to a pure parliamentary model; not only was the new premier (neo-Gaullist Edouard Balladur) backed by an extraordinary majority, but the president's poll ratings were low, he seemed like a lame duck, and his party was in disarray.[78] On the other hand, Mitterrand continued to assert "reserved domain" powers (e.g., he appeared without Balladur at the July 1993 Tokyo summit), and the primacy of the presidency as both an office and a political prize was underscored in a remarkable manner: Jacques Chirac, frustrated in two prior attempts to make the premier's position at least temporarily supreme, declined to accept the Matignon role in 1993 (despite an 80% majority in the Assembly!), the better to prepare himself for another run at the Elysée in 1995.[79] It is difficult to imagine a more vivid testament to the political power and status of the presidency in the Fifth Republic.

CONCLUSION

The central conclusion we can draw from this analysis of the development of the Fifth Republic is that institutions matter but that institutions do not make their own history. As Weaver and Rockman note, while institutions affect governmental capabilities, "their effects are contingent." The French case vividly confirms that the impact of institutional arrangements tends to be "strongly mediated by . . . noninstitutional factors."[80]

In many respects, the Fifth Republic merits its reputation as a successful regime worthy of emulation abroad. However, would-be importers should note carefully how the regime's institutions acquired their actual meaning and should recognize how difficult it would be, in another societal context, to replicate the effects often attributed to these institutions.

To what extent did the institutions of the new regime make possible the resolution of the Algerian crisis? Some of the assets it gave the president (e.g., the power to hold referendums; Article 16) facilitated de Gaulle's efforts. However, de Gaulle's success in this case was clearly due to his unique personal authority and the related fact that other actors, desperate for an end to the crisis, allowed him to ignore or maneuver around institutional constraints. He was thus allowed to wield nearly dictatorial power during his first eight months in office and, later—with minimal protest—to extend emergency powers longer than seemed justified. He was also able to inspire loyal cooperation from his premier, even when the two men disagreed, and to overcome potentially problematic formal limits to his presidential powers by "indirectly" exercising those of his prime minister.

To what extent can the regime's institutions be credited with enhancing governmental stability and governing capacity in the period since the resolution of the Algerian crisis? Clearly, the strengthening of the presidency contributed to these outcomes. However, it was less the letter of the constitution than the behavior of key political actors that enhanced the powers of the presidency. De Gaulle's role was central, of course, but others played major supporting roles. As prime minister, Michel Debré helped "amend" Article 8 by allowing the president to fire him. A different individual faced with a different president obviously could have resisted and altered the course of regime development (for this reason, some other systems largely modeled on the Fifth Republic—such as that of Sri Lanka—explicitly give the president the right to dismiss the premier; by the same token, the presidents of both Poland and Ukraine have proposed constitutions explicitly granting them that power).[81] Later French premiers followed suit, but they would have been unlikely to do so if the 1962 amendment had not ensured that de Gaulle's successors would be the acknowledged leaders of their parties and coalitions. That crucial amendment passed, only because both the general public and the Constitutional Council were willing to tolerate a violation of constitutional procedure. The extent of presidential dominance associated with the Fifth Republic also resulted from such factors as unwritten rules (e.g., acceptance of the "reserved domain"), an ethos of deference to the executive on the part of the president's party in the National Assembly, and the public's failure to elect candidates who might have interpreted the chief of state's powers in a restrictive fashion.[82] Finally, as the recent cohabitation experiences have shown, presidential dominance can be undermined by a citizenry willing to elect a National Assembly majority opposed to the president.

There can be no doubt that certain other institutional features of the new regime strongly increased the probability that the Fifth Republic's governments, whether dominated by the president or the premier, would be more stable and effective than those of the Fourth. The "rationalization" of parliament and the arming of the executive with an arsenal of "constitutional weapons" were expected to make a substantial impact, and they have indeed. The move to a two-ballot electoral system for the National Assembly was important as well, serving to reduce the number of parties in parliament and to increase the chances of obtaining coherent majorities.[83]

Important though all of these institutional changes were, they alone are hardly responsible for the stark contrast in outcomes achieved by the two postwar French Republics. The Fourth Republic was forced to cope with "a period of unprecedented social and political tension" dominated by the divisive wars in Indochina and Algeria.[84] The year that marked the "routinization" of the Fifth Republic, 1962, was also the year that France's colonial nightmares ended.[85] A post-Algeria Fourth Republic would not have matched the Fifth for stability and efficacy, but it almost certainly would have functioned better than it did between 1946 and 1958.[86]

Two final caveats should be added here, especially for prospective importers. First, there are some costs to the institutionally induced stability and effectiveness of the Fifth Republic. In any of the three modes in which it has functioned since 1962, the French semipresidential system precludes the major problem associated with pure presidentialism: American-style deadlock. The executive's power vis-à-vis the rationalized parliament ensures that even a relatively weak president such as Giscard will be able to achieve many of his policy goals. However, the other side of this coin is that the French system, unlike regular presidentialism, fails to ensure limited government through a genuine separation of executive and legislative powers. The recent enhancement of the Constitutional Council's role has attenuated this problem somewhat, but the persistent weakness of parliament remains an issue in French politics, especially in an era when constitutional weapons have been deployed against it with unprecedented frequency.[87]

Second, the prospect of cohabitation always carries with it the potential for instability and governmental ineffectiveness, from which the Fifth Republic has so far been spared. While the premier-presidential model has worked fairly well to this point, this has been possible in large part because of a fortuitous consensus on important foreign policy matters. There can obviously be no guarantee of such consensus in the future, and the Fifth Republic system thus remains most vulnerable to policy stalemate on precisely those issues featuring the greatest national stakes.[88]

PART III

The Latin American Context
Rebuilding Presidential Institutions and Democracy

CHAPTER 5

Hybrid Presidentialism in Bolivia

Eduardo A. Gamarra

Governing Bolivia in the last dozen years has been a very complicated undertaking. There is a temptation to explain these difficulties as rooted in the presidential nature of the Bolivian system. To overcome similar crises of governability elsewhere in Latin America, numerous authors have proposed the adoption of parliamentarism.[1] Following this general trend, a number of analysts have proposed a similar solution to Bolivia's recurrent impasses between executives and legislatures.[2]

While Bolivia confirms many of the perils associated with presidential systems, other structural realities have shaped the problems of governance. These include a severe pattern of economic dependence and recurrent periods of economic crisis; a weak political party system tied almost exclusively to patronage; a small private sector; and a middle class dependent on the state for employment. To understand Bolivia's problems of governability, it is important to focus on how the country's institutional arrangements have dealt with specific crises, given the constraints imposed by these structural realities. Broader structural realities have limited the options available to policy makers to respond to crisis situations.

This chapter explores how Bolivia's institutional framework dealt with the severe challenges of democratizing the country while simultaneously attempting to impose harsh austerity measures. A principal conclusion is that political institutions have fundamentally shaped policy outcomes. These policy outcomes, which include profound structural reform of both the economic and political systems, were possible primarily because of the presidential institutional arrangements in Bolivia.

BOLIVIA'S HYBRID PRESIDENTIALISM

Bolivia's political system is not strictly presidential because it includes certain features normally associated with parliamentarianism. The most important difference from other contemporary Latin American presidential systems lies in the election of the Bolivian president. When no candidate achieves an absolute majority, the National Congress must elect the chief executive from among the top three finishers.[3]

While selection of the chief executive by the legislature is often seen as a positive aspect of parliamentarianism, in Bolivia it has at times served to weaken, and even to destabilize, executives. When coalitions in the National Congress are stable, however, the congressional election of the head of state has also served to strengthen the executive. Although Congress elects the president, there is no dependence of the executive branch on parliamentary confidence. Thus, Bolivia's system is a hybrid that combines features of both presidentialism and parliamentarianism.

Unlike most presidential systems, Bolivia's system allows members of Congress to serve in the cabinet. There is also a provision for interpellation of cabinet ministers; however, a vote of censure must be passed by a two-thirds majority, and even then it does not force the president to accept the resignation of the minister.

Bolivia's hybrid presidential system can be traced to the latter part of the nineteenth century. Between 1880 and 1930, presidentialism in Bolivia emulated many of the features commonly associated with presidential democracies elsewhere in the world during that period. One of the most salient features of the Bolivian system was a provision for malfeasance trials (*juicios de responsabilidades*), which granted the National Congress an oversight capability beyond those of other presidential systems. Through malfeasance trials, the legislature has the power of impeachment over not only members of the executive branch but over members of other branches as well.

Owing to an electoral system based on a single-member district for the election of members of Congress, the full hybrid nature of the system did not manifest until after the 1952 revolution led by the Movimiento Nacionalista Revolucionario (MNR). Key reforms, such as the adoption of a proportional representation electoral system, were instrumental in debilitating the capacity of presidents to control the National Congress. Paradoxically, electoral reforms ran counter to the logic of the MNR to strengthen executive power and to subordinate the legislature.

The military government of General René Barrientos, which followed the MNR's 1964 overthrow, exacerbated a specific contradiction of Bolivia's hybrid system: a state-centered development strategy that called for a strong executive, and electoral laws that encouraged the proliferation of political parties, thereby undermining the capacity of the executive to control the National Congress. Military-based authoritarian regimes institutionalized the paradox by introducing legislation, such as a 1966 electoral law, that weakened the executive branch. The institutionalization of proportional representation led to a full-blown hybrid presidential system.

In the late 1970s, following almost two decades of military rule, Bolivia moved toward democratization. As the nation lurched through abortive elections, coups, and countercoups it became evident that many of its problems were rooted in the conflict between the imposition of economic stabilization measures and the country's hybrid presidential system.

PRESIDENTIALISM AND DEMOCRATIC TRANSITION, 1979–1985

In the late 1970s, Bolivia's hybrid presidential system was one of the least prepared in Latin America to undertake the process of democratization. When the military opted to disengage from politics, Bolivia was a nation plagued by deep-seated regional, class, and political conflicts. Weak institutions and an atomized political society exacerbated tensions built into the system over years of intense political struggles. Consequently, the tumultuous round of coups, countercoups, and aborted elections that followed the military's withdrawal should not have been surprising. Between 1978 and 1982, seven military and two weak civilian governments ruled the country.

Numerous conflicts and contradictions arose during this period, revealing the weaknesses of Bolivia's hybrid presidential system. Every government between 1978 and 1985 demonstrated that presidents lacked the capacity to govern mainly because of structural constraints. Because no government was able to address an impending economic crisis, the country edged slowly toward hyperinflation.

In deeply divided societies like that of Bolivia in the late 1970s, democratization faced an even greater challenge; when the military lifted proscriptions on political parties, more than seventy made their appearance on the scene. The number of parties reached such an extreme that Bolivians derisively referred to them as "taxi parties": organizations so small they could hold their national conventions in a taxicab. At least thirty of these parties were identifiable factions of the MNR.

Three principal contenders emerged during the transition process: the Unidad Democrática y Popular (UDP), a coalition of the Partido Comunista Boliviano (PCB), and the Movimiento de Izquierda Revolucionaria (MIR). Hernán Siles Zuazo's Left faction of the MNR (MNRI) was the front-runner in the 1978, 1979, and 1980 elections. Víctor Paz Estenssoro headed the largest faction of the MNR, luring other members of Bolivia's political class. Facing an onslaught of civilian investigations into his seven-year tenure as president, General Hugo Bánzer Suárez founded Acción Democrática y Nacionalista (ADN) to help fend off charges of human rights violations and corruption. These three groups have dominated the political arena since 1978.

The proliferation of political parties in Bolivian politics exacerbated what has been described as the problem of dual legitimacy.[4] Although this duality was less of a problem than in, for example, Peru, it was rooted in the way in which Bolivian presidents are elected. Under the terms of Article 90 of the Bolivian constitution, when no candidate achieves an absolute majority, the National Congress must elect a president from the top three contenders. With as many as twenty-seven political parties present in the Chamber of Deputies, this proved to be a most difficult task. Whichever candidate was able to put together a coalition to win the presidency was soon in a chronic conflict with the legislature.[5]

The real task facing every president elected by the legislature was to maintain a coalition in place long enough to support his or her policy initiatives. By virtue of Article 90, members of Congress believed that, because they elected the chief executive, they also had the power to oversee each and every activity of the president. Claiming the National Congress was the only truly representative institution, the *fiscalización* of executive actions continued apace. It is noteworthy that, since 1978, Congress has elected presidents who obtained less than 35 percent of the popular vote, and in two of the last three elections, the winner of the popular plurality was not the winner of the congressional round. For example, Jaime Paz Zamora, Bolivia's former president, won less than 20 percent in 1989 and placed third in the popular balloting. This situation exacerbated dual claims to legitimacy. Presidents claimed to enjoy a popular mandate, while the National Congress argued that legitimacy rested in that body. The result was an intense and bitter interinstitutional dispute. In short, throughout this democratizing period, Bolivia moved gradually toward a political system characterized by a resurgent and dominant Congress and an extremely weak executive branch.

Competing claims to legitimacy were only one dimension of the governance problem faced by Bolivia's presidents. Disputes over the distribution of state patronage were an even graver issue. Political parties in the National Congress demanded patronage in exchange for their legislative support; however, because the size of the patronage pot was limited, even members of the president's own party were excluded. The result was an almost immediate assault on the executive for a greater share of the patronage pool. In Congress, political parties and factions immobilized the executive branch through congressional investigations, "constitutional coups," and the like.[6]

Bolivian presidents were also incapable of asserting authority over the sprawling bureaucratic apparatus housed in the executive branch. As presidents handed out posts in the bureaucracy in exchange for support, the state bureaucracy became the captive of a series of rival patron-client networks. Because these patron-client networks in control of state agencies and corporations consumed all surplus extracted from society, little if anything was left over to finance public policy. In short, presidents were forced to deal not only with assaults from Congress but also with an inefficient and parasitic bureaucracy. As a result, presidents were incapable of resolving even the most simple problems of governance.[7]

These conflicts illustrate another dimension of hybrid presidentialism in Bolivia. The fixed terms to which presidents are elected exacerbate tensions between branches of government. Because they elected the chief executive, members of Congress believed they also had the right to revoke his or her mandate, either through impeachment, malfeasance trials, or constitutional coups. To overcome these maneuvers and legislative inaction, Bolivian presidents resorted to decree laws, which in turn brought charges of unconstitutionality from the legislature (a situation particularly evident during the 1982–85 Siles Zuazo period). Bolivian presidents were thus rendered totally ineffective in dealing with any crisis. They were particularly helpless, however, in dealing with the economic crisis. While this can be viewed as a problem of presidentialism, the problem also lies in the nature of the party system and the form of proportional representation used to elect the Congress.[8] This problem became apparent with the explosion of parties and factions that occurred during the transition to civilian rule.

In 1956 the MNR government adopted closed-list proportional representation according to the system of a simple quota and the largest remainders. The average magnitude of legislative districts is 14 representatives, with five of the nine districts being very large. Because this allocation formula is favorable to smaller lists[9] and because of the large magnitude, very small parties can easily gain representation. Moreover, the closed-list system applies not only to Congress but also to the relation between Congress and the president. That is, voters may not split their tickets but, rather, must cast a single vote for one party in both the presidential and congressional races. This means that small parties cannot endorse a major party presidential candidate and still keep their own identity in the congressional election; they must run a presidential candidate. This proliferation, in turn, reduces the likelihood of one presidential candidate winning a majority of the votes, thereby enhancing the hybrid nature of the system.

Because of the closed lists, the MNR (and other parties) handpicked their supporters; party factional leaders selected the individuals and the order in which they would appear on the ballot. Not surprisingly, party discipline in the legislature was tied to patron-client networks: as long as patronage was available, discipline in the legislative assembly was possible. However, when the spoils were scarce, legislators often turned on the very individuals who had nominated them for the ballot in the first place.

The military government of General René Barrientos (1964–69) introduced few modifications to the 1956 electoral law. Apart from allowing a greater number of political parties to run for office, the proportional representation system remained virtually intact. This was the electoral system employed in 1978 when the military convoked elections. When General Bánzer lifted proscriptions (not found in the electoral law), his government faced an uncontrollable phenomenon—not only did dozens of parties register with the national electoral court, but the same old tired faces of Víctor Paz Estenssoro, Hernán Siles Zuazo, and Walter Guevara Arze, the old MNR titans, emerged as the front-runners.

Given this peculiar set of circumstances, Bolivia's political elite recognized the problem with electoral mechanisms as early as 1979. Reforms of the electoral law aimed at preventing proliferation of the so-called taxi parties. Under the terms of these reforms, parties that did not achieve a fifty-thousand-vote minimum were forced to pay their share of printing the ballot. To guarantee minority representation, the electoral law allowed alliances and coalitions. A new multicolor and multisign ballot helped end the practice of ballot stuffing by political parties; until 1979 parties printed their own ballots.[10]

Because the 1979 and 1980 electoral laws allowed alliances and coalitions, smaller parties threw their support to the principal presidential candidates in exchange for a place on the ballot. Despite controlling only a few seats in Congress, these smaller parties became the key to electing a new president. Owing to the fact that a single seat might be crucial to ending impasses, minority parties became important instruments both to block and to oversee executive initiatives. In short, the proliferation of parties in the legislature contributed greatly to the hybrid nature of Bolivia's presidential system.

The party system, however, maintained the same characteristics: patron-client networks were responsible for the selection of individuals to party lists. Beyond these tenuous links, no guarantee of party discipline in the legislature was available. Beyond providing a seat in the legislature, party coalitions could do little else for the individuals who rode into Congress on the coattails of a conjunctural alliance. As a result, party discipline in the National Congress was lax, often lasting less than a few days after the inaugural session.[11]

A basic and recurrent pattern dominated all elections in Bolivia between 1979 and 1989: presidential candidates went through three distinct coalition-forming stages. First, electoral coalitions were formed to contest the elections to secure a position for the critical second round. Second, in Congress a round of maneuvering and coalition building took place to elect a president. Third, when Congress finally elected a chief executive, that coalition broke down as presidents scrambled to form a governing coalition.

This hybrid presidential system is a product not only of institutional constraints but also of factors common to several Latin American nations but acutely present in Bolivia. These factors, which were brewing beneath the surface during the military period, came to the fore during the transition period and have yet to be resolved.

One of the principal problems Bolivian presidents faced during the transition was to respond to demands from social groups and movements without the mediation of political parties or the National Congress. Several conflicts manifested simultaneously. An intense struggle arose between the private sector, represented by the Confederación de Empresarios Privados (CEPB), and the Central Obrera Boliviana (COB), over the implementation of economic stabilization. Class conflict was complicated by intereconomic sector tensions, which set traditional peasants against the urban sectors and the newly emerging agroindustrial interests of the eastern lowlands. Finally, a very intense process of interregional rivalry to control national policy and resources unfolded as regional "civic committees" moved to advance local interests.[12]

Political parties and Congress played little or no role in mediating the impact of these conflicts on weak presidential structures. Parties, in fact, were largely disconnected from the main interests of class or regional groups. As a result, the primary organizations expressing the interests of society were the regional civic committees, peasant unions, and syndicates. Each group bypassed the legislature and political parties and pressed their demands directly on the executive. These conflicts forced presidents to avoid unpopular initiatives, especially in economic policy, and to present watered-down versions of economic stabilization programs. The result was an economic crisis of major proportions.

The general pattern revealed itself in a rather dramatic fashion during the 1982–85 Siles Zuazo government. When Siles was sworn into office, Bolivia was already experiencing the worst political and economic crisis of its history. Siles attempted to govern at the head of the UDP, a multiparty coalition built around his Left faction of the MNR (the MNRI), the MIR, and the Communist Party (PCB). Siles never controlled his coalition, particularly in the National Congress, which almost immediately began to conspire against him. The instability of the period was reflected by the numerous cabinet crises, the recurrent interpellation, and the censure of cabinet ministers. Between 1982 and 1985, more than eighty individuals served in the cabinet.

Led by the COB, organized labor vigorously pressed the weakened president to resolve the demands of the popular classes. Simultaneously, the private sector, regional civic committees, and other groupings exerted untenable demands on the Siles presidency. Siles's problems with these groups were made worse by the lack of an institutional mechanism to respond to crisis situations. As a result, the hapless Siles government was unable to achieve a coherent economic program, and the economy plunged into a crisis of catastrophic proportions, characterized by a hyperinflation rate that reached 26,000 percent in 1984–85.

By the end of 1984 politicians threatened to impeach Siles, labor took to the streets in month-long strikes, the military threatened to launch a coup, and other groups pressed for the president's resignation. Facing an imminent collapse of the economy and a derailment of Bolivian democracy, these forces came together to force Siles from office a year early and to organize another attempt to find an electoral way out (*salida*) of the profound political impasse.[13]

The July 1985 elections once again did not produce a government, and for the third time since 1979, the task to elect a new president fell upon the National Congress. Although General Bánzer's ADN won a slight plurality, a coalition between the MNR and MIR prevented his ascension to the presidency. At age seventy-eight, Víctor Paz Estenssoro was elected to his fourth presidential term. A significant turning point came on August 6, when General Bánzer accepted the outcome and pledged support for the democratic process.[14]

THE PACTO POR LA DEMOCRACIA

Reestablishing presidential supremacy entailed filling a power vacuum at the center of the Bolivian political system. Because Congress was again dominated by the opposition and organized labor was poised to prevent the imposition of harsh austerity measures, this was a difficult task. Nevertheless, Paz Estenssoro set in motion a pattern of governance that allowed his government to both impose economic stabilization and control opposition from Congress and labor. The relative success of Paz and the MNR suggests that Bolivia's hybrid presidential system can produce the mechanisms to overcome crisis situations.

On August 29, 1985, through Decree 21060, the government introduced the Nueva Política Económica (NPE). Surprising the Left and the groups that had supported his election in Congress, Paz Estenssoro announced a program that restructured the development strategy established thirty-three years earlier by the populist MNR. The NPE sought three basic objectives: the liberalization of the economy, the ascendance of the private sector as the central actor in economic development, and the recuperation of state control over key state enterprises captured by factional cliques and labor groups. The NPE put in place a shock therapy, reducing fiscal deficits, freezing wages and salaries, devaluing the currency, and drastically cutting public sector employment. The government also announced the privatization of state enterprises and other similar measures.[15]

In one year, the NPE was credited with reducing inflation to 10 percent. Government officials claimed that the foundations for economic recovery had been established. Internationally, Bolivia's NPE became a showcase, as international financial institutions and foreign governments lavishly praised the program. Bolivia's economic recovery, however, did not proceed rapidly. The collapse of the tin market in October 1985 and the decline in the price of natural gas (the country's only sources of hard currency) threatened to derail the NPE. In 1987—for the first time in the 1980s—the economy finally showed signs of growth.

Considering the extreme crisis faced by the Paz Estenssoro government in 1985 and the structural weaknesses of Bolivian presidentialism, the success of the NPE must be explained in more detail. To neutralize labor, the MNR government launched a state of siege, banishing hundreds of labor leaders, including COB leader Juan Lechín Oquendo, to remote jungle towns. The COB sabotaged every attempt by the Siles government to impose austerity. In addition, organized labor eroded the effectiveness and legitimacy of strikes. Thus, when twenty-three thousand mine workers were fired, the COB barely mustered enough support to call a general strike.

As in most presidential systems, the continuation of a state of siege in Bolivia depends on congressional approval.[16] Almost immediately, opposition groups in Congress set in motion interpellation maneuvers to counter the launching of the NPE and the state of siege. Owing to its association with Siles and the UDP and its humiliating defeat in the general elections, the Left received little popular support for their congressional maneuvers. The only left-of-center party of significance was Jaime Paz Zamora's MIR, which had shrewdly abandoned the UDP and recast the party in more acceptable social democratic circles. In short, left-of-center groups in Congress lacked the votes to overturn the state of siege.

The only real threat in Congress came from General Bánzer's ADN. Shortly after launching the NPE, Paz Estenssoro moved to form the Pacto por la Democracía, which aimed mainly at securing congressional ratification for the state of siege. Beyond patriotic gestures and democratic rhetoric, the pact provided legislative support for the NPE in exchange for an ADN share of state patronage.[17] A secret addendum (signed in May 1988) provided for alternability, as the MNR pledged to support Bánzer's candidacy in the 1989 general elections. On a smaller scale, the Pacto por la Democracía introduced elements similar to those present in Colombia's governing pact between *liberales* and *conservadores*: a share in state patronage and a mechanism to ensure the rotation of the presidency between the MNR and the ADN. In short, the *pacto* was a significant attempt at institutionalizing a governing arrangement between the government and the principal opposition party.

The Pacto por la Democracía revealed a basic reality about multiparty presidential systems. To govern, presidents must be able to form and sustain coalitions in Congress to support their policy initiatives. Because the pact granted the executive a majority in Congress, decision-making authority was concentrated in the executive branch, at the cabinet level.[18] The pact allowed the president to overcome the severe conflict between weak executives and an opposition-controlled legislature. As was evident during the Siles Zuazo period, this tension made the parliamentary characteristics of the system more salient. Although this conflict was temporarily resolved by the *pacto*, unless this contradiction is resolved through constitutional amendments or electoral reforms, every future president will be forced to replicate a version of the pact in order to govern. Paradoxically, this is both the principal strength and the principal weakness of the system.

One of the most significant aspects about the pact was that it allowed Paz Estenssoro to overcome the problem of dual legitimacy, which had plagued Siles Zuazo. Defenders of the arrangement argued that, because the first- and second-place finishers in the 1985 elections entered into the pact, approximately 55 percent of the electorate was represented. That the MNR placed second was an important consideration in Paz Estenssoro's decision to enter into a governing pact with the winner of the elections. The key to forming and sustaining the pact rested mainly on the ability of Paz Estenssoro and General Bánzer to control their respective parties and to maintain discipline in the coalition.[19] Owing largely to their stature, no faction could significantly challenge the grip of these two men over their respective parties. Thus, a crucial factor in the formation and maintenance of this pact was the role of statesmanship and old-fashioned *caudillismo*.

As some argue, the pact resolved the institutional dilemmas of Bolivia's hybrid presidential system but ratified the significance of patronage.[20] Paradoxically, the pact increased party patronage pressures on public employment despite the high-flown neoliberal rhetoric of reducing the size of the state. This logic also undermined the president's ability to assert authority over the state bureaucracy.[21] In short, Paz Estenssoro's government faced Bolivia's most pressing problem: the need to provide employment to the dependent middle classes. In Bolivia, in other Latin American nations, *empleomanía*, or job factionalism, drives the logic of political party competition and is crucial to the survival of presidents.

To implement the NPE, President Paz Estenssoro established an economic cabinet team headed by Gonzalo Sanchez de Lozada, the "super" minister of planning, who became a de facto prime minister for economic affairs. Paz also established a political cabinet, headed by Foreign Affairs Minister Guillermo Bedregal, to control party discipline. In setting up two quasi prime ministerial posts, Paz Estenssoro insulated himself from the day-to-day party squabbles constantly faced by the economic team. While this style proved successful for Paz Estenssoro, it would be difficult to replicate.[22]

From the perspective of institutionalizing this style of governing, the key was to reform the electoral mechanisms that had given birth to Bolivia's complex multiparty system. ADN and MNR strategists envisioned a two-party dominant system. The opposition, headed by Jaime Paz Zamora's MIR, charged the two allies with attempting to establish a new, hegemonic party; the MIR proposed instead, a new electoral court staffed by members of the top three vote getters of 1985. In a round of horse trading, the MIR's electoral reform proposals were accepted in exchange for its support for a new tax code. The principal objective of the 1986 electoral law was to concentrate parliamentary representation in a few parties (ADN, MNR, MIR) through the revision of the allocation formula.[23] The authors of the new law believed that the reforms could prevent the atomization of political parties and would make the National Congress into a more efficient legislative body. In short, these electoral reforms aimed to reestablish presidential supremacy through enhancing the advantage of the larger parties. Time would show that the electoral reforms, especially the makeup of the national and departmental electoral courts, only added to the problems of electing presidents. Because Congress was given the authority to elect the members of the electoral court, the new law paradoxically positioned the ADN and the MIR for a joint assault on the MNR during the 1989 general elections.

The May 1986 approval of the electoral reforms marked an important turning point for Bolivia's hybrid presidential system. After these reforms were signed into law by Paz Estenssoro, the MIR announced it would carry out a "constructive" opposition in Congress. This announcement could be interpreted as the MIR's official endorsement of the 1985 neoliberal reforms. For the next three years, the Pacto por la Democracía and the MIR's mild opposition allowed Paz Estenssoro's presidency to impose two more congressionally sanctioned states of siege, delivering punishing blows from which organized labor has yet to recover.[24] The pact also allowed the imposition of NPE-related legislation, including the new tax code and three successive national budgets.

Although the Pacto por la Democracía demonstrated that formal congressional coalitions are essential to stability and effective government under presidential systems, it also revealed that governing pacts seldom are flexible enough to become viable electoral coalitions. Despite the pact's success in forcing through the NPE and related legislation and the fact that popular support for the policy initiatives of the MNR government was quite high, the pact could not survive the 1989 election campaign. At issue was the refusal of the MNR to live up to the terms of the secret May 1988 addendum, which had assured support for General Banzer's candidacy. Once again, the patronage logic of the political parties destabilized the Bolivian political process. Despite the "modern" tone, old ways of doing politics—specifically, the determinant role of patronage and clientelism—survived, as political parties revealed that they were interested more in controlling state patronage than in ruling effectively.

Based on the belief that popular support for the NPE could lead the MNR to an outright victory in the elections, the MNR named as its candidate Gonzalo Sánchez de Lozada, the "super" minister of planning and one of the principal architects of the 1985 stabilization measures. Sánchez de Lozada promptly broke the pact with the ADN and conducted a bitter negative campaign, which mimicked the worst of American presidential campaigns.[25]

The decision to break the pact and the MNR's campaign style proved fateful. Although Sánchez de Lozada won a slight plurality—23.07 percent, to Bánzer's 22.7 percent and Paz Zamora's 19.6 percent—neither the ADN nor the MIR would contemplate supporting the MNR's claim to the presidency. The insult of breaking the pact, compounded by the tone of the campaign, contributed to the MNR's isolation.[26] As a result, between May and August 1989, Bolivia lurched through three months of both intense negotiations between the ADN and the MIR and of futile attempts by the MNR to strike a deal. On the eve of the convening of Congress to elect the next president, as he ordered his party to support Paz Zamora's bid for the presidency, Bánzer revealed that the least likely outcome had prevailed.

THE ACUERDO PATRIÓTICO

The Paz Estenssoro period provided several lessons for Jaime Paz Zamora, who ruled Bolivia between August 1989 and August 1993 with the support of General Bánzer's ADN. Before assuming office, Paz Zamora entered into a past, the Acuerdo Patriótico, with General Bánzer, all the while claiming that they would not sign a document formalizing the arrangement because both leaders had pledged their word of honor.[27]

The new pact emulated many of the dimensions of the MNR-ADN pact. First and foremost, its role was to push through Congress legislation designed to deepen NPE economic reforms. But the Acuerdo Patriótico's major problem was to find an "economic personality" of its own. Pushing through NPE-related legislation gave the new government no distinctive flavor to distinguish it from the MNR period. In January 1990, to overcome this situation Paz Zamora announced Decree 22407, replacing Decree 21060, which had introduced the NPE in 1985. Apart from calling for a privatization law and new mining and hydrocarbon investment codes, the new decree was simply a ratification of the main premises of the political economy of the Paz Estenssoro government.

Taking a page from the Paz Estenssoro government, Paz Zamora also declared a state of siege to control organized labor's opposition to economic policy. In November 1989, the Acuerdo Patriótico arrested hundreds of union leaders and banished them to remote jungle towns. Unlike his predecessor, however, Paz Zamora could not seek congressional approval for his government's actions. Although the Acuerdo Patriótico controlled a majority in both houses of Congress, it did not command the two-thirds majority required to approve a state of siege.[28]

Utilizing similar mechanisms, the Acuerdo Patriótico also rolled over opposition in the legislature to the approval of controversial policies, such as new investment laws allowing for the privatization of the hydrocarbon and mining industries. The MNR-led opposition charged the government with resorting to extraconstitutional measures to pass these laws.

With no clout in Congress, the opposition resorted to the Supreme Court, whose entire membership had been named by the previous MNR government.[29] This is another key dimension that weakened and undermined the effectiveness of the Acuerdo Patriótico. The judiciary became the focus of political conflict, as individuals and political groups pressed the Supreme Court to review not only all recent economic policy but also political decisions of president Paz Zamora.[30] The conflict stemmed from a Supreme Court ruling declaring unconstitutional a tax on breweries. Claiming that the ruling was the product of corruption—namely, the bribing of the justices by the two largest brewers in Bolivia—the executive refused to accept the court's decision. Instead, the Acuerdo Patriótico initiated a malfeasance trial in the National Congress against eight Supreme Court justices. The MNR escalated the conflict by resubmitting a lawsuit demanding that the court declare the 1989 elections null and void.

The impasse became one between, on one side, Congress and the executive, which were controlled by the Acuerdo Patriótico, and, on the other, the judiciary, which was controlled by the opposition. As in the past, the preferred outcome was a short-term unconstitutional *salida*. On February 5, 1991, a tentative agreement was reached with the opposition whereby the justices would be forced to step down in return for a new electoral law. When the government appeared to renege on its promises to reform the electoral law, the arrangement temporarily broke down.[31] Faced with declining popular support and accusations of deep-seated corruption, in mid-May 1991, the government allowed the eight suspended Supreme Court justices to return to their posts, and a new electoral law was accepted.

Many of the problems facing the Acuerdo Patriótico had to do with the nature of this governing pact. In contrast to the Pacto por la Democracía, the Acuerdo was a pact between two parties exercising control over the executive branch. It did not constitute an arrangement between a ruling party and the principal opposition force but an arrangement between two ruling parties to share power. The opposition was shut out of virtually all major decisions and leadership posts, including membership on congressional committees. This was the key dimension that rendered President Paz Zamora's governing style ineffective.

Unlike the Pacto por la Democracía, the Acuerdo Patriótico gave the presidency to the third-place finisher, thereby excluding the MNR, which won a plurality in May 1989. Although Bánzer won the 1985 elections, the pact with the MNR and the resulting distribution of patronage ended contending claims to legitimacy from the legislature. Moreover, the subsequent informal entry of the MIR as a "loyal" opposition had much to do with the duration and stability of the three-year pact. In contrast, and to reiterate a point made above, the Acuerdo Patriótico excluded the MNR and most opposition parties from any patronage spoils.[32] The MNR, in turn, challenged the legitimacy of the ADN-MIR government, arguing that it was deprived of the presidency by virtue of electoral fraud.

The distribution of patronage among members of the Acuerdo Patriótico, however, ran deeper than was the case under the Pacto por la Democracía. While the government announced a new round of firings in the state mining corporation, the patronage requirements for the political class resulted in the establishment of three new ministries and sixteen vice ministerial posts.[33] Again, the political needs of the pact ran counter to the neoliberal logic of reducing the size of the state. But the main political conflict had little to do with the economic logic of stabilization and everything to do with the exclusion of the MNR and other opposition parties from patronage spoils.

Along these lines, the critical conflict was the Acuerdo Patriótico's refusal to live up to its promises to reform the electoral law.[34] Blocking the MNR's attempts to reform the law in the legislature, the ADN-MIR coalition crafted an alliance formula aimed at carrying General Bánzer to the presidency in 1993. As proposed by the leadership of both ruling parties, the presidency would rotate between the ADN and the MIR for the remainder of the 1990s. The opposition interpreted these maneuvers as attempts by the Acuerdo Patriótico to establish a facade two-party system disguising a de facto single-party structure.

As others note, locking the opposition out of the rotation of patronage does not bode well for the continuity of the democratic process.[35] In Bolivia, these maneuvers by the ruling alliance led to a discussion of scenarios where the opposition resorts to antidemocratic mechanisms to inject itself back into the power and patronage game. Whatever scenario plays itself out, Bolivian presidentialism must address the issue of patronage rotation among sectors of the dependent middle class.

As the situation stands in the mid-1990s, the principal political institutions in Bolivia have little or no public support.[36] Toward the end of the 1980s, because political parties, Congress, and the judiciary had extremely low confidence ratings, nontraditional quasi-populist parties and leaders made their appearance in dramatic fashion. Max Fernández (Unión Cívica Solidaridad, UCS) and Carlos Palenque (Conciencia de Patria, CONDEPA), a controversial brewery owner and a radio and television station owner, respectively, became the front runners in many public opinion polls.[37] Much of their support was based on appeals to race and class; however, their strategy was essentially patrimonial.

Fernández traveled extensively around the country, building hospitals, sponsoring sporting events, and building patron-client networks. In the eyes of aspiring mestizo or *cholo* entrepreneurial sectors, Fernández became Bolivia's Horatio Alger: he was a poor *cholo* man from Cochabamba who worked his way up from delivering beer to owning the country's largest brewery. The emergence of "*cholo* capital" is quite significant because it represents a challenge to the traditional white, *k'ara*, capital, which has dominated Bolivian politics.[38]

Palenque, on the other hand, represents what could be termed "lumpen capital," or the marginal sectors of the city of La Paz. He has become a powerful broker in national politics, although his power base is still La Paz. In many ways, Palenque's television and radio programs have become small claims courts where La Paz's marginal, but large, Aymara-speaking population finds a quick resolution to personal problems it cannot possibly hope to resolve in Bolivia's overburdened, corrupt, and discriminatory justice system.[39] In short, Fernández and Palenque positioned themselves to become powerful political contenders in the 1993 national elections.

PRESIDENTIAL AUTHORITY UNDER SIEGE: THE MNR'S RETURN TO OFFICE

The June 1993 elections brought Gonzalo Sánchez de Lozada into power. This time around, the MNR's candidate garnered 35 percent of the vote, which translated into a majority in the National Congress. The results were not enough to win the presidency outright but sufficient to prevent the Acuerdo (which came in second, with less than 25 percent) and any other party from laying claim to the office. On August 6, Sánchez de Lozada won the congressional round and was sworn into office.

One of the most significant dimensions of the MNR's return to office was the electoral coalition with Víctor Hugo Cárdenas of the Movimiento Revolucionario Tupac Katari (MRTK), an indigenous party. During the campaign, Sánchez de Lozada and Cárdenas were portrayed as "children of the revolution," in a calculated attempt to tap those social sectors once strongly identified with the MNR, such as the peasantry, but which had long ago abandoned the party. As the first Aymara to achieve such high office, Cárdenas brought with him a great deal of expectations in the indigenous sectors of Bolivia. Cárdenas delivered to the MNR a huge voting bloc of mainly rural Aymara campesinos. Moreover, Cárdenas represented the most important hope for bridging ethnic and linguistic cleavages and for extending Bolivia's young democracy to the indigenous masses.[40]

Although Sánchez de Lozada and Cárdenas controlled a majority in Congress, they still required coalitions to ensure smooth sailing for the implementation of Sánchez de Lazada's ambitious reform agenda. The key now, as in the past, was to build a coalition with opposition parties. In contrast to the Pacto por la Democracía and the Acuerdo Patriótico, however, the MNR did not have to enter a pact with the second or third-place parties.

Sánchez de Lozada's search for a governing partner culminated in two surprises. On July 2, the MNR struck a deal, (dubbing it the Pacto de la Gobernabilidad, or Governability Pact) with Max Fernández, Bolivia's controversial beer baron and chief of the UCS. As in all previous pacts, the distribution of key government posts in exchange for the UCS's twenty-one seats in Congress sealed the agreement.[41] Moreover, Sánchez de Lozada brokered the first visit by Fernández with the U.S. ambassador since accusations surfaced of his alleged ties to narcotics trafficking. The MNR's deal making did not end there. On July 7, Sánchez de Lozada signed the Pacto por el Cambio (Pact for Change) with the MBL (Movimiento Bolivia Libre) doling out yet another set of government posts.[42]

A FRAGILE RULING COALITION

President Sánchez de Lozada made institutional reform the centerpiece of his government. The basic theme of the new government was that the process of reform initiated in the mid-1990s under the NPE had suffered a severe setback under the Acuerdo Patriótico government. Political institutions were not modernized, and economic reforms were not consolidated.

Sánchez de Lozada put forth the Plan de Todos, which promised a social-market economy alternative to the rigid continuity of the new economic policy. The plan included seven pillars: attracting investment, creating jobs, ensuring economic stability, improving health and education, encouraging popular participation, changing the role of government, and combating corruption. The key to the MNR's investment proposal rested on the capitalization of public enterprises, a significant departure from earlier privatization schemes. In February 1994, the MNR-MBL-UCS coalition in the Congress approved a capitalization law, which essentially authorized a joint venture association in which a state enterprise would contribute its assets and a private investor would contribute an equivalent amount in capital. In theory, this would double the original value of the enterprise. Once an enterprise was capitalized, the investor would receive 50 percent of the company's stock and sole management control. The remaining stock would be distributed evenly among the 3.2 million Bolivians over the age of eighteen years.[43] The government also claimed that this program would result in the creation of a half million new jobs. The capitalization law also promised that revenue from the sale of state enterprises (expected to reach about US$8 billion) would be deposited in a pension fund for all Bolivians over the age of eighteen years. Government economists argued that the capitalization of state enterprises would be equivalent to investing approximately 35 percent of Bolivia's gross domestic product.

While turning ownership of state assets over to Bolivian citizens and workers and establishing a pension fund were important shifts from pure privatization, their implementation was extremely difficult. In 1995, the government sold ENTEL (telecommunications), ENDE (electricity), and LAB (airlines) to foreign investors. Nevertheless, the capitalization scheme stirred great passions, ranging from labor's claims that workers would be fired en masse to ADN's claim that the government was giving away Bolivian assets to foreigners. The government's scheme for a private pension plan was met with equal suspicion. Most controversial, however, was the attempted capitalization of YPFB (hydrocarbons), which was postponed until mid-1996 because of opposition from labor and others.

THE PLAN DE TODOS

Implementing the government's reform agenda and governing Bolivia proved more difficult that Sánchez de Lozada anticipated. His problems in governing were rooted mainly in two significant factors: the fragility of his coalition and the timing of his reform attempts.

First, the ruling coalition faced difficulties controlling its ranks, as both interparty and intraparty feuding proved destabilizing. A severe conflict between the president's party and the members of the cabinet was especially problematic. As often happens in presidential systems where a president controls the patronage in the cabinet, leaving control over the legislature to old party hacks, Sánchez de Lozada named an independent cabinet made up of technocrats and businessmen and left Congress in the hands of the MNR's old guard. A joke circulating among the opposition in the early months illustrates the problem: Sánchez de Lozada forgot that to govern Bolivia one must always make a pact with the MNR. These tensions eventually produced a cabinet crisis in March 1994, forcing Sánchez de Lozada to replace the most prominent private sector ministers with members of the MNR. Another cabinet shift in September 1995 had similar characteristics.

The ruling coalition proved to be extremely unstable because of numerous outbursts from Max Fernández and the UCS. On any given week, unsubstantiated rumors abounded about a UCS departure from the cabinet. Fernández, who felt excluded from the decision-making process, lashed out against the MBL and finally withdrew from the coalition in December 1994 only to rejoin and depart again in a huff in mid-1995. His party retained control over the Ministry of Defense and, in September 1995, was granted the Ministry of Sustainable Development. The reality of the situation, however, was that, beyond the specific and very limited role it played in the cabinet and the crucial votes it provided in the National Congress, the UCS was not very significant.

Max Fernández's untimely death on November 26, 1995, in an airplane accident may signal the end of the UCS. Despite a rather significant increase in support for the party following Fernández's death, without the caudillo this party will likely disappear and its members will seek accommodation within the MNR or other larger parties.[44] Its followers are up for grabs, and because they shared a similar constituency, only CONDEPA is likely to sway them.

By the same token, the MBL found itself in the difficult position of having to defend policies it opposed over the past eight years, such as U.S.-designed counternarcotics programs and deepening "neoliberal" economic reforms. Only a national summit in January 1994 with Sánchez de Lozada cemented the MNR-MBL relationship. Antonio Araníbar, the MBL foreign minister, performed a crucial ceremonial role and, at least according to some opinion polls in early 1994, was the most popular member of the cabinet. A more accurate picture would reveal that the MNR engulfed both the MBL and the UCS and that their fate rested entirely on Sánchez de Lozada's. Despite attempts by members of the MBL to retain their identity independently of the MNR, the fact remains that the future of this small band of well-intentioned leftists is tied intimately to the fortunes of the MNR government.

Second, the Sánchez de Lozada government raised numerous expectations that it would alleviate the social costs of economic reform and impose some sort of social market model. In his first two years, however, to prevent an economic crisis the government was forced to tighten austerity. In contrast to the 1980s, however, social tolerance for austerity had decreased considerably. In the context of a fragile ruling coalition, the government was incapable of pushing ahead without facing resistance from labor, students, regional groups, and opposition political parties.

President Sánchez de Lozada faced an all-out battle with opposition political parties from the very day he took office. In November 1993, for example, a few members of the two former ruling parties

(ADN and MIR) called for his impeachment or the convocation of early elections. Then in December, when the MNR-controlled National Congress amended the electoral law, the opposition parties charged Sánchez with attempting to rig the rules of the game to favor his party.

But these moves were not significant, as these parties faced severe internal crises and charges of corruption.[45] The unraveling of the opposition warrants more concern because it is intrinsically linked to the explosion of political corruption that plagued Bolivian democracy and has had serious repercussions for the governability of the country. Since leaving office in August 1993, the ADN party became engulfed in tremendous internal political battles that forced General Bánzer out of retirement. Bánzer's return from early retirement confirmed the institutional weaknesses of the ADN, especially its inability to name a viable successor. No single individual other than Bánzer appears capable of bringing the party together in time for the 1997 elections.

In many ways, ADN's internal crisis was fueled by speculation of widespread corruption during 1989–93. Concern for corruption in office became the single most significant factor in the almost total collapse of the MIR. Beginning in August 1993, former president Paz Zamora has attempted to distance himself from his party and to pursue lofty international objectives, including stints at the Wilson Center in Washington, D.C., and on the International Peace Commission in Chiapas, Mexico. These goals, however, were dramatically altered with the March 1994 accusations by the Special Counternarcotics Force (Fuerza Especial de Lucha Contra el Narcotráfico, FELCN) that widespread linkages between the MIR and narcotraffickers have existed since at least 1987.[46] These accusations extended to the entire leadership structure of the MIR and all but ended the party's quest for a return to political office at middecade. In a dramatic sequence of events, drug traffickers outlined in painful detail before a congressional committee the manner in which Paz Zamora and the MIR had allegedly come to rely on the cocaine industry to finance their 1989 electoral campaign. The impact of these accusations was great. On March 25, 1994, Paz Zamora resigned from politics, claiming that "errors were made during his administration but no crimes occurred." In December, Oscar Eid Franco, the party's principal strategist, was arrested and as of this writing has not been released.

The MNR has not been exempt from charges of corruption. In September 1995, the government was rocked by allegations that several high-ranking members of the party had close relations with a trafficker who shipped four tons of cocaine in a DC-6 to Mexico from the country's principal airport. The planeload of cocaine was intercepted in Lima, Peru, only after U.S. Drug Enforcement Administration authorities in Bolivia alerted Peruvian police. Although the party dodged the accusations, few doubted that the "narcoavión" scandal, as it was named, would have a serious impact on the MNR's chances in 1997. There is already talk that a few potential candidates for office are tainted by the scandal. If this is the case, the MNR could very well follow the MIR.

With the demise of the Acuerdo Patriótico, the troubled future of the ADN and the MIR, and the implications of the *narcoavión* scandal, the main opposition appears to be CONDEPA, the populist party headed by Carlos Palenque, which in the December 1993 municipal election managed not only to expand its support outside of the department of La Paz but also to again win the mayor's office in the capital city. It is extremely unlikely, however, that CONDEPA will pose a serious challenge outside of La Paz. In this context, a return to the presidency by General Hugo Bánzer in 1997 is not out of the question.

REFORMS TO BOLIVIA'S HYBRID PRESIDENTIALISM

Despite the weaknesses of the ruling coalition, the first twelve months of the Sánchez de Lozada government witnessed the congressional approval of five significant laws: the cabinet restructuring law, the capitalization law, the popular participation law, the education reform law, and the constitutional amendments law. As far as government officials were concerned, this body of legislation provided a reform agenda as far-reaching as Bolivia's 1952 national revolution. But the difficulties in securing approval were numerous and revealed both the weakness of the coalition and the government's inability to sell its message.

In August 1994, thirty-five articles of the constitution were amended through the constitutional amendments law, including the direct election of half the members of the lower house of Congress from single-member districts; an increase in the terms for presidents, members of Congress, mayors, and municipal council members to five years, with general and municipal elections alternating every two and a half years; the direct election of the president and all mayors; a lowering of the voting age to eighteen; an increase in the powers of departmental prefects; the establishment of an independent human rights ombudsman; and the establishment of a constitutional tribunal.

These reforms are significant and warrant an extended discussion beyond the scope of this essay. For our purposes, the most significant reforms have to do with the way in which both presidents and members of the lower house will be elected, beginning in 1997. Under the terms of the current reform, if no candidate achieves 50 percent of the vote, the congressional runoff will be decided between the top two candidates. This modification may prevent the impasses that characterized nearly all elections since the transition and may ensure the quick election of a president.

The manner in which members of the lower house will be elected may force legislators to develop closer bonds with the districts they ostensibly represent. Single-member district representatives will be forced to campaign in their respective districts and may not be as tied to the party patronage structure as is currently the case. Charges abound, however, that two types of legislators have been created; those elected through single-member districts, who will see themselves as true representatives, and the rest, who will be seen as party hacks. Moreover, although its supporters claim that this new system will ensure the election of a majority, there is no guarantee that this reform will foster coalition building, the only strength of the Bolivian system. The results of these reforms will not be felt until the end of the decade.

GOVERNABILITY UNDER THE NEW RULES

President Sánchez de Lozada's term has been marked by a series of confrontations with labor, students, coca growers, regional organizations, and the opposition. Throughout 1995, the government faced numerous strikes by the COB, a teacher's strike and university student demonstrations demanding an end to educational reform, an incipient separatist movement from the southernmost department of Tarija, and a potential insurrection by coca-growing peasants in the Chapare Valley.

Two explanations may account for the resurgence of social conflict in Bolivia. First, the fragility of the ruling coalition has emboldened both the opposition and the numerous groups that have challenged the government. Second, the economic strategy has done little for the Bolivian working class, which, after ten years of neoliberalism, is expecting greater results. Whatever accounts for the resurgence of social conflict, the result has been the same. The government resorted to the same mechanisms of the past ten years to control labor and peasant unrest. Sánchez de Lozada declared a state of siege on April 18, 1995, for a ninety-day period. In July it was extended for another ninety days. When the state of siege was finally lifted, social unrest continued, with students, coca growers, members of opposition parties, and others still on the warpath. The state of siege option may no longer be the one required to control unrest.

CONCLUSION

Bolivia's hybrid presidential system created mechanisms that enabled at least three presidents to overcome institutional crises. Ruling coalitions have not been enough, however, to overcome constitutional and electoral mechanisms that give the Bolivian National Congress the power to elect the president when no candidate obtains a majority. As a result, three distinct types of coalitions have been formed: electoral coalitions, which allow parties to establish a broad platform to appeal to wider segments of the electorate; congressional coalitions, which enable the election of a president; and a ruling coalition to govern the country. These characteristics anchor the entire system in political parties and Congress. As long as this is the case, Bolivia's system will not be strictly presidential but a hybrid, where the legislature plays a critical role.

One way to overcome the dilemma of reconstituting alliances is to convert a ruling coalition into a viable electoral vehicle. As the breakdown of the Pacto por la Democracía revealed, ruling coalitions lack the flexibility to become viable electoral alliances, because alternating positions in the executive branch among members of the coalition entails recomposing and redistributing patronage. Moreover, to win elections political parties must form broad conjunctural alliances and propose populist platforms. By the same token, converting an electoral or congressional coalition into a viable governing coalition has proven extremely difficult.

One of the keys to institutionalizing the present system will be to form effective governing alliances that can fare well during electoral battles. Alliances must able be able to transcend postelectoral bargaining. These objectives must take into consideration that, in Bolivia, the principal function of elections has been to allow competing leaders to periodically restructure patronage networks. In short, the recomposition and redistribution of political patronage is the Achilles tendon of Bolivia's hybrid presidential system.

The critical issue raised by the Bolivian experience is the impact on policy outcomes of the method of selecting the executive. Owing to this fact, a recurrent need to form coalitions has paradoxically become both the strength and the weakness of the system. Coalitions, such as the Pacto por la Democracía, the Acuerdo Patriótico, and the Pacto por la Gobernabilidad have enabled executives to overcome recalcitrant congressional opposition to impose economic stabilization measures. By demonstrating a capacity to enter into long-term pacts, these coalitions also reveal a degree of political maturing of Bolivia's political class. As recently as the mid-1980s it would have been improbable and even absurd to suggest the possibility of a coalition between the ADN and the MIR; this capacity to form coalitions gave the system a much needed dose of political stability. It is noteworthy, therefore, that Bolivia's hybrid presidential system does possess the capability to proceed with democratization while simultaneously implementing draconian austerity measures. The permanency of these trends, however, is still questionable, as evidenced by events under the Sánchez de Lozada administration.

Coalitions have also served to shut out the opposition from the patronage spoils of the system and from the decision-making process. In domestic policy, the opposition has been excluded from participation in (or discussion of) the enactment of key legislation, such as mining codes and investment laws. This situation has also revealed itself rather dramatically in the manner in which the government has negotiated foreign policy, especially counternarcotics agreements with the United States. Owing to this exclusionary style, Congress has demonstrated a lack of knowledge regarding the details of the international agreements it must approve as well as the technicalities of economic policy. This exclusionary pattern does not bode well for the future, as opposition groups consider extrasystemic ways to influence policy making.

What can be learned from the recent Bolivian experience? First, we now know that imposing and sustaining market-oriented reforms in a small and poor country is a very difficult task, indeed. A decade after the imposition of Decree 21060, Bolivia reached a critical juncture. Although the country's economy grew steadily—averaging 2.5 percent per year—this was not enough to deal with declining socioeconomic conditions. Three democratically elected governments since 1985 imposed states of exception to deal with labor and other social unrest. In the process, they relied on the armed forces to engage in public security missions.

Second, the Bolivian experience suggests that decision making must be largely centered in the executive, with legislatures playing little or no legislative role other than approving executive initiatives. To achieve this, stable ruling coalitions are essential to avoid executive-legislative impasses. In some sense, however, this style of rule has resulted in a profound crisis for all major political institutions. Political parties are perhaps more disconnected from society in 1995 than at any time since the transition to democracy in 1982. The legislature and the judiciary rank at the bottom of citizen confidence.

Third, the Bolivian case suggests that profound constitutional reforms are difficult to enact but even more difficult to implement. The Sánchez de Lozada administration's promise to resolve age-old problems of representation and administration of justice will take time to be realized. Few in Bolivia, however, are willing to give the reforms a chance to succeed, as the only term of significance is the short term.

Over the past decade, Bolivian governments have done much to fit into the neoliberal wave that has engulfed the Americas. Yet, the relative insignificance of the country in regional affairs has resulted in little international interest or, more importantly, investment. Innovative ideas such as the capitalization initiative of the current government have received extensive praise from international financial institutions, but the program cannot survive on praise alone, especially given the domestic political opposition.

CHAPTER 6

Brazilian Presidentialism
Shifting Comparative Perspectives from Europe to the Americas

Kurt von Mettenheim

Presidential institutions have been critical for political development and democratization throughout modern Brazilian history. To understand the context and content of Brazilian presidentialism, scholars must shift away from theories and concepts derived from European history, such as parliamentary government, rigidly organized party systems, and associated patterns of polarization that produced democratic breakdown and fascism. In their stead, classic analyses of political development in the United States can provide fundamentally new perspectives. The U.S. experience, Brazilian history, and the recent events of transition from military rule suggest that Brazilian presidentialism can reconcile the heady popular appeals of mass democracy with more sober liberal notions of indirect representation; that direct executive elections can generate significant political change through critical elections and party realignments; and that, once elected, presidents can deftly renegotiate legislative coalitions because they are free to appoint professional politicians to administrative posts.

This new comparative perspective is compelling because party-electoral politics in Brazil today are strikingly similar to the U.S. experience of precocious democratization and political reform a century ago.[1] During the rapidly shifting events of transition from military to civilian rule, the Brazilian presidential and federal system facilitated the rapid organization of mass politics in two ways: first, such a system encouraged broad popular appeals during campaigns for executive office; and second, once in office, executives were free to nominate party professionals to thousands of administrative posts. Far from exceptional, this pattern is typical of party development in presidential and federal systems throughout the Americas. And far from dysfunctional, this pattern produced a rapid and sweeping organization of political parties through a complex series of alliances between new national political elites and patronage machines. Although comparative analysis of recent events may be premature, the movements for the moralization of Brazilian public life, which produced the impeachment of President Fernando Collor de Mello in late 1992 and the election of President Fernando Henrique Cardoso in 1994, suggest that further comparisons between the United States and Brazil may be appropriate. The Progressive-era reforms that reacted to the brazen corruption and political monopoly of party machines in early twentieth-century America may provide comparative references for understanding political reform and democratization in Brazil.

Scholars who criticize presidential institutions in Brazil for exacerbating populism, patronage, party indiscipline, corruption, and a weak congress (like advocates of the responsible party system model in the United States more than four decades ago) fail to recognize the positive place of these realities in the typical trajectory of democratization in presidential and federal institutions.[2] A central argument of this chapter is that the U.S. experience is a more productive reference for comparative analysis of political development and democratization in Brazil. From the acute observations of Max Weber and James Bryce in the first decades of this century to "new political historians" more recently, central aspects of American exceptionalism have been defined in terms of the impact of presidential instead of parliamentary institutions, the precocious emergence of mass democratic politics and parties, the predominance of pragmatism, patronage, and pork barrel politics over ideology and party organization, and the importance of federalism in a new and large country.[3]

In contrast to the widespread criticism of presidential institutions in Brazil, American scholars recognize that the rapid organization of mass parties in the nineteenth-century United States occurred through the plebiscitarian appeals of direct presidential elections and the power of presidents to nominate party professionals to administrative posts (thereby creating alliances with the patronage systems of senators).[4] Recent debate among political scientists and historians such as Walter Burnham, Philip Converse, Paul Kleppner, and Jerrold Rusk has focused once again on the cultural, historical, social, and political dimensions of rapid democratization in nineteenth-century America. But a fundamental theoretical shift has occurred: debate among U.S. scholars now occurs within a new understanding of presidentialism in their country, which rejects traditional theories based on European parliaments and well-organized, ideological parties.

These new theories of presidential institutions and political development in the United States also produced fundamentally new conceptions of American democracy. For scholars such as William Chambers, Burnham, Theodore Lowi, Samuel Hays, and others, the populist appeals of direct presidential campaigns matter more than party programs or ideologies, and the electoral practices of party professionals matter more than the formalities of party organization.[5] And despite corruption in urban America, these scholars argue that the patronage machines of urban immigrants were linked to political parties through shifting alliances with executives. Burnham extends this perspective by arguing that V. O. Key's pathbreaking concept of critical elections provides a broad theory of political change in American history and that the wave of populism and party mobilization in the late nineteenth century (reversed by Progressive-era legislation) was a lost opportunity for party building and popular inclusion.[6] Lowi argues that the peculiar combination of formal party continuity alongside substantive electoral and policy change throughout American history is based on the powerful constituent function of direct presidential elections in the United States.[7] Finally, Hays notes that the classic sociological distinction between community and society was articulated within party-electoral politics in the United States. Citizens resisted northeastern liberal visions of modern capitalist society by reinforcing patronage machines in local communities.[8] In sum, the American experience suggests that presidential institutions provide a series of opportunities for political development and democratization.

This chapter attempts to understand the impact of presidential institutions during and after the transition from military to civilian rule in Brazil (1974–1994) by clarifying the similarities and differences between the American and Brazilian experiences. A brief review of several differences between American and Brazilian presidentialism and a sketch of the origins and development of party-electoral patronage and executivecentric federalism in Brazilian history preface the analysis of recent events of democratic transition. Significant evidence from the past and present suggests that the broad popular appeals of direct presidential elections can deepen democratic politics in Brazil, that presidents can deftly renegotiate legislative coalitions by directly nominating professional politicians to administrative posts, and that policy initiative and creativity is encouraged by the clarity and personalism of presidential leadership.

BRAZILIAN PRESIDENTIALISM AND LATE PARTY DEVELOPMENT

Far from applying theories of American presidentialism to Brazil *tout court*, the American trajectory of political development provides an extremely useful point of departure for analysis of similarities and differences. Perhaps the most critical difference is that emphasized by Hans Daalder for Europe: "It was of profound significance whether an articulated party system developed before, after, or concurrently with the rise of bureaucracy."[9] This difference is less a question of state or party strength than timing. Mass parties emerged in the United States during the nineteenth century, before the emergence of central government bureaucracies and state intervention into the economy in the 1930s. In Brazil, competitive mass politics first appeared during the 1945–64 period, well after modern state bureaucracies were centralized and immediately following a period of extensive state intervention under the Estado Novo of Getulio Vargas (1937–45).

For Daalder, the relative timing of party and bureaucratic development in Europe determined both the extent of party control over government and broader prospects for stability.[10] The differences between American and Brazilian politics confirm the first part of Daalder's argument. Precocious political development throughout nineteenth-century America took the form of party empowerment over government bureaucracies (before civil service reform and other Progressive-era measures weakened their grip). In comparison, both Giovanni Sartori and Maria do Carmo Campello de Souza argue that Brazilian politics lack the characteristics associated with fully consolidated party systems because Brazilian party elites remain dependent upon state structures.[11] In sum, the first part of Daalder's argument holds. The late development of mass party politics in Brazil produced parties with less control over government bureaucracies.

The second part of Daalder's argument, which suggests that late party development generates political instability, requires greater attention. While Brazilian parties lack the formal organization, parliamentary discipline, and ideological clarity of some European parties, one cannot thereby infer scenarios of instability. Instead, Douglas Chalmers argues that "the aspects of parties often identified as faults—absence of a solid, independent organizational network, presence of personalist leadership, weakness of ideological or programmatic content, rapid rise and fall of ad-hoc parties, lack of sharp identification with class or other specific interests—are clearly the product of the Latin American socio-political structure. More important is the fact that *it is these characteristics which make parties functional* within that structure."[12] Arguments that a dysfunctional or weak party system (organizational fluidity, corruption, patronage, shifting electoral alliances and legislative coalitions, and poorly disciplined party elites) caused the Brazilian crises that led to instability and democratic breakdown in 1964 are misleading because they fail to consider the alternative trajectory of party development within presidential institutions.

Scholars of the United States suggest that party-electoral change occurred in their country through a sequence of critical, realigning elections that produced new policy constellations.[13] The stakes of Brazilian elections are even higher because of the greater centralization of powers in the central government and the executivecentric character of its federalism. Consequently, party systems in Brazilian history were not redefined by critical elections and policy realignments, as in the United States, but were reconstructed after matters of political inclusion-exclusion or policy change were redefined through other (usually military) means. Instead of a sequence of electoral realignments as constituent political acts that redefine the political power of new and old groups, the succession of party systems in Brazil can be seen as a sequence of averted realignments: refusals to include claimants and the authoritarian reorganization of the party-electoral sphere.

Because of late party development, Brazilian populism also differs considerably from American populist movements of the nineteenth century. Unlike the social and agrarian character of American and European populist movements, populism emerged in Brazil as a political movement organized by state elites geared primarily toward urban groups.[14] The vision of the state as a multiclass national front against the domination of foreign capital and imperialist interests is a unique element of Latin American populism.[15] This different, more statecentric, and urban-oriented character of Brazilian and Latin American populism is a widely recognized result of the greater role of the Latin American state in dependent economic development. In sum, late party development within Brazilian presidential institutions increased the stakes of electoral politics and contributed to this nation's statecentric tradition of populism.

PRESIDENTIALISM IN BRAZILIAN HISTORY

The central argument about presidential institutions in Brazilian history is that competitive politics between 1945 and 1964 embodied the elements of American political development outlined above. The broad popular appeals of direct executive elections and the ability of presidents, governors, and mayors to directly appoint party politicians to administrative posts permitted the rapid reorganization of corporatist and patronage machines into competitive political parties (PSD, PTB, UDN). These three parties dominated electoral politics until military intervention in 1964. However, before turning to the 1945–64 period, a few remarks are in order about the origins of both party-electoral patronage during the Brazilian empire (1822–89) and the organization of the extremely executivecentric character of Brazilian federalism during the Old Republic (1889–1930).

Reviewing the origins of party-electoral patronage in nineteenth-century Brazil helps clarify subsequent patterns of political development in the twentieth-century.[16] For, unlike the wars and discord that wracked the newly independent states of Hispanic Latin America, effective bureaucratic institutions, a prince and parliament, and powerful military forces were built at the center during the Brazilian empire. Much of this exceptional trajectory of Brazil in Latin America is due to the manner in which the national political institutions of the empire were built upon complex patterns of party-electoral patronage. Patronage linked central imperial institutions to the variety of provincial and local institutions throughout the vast Brazilian territory.

Far from a static characteristic of social structure or Ibero-American culture, patronage during the Brazilian empire is of interest here because of its changing content in response to party-electoral politics. The work of Brazilian political analysts Oliveira Vianna and Paula Beiguelman suggests that three critical moments define the organization of patronage during the sixty-seven years of parliamentary monarchy.[17] First, a grant of free-male suffrage with low income requirements by Dom Pedro I upon independence in 1822 quickly transformed the paternal clans that ruled the large farms (*fazendas*) and vast rural areas of Brazil into political clans. Second, once electoral resources were thereby established, the decentralizing Criminal Code of 1832 encouraged these newly empowered leaders of political clans to resolve conflicts with their counterparts and build institutions on the county level. Finally, when power was centralized once again (beginning with the Additional Act of 1836 and culminating in the 1841 regency), political alliances for and against centralization emerged on the national level between existing county (*municipio*) and provincial party-electoral machines. These national political alliances became the Liberal and Conservative Parties, which dominated imperial politics until 1889. In sum, party-electoral patronage developed during the Brazilian empire in a cumulative sequence of responses to the adoption of liberal and monarchic rules and procedures from abroad.

Executivecentric federalism is the second historic element of Brazilian politics critical for understanding its presidential institutions.[18] The authors of Brazil's first republican constitution in 1891 sought to reverse the centralization of state power during the empire by establishing state's rights to contract foreign loans, levy export taxes, write constitutional, criminal, and electoral law, and form autonomous military organizations.[19] Unusual gubernatorial powers were grafted onto this constitutional design when President Campos Salles attempted to avert further civil wars between political factions within states by ruling that federal deputies would be seated only if they were approved by their respective state governors. Governors retained this legal prerogative to seat their congressional delegations throughout the Old Republic. Single parties thereby tended to predominate within states, and governors dominated negotiations of electoral alliances and legislative coalitions between single state parties on the federal level. Although Brazilian governors lost the prerogative to seat congressional delegations in 1930 and never regained it, their influence in electoral and party politics on the state and federal levels remains critical today.

PRESIDENTIAL INSTITUTIONS AND MASS POLITICS, 1945–1964

For the first time in Brazilian history, the postwar period fully combined the mechanisms of precocious democratization through the party-electoral politics emphasized by scholars of nineteenth-century America. Direct elections for president, governor, and mayor were held throughout the 1945–64 period. Once elected, executives freely appointed party politicians to administrative posts. Governors, regional party politicians, and new state elites from Getulio Vargas's Estado Novo thereby linked local patronage machines to create regional and state party-electoral organizations. In turn, the organizations were linked to the broad popular appeals of presidential and gubernatorial elections through electoral alliances, legislative coalitions, and administrative nominations typical of spoils systems.[20]

Despite the innovative historical research on this period, political scientists still describe events from 1945 to 1964 by using concepts, theories, and models based on European experiences with parliamentary government, polarized pluralism, and democratic breakdown.[21] These comparisons misrepresent the causal place of presidential institutions and democratic politics in the crises of pre-1964 Brazil because they either cling to an idealized image of Westminster parliamentary government (and related models of ideological, well-organized party systems and disciplined, effective parliamentary elites) or draw unfounded analogies with the polarization in European parliamentary systems, which produced democratic breakdown and fascism in the 1920s and 1930s. If one instead compares Brazilian party-electoral politics from 1945 to 1964 to the American experience, one can better describe how popular pressure, machine politics, plebiscitarian appeals, and the constraints on change in capitalist society generated political crisis and military intervention by 1964.

Souza's pathbreaking work entitled *Estado e Partidos Politicos no Brasil, 1930–1945,* provides an explanation for the pre-1964 crisis that avoids problematic comparisons to European parliamentary systems. Souza focuses both on structural problems of pre-1964 party competition and the prospects for overcoming those problems through the mechanisms that drive politics in the Brazilian presidential system: the popular appeals of direct executive elections and the links between executives and the patronage machines that control local politics. Souza's central claim is that politics in the pre-1964 presidential system produced crisis and military intervention precisely because it generated the outcomes normally associated with political development and democratization: "Our central hypothesis . . . is that the critical character of the [pre-1964] conjuncture derives from the simultaneous strengthening of the state and the party system, presenting in an immediate way the following dilemma: State without parties or party government."[22] Military intervention occurred in 1964 because the plebiscitarian appeals of presidential elections generated both popular expectations of political change and a conservative reaction typical of the constraints on change in capitalist society. Souza thereby offers a compelling account of how Brazilian presidentialism shaped political development, democratization, and the crises that led to the breakdown of democracy in 1964.[23]

Both electoral trends and data on party representation in congress from 1945 to 1964 support this interpretation and refute analyses that explain military intervention in 1964 as resulting from polarized pluralism or electoral fragmentation. At first glance, congressional elections between 1945 and 1962 appear to present evidence of an electoral decline in the fortune of the major parties PSD, UDN, and PTB, which would support theories of fragmentation or polarization (see table 6.1). Votes for the PSD and the UDN declined between 1945 and 1962. After the PTB peaked in the 1950 election (when Getulio Vargas won the presidency), the party declined in the 1962 elections.

But these trends fail to indicate polarization or fragmentation, because votes were not displaced to minor parties. The percentage of votes obtained by minor parties running candidates in isolation fell from 17.2 percent in 1945 to 4.9 percent in 1962.[24] Instead, voters shifted their preferences to party alliances, which increased their share of the total congressional vote from 22.9 percent in 1950 to 39.7 percent in 1962. Hence, the argument about electoral trends shifts to the problem of an increasing number of electoral alliances among congressional candidates. For those intent on comparing the Brazilian experience with the electoral fragmentation and polarization that produced fascism in Europe, this increasing number of electoral alliances appears dysfunctional because it would impede the formation and maintenance of coalition governments. But if the

Table 6.1 Official Results for Federal Chamber Elections in Brazil,
1945–1962 (percent of total vote)

Political Party	1945	1950	1954	1958	1962
PSD	42.6	30.5	21.6	18.1	15.0
UDN	26.5	19.2	13.3	12.9	10.8
PTB	10.1	18.6	14.6	14.4	11.6
Party alliances		22.9	25.2	32.6	39.7
Other parties	17.2	21.7	18.5	12.6	4.9
Blank or null					
votes	3.3	0.8	6.6	9.1	17.7
N	5,934,332	6,763,273	9,889,827	12,687,997	14,747,221

Source: Estatisticas Historicas do Brasil (Rio de Janeiro: IBGE, 1990).

comparative perspective is shifted away from Europe to the presidential and federal systems typical of the Americas, the increase in electoral alliances can be interpreted as a process of realignment among congressional, state, and local party elites responding to electoral change under way on the national level. And far from dysfunctional, the patronage, corruption, and ad hoc character of party identities in pre-1964 Brazilian politics can be seen as facilitating this realignment.

Another apparent paradox for theories based on the rigid party organizations found in European parliamentary systems appears in the data on the party membership of Brazilian federal deputies.[25] Candidates for federal deputy did indeed enter into an increasing number of party alliances during the 1945–64 period. However, few deputies declared formal affiliation with minor parties after taking office. In 1945, deputies representing the three major parties (PSD, UDN, PTB) totaled 89.5 percent of the federal chamber. In 1962, the three parties controlled 83.5 percent of the chamber. A decrease of 6 percent over seventeen years is hardly sufficient to suggest major party decline, electoral fragmentation, or polarized pluralism.

Trends in presidential elections from 1945 to 1964 also support the idea of electoral realignment and fail to confirm theses of major party decline, electoral fractionalization, or polarized pluralism. The percentage of direct popular vote for the PSD-PTB alliance, which elected three successive presidents, did indeed fall from 54.1 percent in 1945 to 28.5 percent in 1960. But the UDN, which polled roughly 30 percent of the popular vote in the first three presidential

Table 6.2 Official Results for Presidential Elections in Brazil, 1945–1962 (percent of total vote)

Presidential Vote	1945	1950	1955	1960
PSD-PTB alliance	54.1	46.6	33.8	28.5
UDN	33.9	28.4	28.6	41.7
Other parties	9.6	20.6	32.2	16.3
Blank or null votes	2.2	4.3	5.2	6.7
N	6,003,209	8,254,979	9,097,014	12,586,354

Source: *Estatisticas Historicas do Brasil* (Rio de Janeiro: IBGE, 1990).

elections, won the presidency in 1960, with Janio Quadros receiving 41.7 percent of the vote (see table 6.2). Perhaps more important, minor parties fared poorly in the 1960 election. Finally, the three major parties of the pre-1964 period together polled 75 percent in the 1950 presidential elections. By 1960 their hold on the presidential contest remained at 70.2 percent. This decrease of less than 5 percent of the electoral vote is insufficient to support theses of major party decline, fragmentation, or polarized pluralism.

If the comparative perspective is shifted from Europe to the Americas, Brazil's 1945–64 experience with democratic politics can be interpreted in a very different light. Political crisis and democratic breakdown occurred by 1964 because the mechanisms of political development typical of presidential and federal systems threatened to, in Souza's words, "simultaneously strengthen the state and party system."[26] Indeed, the major populist party of the period (PTB) more than quadrupled its representation of deputies in the federal chamber, from 22 in 1945 to 116 by 1962. The representation of the PSD and UDN in the federal chamber did indeed fall— from 52.8 to 30.3 percent and from 29.0 to 23.4 percent, respectively —but this realignment of federal deputies from the statecentric PSD and conservative UDN to the populist PTB cannot be considered a process of major party decline, fractionalization, or polarized pluralism. Instead, the process appears to be a significant realignment of party elites toward "a party with governing capacity."[27]

Shifting comparative perspectives on pre-1964 party-electoral politics also suggests that the prospects for governance were considerably greater than concepts of polarized pluralism and power vacuum (which describe the European descent into fascism) would suggest. First, the rapid reassertion of presidential authority by Goulart through a direct referendum in 1962 is similar to de Gaulle's statecraft in France (both his inauguration of the French Fifth Republic in 1958 and his call for introducing direct presidential elections through a national referendum, also held in 1962). Second, the increasing number of party alliances is consistent with the claim that a major party-electoral realignment was under way. Finally, the 1964 military intervention was a means of averting populist-led political change.

While analysts differ about the content of populist mobilization in both the United States and Brazil, the demobilization and exclusion that followed the periods in question may indicate the degree of change. In the United States, the period of precocious political development in the late nineteeth-century was followed by Progressive-era reforms designed to weaken parties, defeat new mass party elites, and demobilize popular participation. Electoral redistricting attempted to weaken party machines and split immigrant voting patterns in urban areas. Poll taxes, literacy tests, and other restrictions on voting were imposed. The Australian ballot was introduced to deprive parties of the right to distribute ballots. The direct primary system was introduced to weaken the control of party elites over candidate nominations. Finally, by reducing the number of presidential appointments, civil service reform attempted to weaken the grip of parties on state agencies, to depoliticize government, and to exclude popular sectors.[28] Popular demobilization and the disorganization of parties in America was inspired by the Progressive movement and was achieved through legislation. In Brazil, popular demobilization, the weakening of parties, and the defeat of party elites occurred only after military intervention in 1964.

In sum, electoral trends, the composition of legislatures, and the course of events that led to military intervention in 1964 are inconsistent with arguments that insist on comparing the Brazilian experience with the decline of centrist parties, ideological radicalization, and the descent of European parliamentary systems into fascism after World War I. Concepts based on these experiences in Europe, such as polarized pluralism and major party decline, fail to explain the place of complex electoral alliances in Brazil, the constant share of major parties in both presidential elections and the federal chamber from 1945 to 1964, and unexpected events such as the UDN victory in the 1960 presidential election. New concepts based on experiences in presidential and federal systems, such as critical elections and party realignment, provide a better point of departure for developing new perspectives on the escalating political conflict that led to military intervention in 1964.

BRAZILIAN PRESIDENTIAL INSTITUTIONS, 1974–1994

One of the most important theoretical observations about transitions from authoritarianism to democracy is that the rapidly changing circumstances of transition rapidly alter the value of power resources.[29] From 1974 to 1994, Brazilians witnessed a parade of elites apparently destined to control party organizations and dominate elections.[30] Early on, with authoritarian legislation still in place, state elites simply manipulated electoral outcomes through executive decree. Later, when control of state patronage resources appeared the key to electoral success, ministers and governors from the authoritarian state became regional party leaders. However, once military and authoritarian state elites lost control of the federal executive in 1985, few were able to win elections or retain control of party committees.

A new generation of opposition intellectuals also seemed to determine the future of Brazil during the symbolic void left by a crumbling regime and an uncertain transition. However, once electoral politics became routine, most intellectuals failed to sustain their presence in party committees, convention floors, and other day-to-day tasks of party-electoral organization. The first elections under civilian rule thereby appeared to confirm the most dire predictions of party sociology, with career politicians and their party-electoral machines apparently prevailing over intellectual elites, business leaders, and other amateur politicians from civil society.[31] However, precisely when the cynicism of party sociology appeared to prevail, widespread corruption generated unexpected social movements for the moralization of Brazilian public life. These movements for political reform culminated in the impeachment of President Collor in late 1992 and the election of Fernando Henrique Cardoso to the presidency in 1994.[32]

These varying circumstances made for varying institutional contexts. Nonetheless, direct executive elections and fluid alliances among electoral machines still appear to drive Brazilian politics.

For example, opposition to (and support of) military government emerged in 1974, when military rulers liberalized legislative elections.[33] In the beginning, political change was plebiscitarian. However, like the preceding periods of democratic politics, winning elections after 1974 also required alliances with patronage machines. By 1986, the PMDB (party of opposition under military rule and member of the Democratic Alliance that brought civilian José Sarney to power through indirect elections in 1985) won twenty-one of twenty-two contested governorships and majorities in the constitutional congress as well as virtually all state assemblies. This landslide (short-lived, as it turned out) was caused, not by a surge of opposition, but by professional politicians on the regional and local levels allying with the party in expectation of the estimated 130,000 administrative posts it would control after transition to civilian rule.[34]

Scholars who emphasized the empowerment of civil society in opposition to military rule or who advocated parliamentary institutions to stabilize Brazil's new democracy perceived the rapid organization of mass politics through these mechanisms only tangentially. For example, theories of civil society empowerment led scholars to emphasize the plebiscitarian character of opposition to military rule in Brazil.[35] But the concept of plebiscitarianism refers not only to patterns of opposition but also to patterns of support. Indeed, support for the military government and party, through direct appeals and marketing campaigns, is based in the presidency (despite the lack of direct presidential elections). Theories of civil society empowerment also suggest that local demands and the national struggle against authoritarianism could go hand in hand. But in a country with more than eighty-two million voters, the organization of a local opposition leadership on the one hand, and competitive elections, on the other, are two very different contexts for collective action. Indeed, subsequent analysis suggests that local problems were linked to the national issues of the day, not by opposition groups, but by the patronage practices of professional politicians.[36]

Linkages between direct popular appeals and patronage machines first emerged under military rule. They developed between 1974 and 1985, during the often ambiguous, prolonged, and elite-centric transition, and were shaped by legacies of authoritarianism, the lack of executive elections before 1982 (except select mayorships), and the unfortunate separation of executive from legislative elections during critical moments of transition in 1985 and 1989. Consequently, local and legislative elections from 1974 to 1982 served largely as mechanisms of a transition still controlled by military elites.[37] The direct election of governors in 1982 (while the federal executive remained under military control) also failed to fully reproduce the traditional outcomes associated with Brazilian presidentialism. Juan Linz insightfully describes the consequence of the situation in 1982–85 as one of dual power, or diarchy.[38] Military control of the presidency diminished the capacity of new governors to negotiate with local politicians and implement policies. This lack of resolution continued when the 1984 presidential succession occurred within the rules and procedures set by the military and proceeded as negotiations among party elites in a restricted electoral college, while mass demonstrations of unprecedented magnitude took place. Military elites, party politicians, social activists, and spontaneous popular opposition all influenced the course of events during 1984. However, after congress defeated legislation calling for direct presidential elections, traditional politicians emerged from the electoral college with their electoral, bureaucratic, and party organizational positions strengthened, while social movements and independent political groups were, by and large, weakened.

Civilian rule also failed to fully reintroduce the traditional mechanisms of Brazilian presidentialism. Instead of responding to popular demands for direct presidential elections, Brazil's first civilian government under President José Sarney called elections in 1985 to replace the nominated mayors from capitals and other cities that had been declared national security zones by the authoritarian government.[39] These elections were considerably outside the historical norm. Since 1932, the Brazilian ballot balanced the direct election of executive offices with the proportional election of legislatures.[40] The 1985 mayoral elections failed to do so because they lacked accompanying slates for municipal chambers.

Despite this lack of resolution, links between national party elites and state and local patronage machines were renegotiated rapidly during the Brazilian transition.[41] First, when legislation calling for direct presidential elections was defeated in 1984, several national leaders of the government party (PDS) resigned to form the Democratic Alliance with the opposition party (PMDB) in the restricted electoral college designed by the military. Then, local and regional politicians rapidly realigned from government parties to the PMDB—first in expectation of the 130,000 federal administrative posts after President Sarney's inauguration on January 15, 1985; later, in expectation of perhaps fivefold that number of state-level administrative appointments to be distributed by governors after the 1986 elections.[42] By 1986, many of the mayors and municipal representatives of towns across Brazil that had delivered votes under military rule for the government party had negotiated affiliations with the PMDB. Direct popular appeals, party elite realignments, and the formation of party alliances through the distribution of administrative posts to professional politicians explain much of electoral politics through 1986.

But these developments failed to fully reflect Brazilian presidentialism because a direct election for president was not held until 1989. This election brought mass participation and modern media techniques to the contest after a thirty-year hiatus. Suffrage had expanded more than fivefold under military rule, from eighteen million in 1960 to more than eighty-two million in 1989. However, like the 1985 mayoral elections, the 1989 presidential election was held in isolation from other legislative and gubernatorial contests (once again, outside the Brazilian historical norm of holding executive elections with proportional representation contests for legislatures). Because elections for governor, as well as federal, state, and municipal legislatures were scheduled for November 1990, party alliances and machine politics mattered little in 1989. The careers of politicians were not directly at stake in the presidential election.

Consequently, instead of being forced to negotiate diverse electoral alliances across Brazil, the 1989 presidential campaign occurred almost exclusively on television.[43] A relatively unknown governor from the small northeast state of Alagoas, Fernando Collor de Mello, dominated the first six months of the campaign through television appearances and denunciations of bureaucratic abuse. When Collor reached more than 45 percent in preference polls (in June), he refused to participate in the live television debates of the first round (accurately reflecting the damaging prospects of sustained attacks from adversaries). While Collor's popularity fell steadily after July, endorsement by media personality Silvio Santos reinforced Collor's image after Santos's own last-minute bid for the presidency was rejected by the Supreme Electoral Court (STE). Collor won more than 28 percent in first-round voting, while Luis Inacio da Silva (Lula), the PT candidate, entered the runoff election with 16 percent. While Lula dominated the first television debate of the second round and surged in the polls to tie Collor only ten days before the December 15 vote, he failed to dominate the second debate and was unable to counter the damaging effect of negative advertising in the final days of the campaign. By mounting a series of personal and political attacks seven days before the election, Collor convinced voters that a PT victory would destabilize society and turn Brazil away from the liberalizing world. On December 15, Collor received 35,089,998 votes (42.7 %), defeating Lula, who received 31,076,364 votes (37.8 %).

The logic of party and electoral politics after Collor's election confirms that presidential initiative, direct appeals, and fluid alliances are still critical in Brazil. Brazil's first directly elected president since military rule took office in March 1990, as hyperinflation loomed and the country ended its first decade of negative per capita economic growth since 1945. Nine months later, few doubted the ability of directly elected presidents to initiate and implement policy in Brazil. President Collor reasserted executive authority and shocked investors on March 16, 1990 (the day after inauguration), with a comprehensive plan to reduce inflation, lower the federal deficit, liberalize trade, and modernize the economy. Despite his party's controlling only 5 percent of the federal chamber upon inauguration, President Collor temporarily confiscated an estimated 80 percent of Brazil's liquid financial assets and unveiled a dramatic package of economic reforms. The Collor administration quickly achieved its short-term economic policy goals, producing government surpluses, reducing interest rates, extending the terms for government paper, and stabilizing the exchange rate. Throughout 1990, the new administration received strong support from the media and the public (confiscated savings were returned), faced virtually no congressional and little social opposition, and overrode governors, who were more concerned with consolidating the support of state and local machines for the 1990 elections than organizing national opposition at the end of their term.

The 1990 elections reproduced these mechanisms on the state level. Direct gubernatorial elections endowed twenty-seven governors with immense popularity in their states and, perhaps more important, with the prerogative to nominate professional politicians to thousands of administrative posts. Governors were thereby able to negotiate legislative coalitions within their states across the most diverse parties and personalities. Indeed, because the 1990 elections were driven primarily by state and local politics rather than by national matters, traditional politicians appeared to reassert control over local machines and either abandoned the national parties, which artificially controlled patronage on the federal level during military rule and the Sarney administration, or rebuilt them locally.

FROM THE IMPEACHMENT OF COLLOR TO THE ELECTION OF CARDOSO

Recent events have reaffirmed the centrality of presidential institutions in shaping and deepening democratic politics in Brazil. In late 1992, Brazil's first directly elected president after the transition from military rule was impeached, through constitutional means, on corruption charges. In April 1993, Brazilians voted in favor of retaining their presidential form of government in a plebiscite held on April 21, 1993. And the 1994 presidential campaign brought to the fore two new political leaders—who first emerged as opponents to military rule. The impeachment of Collor, the popular vote to retain presidential government, and the political clarity of the choice between the PT candidate, Lula, and the PSDB candidate, Fernando Henrique Cardoso, in the 1994 presidential contest suggest that significant political change will continue to occur within Brazilian presidential institutions.

On September 29, 1992, the chamber of deputies voted 441 to 38 to suspend President Fernando Collor de Mello from office and initiate a formal trial in the senate, seventy-six of eighty-one senators voted on December 29–30 for impeachment.[44] This unprecedented removal of a Brazilian president began in May 1992, when Collor's brother accused the president of extensive involvement in corruption, the use of campaign funds for private ends, and participation in the extensive influence peddling organized by his 1989 campaign finance manager. The impeachment of Collor in late December 1992 effectively neutralized campaigns for the adoption of parliamentary government in the plebiscite held on April 21, 1993. Instead, 55.4 percent of voters chose to maintain the presidential form of government, while 66 percent chose to maintain a republic.

Soon after the national plebiscite on the form of government, President Itamar Franco (Collor's vice president) called on Fernando Henrique Cardoso to accept the key economic ministry, the

Ministerio da Fazenda (on May 21, 1993), a post he retained until assuming campaign duties full-time in May 1994. Far from proposing dramatic initiatives or unveiling economic packages, Cardoso sought to assure business leaders and the public that their lives and investments would be safe from government plans, which tend to radically alter prices, incomes, savings, currency exchange rates, and investment returns. Indeed, by 1993, Brazilians appear to have tired of dramatic initiatives. Since the transition to civilian rule in 1985, seven major policy packages and innumerable intermediate adjustments had been introduced unexpectedly by the federal government.

Instead, Cardoso adopted a gradualist approach, focusing on fiscal reform, monetary restraint, and the need for more transparency in the economic policy process. Repeated ministerial appearances in the media assured Brazilians that inflation was high but stable, that the government was not going to freeze wages and prices or confiscate savings, that draconian adjustment policies would be averted, and that extensive interventions into financial or currency exchange markets would be avoided. Indeed, the achievements of Cardoso as economic minister were piecemeal, even minor, compared to the dramatic economic packages preceding his tenure. For example, progress on the fiscal front was secured through legislative support for a 15 percent reduction of constitutionally mandated transfers from the federal government to states and municipalities in late February. Cardoso subsequently sought to unify the profusion of financial instruments used as de facto currencies because they index against inflation. The *Unidade de valor real* (real value unit, or UVR) was designed to become a single measure of inflation, which could be readjusted daily by the government.

Focusing the attention of investors and the public on a single government index permitted Cardoso and his economic team to gradually ratchet down inflationary expectations by setting and subsequently meeting realistic fiscal and monetary performance targets. By May 9, Cardoso was able to accompany the announcement that a new currency would be launched on July 1 (made by his successor at the Fazenda). This demonstrated once again that the administration was determined to publicize policy measures well ahead of time rather than attempting to shock inflation out of the economy by suddenly unveiling secret economic packages. The stabilization of the new currency, the real, quickly began to symbolize the success of this gradualist approach in reducing inflation and projected Cardoso into the presidential race. Not only did inflation fall, but real wages increased an estimated 20 percent during the first six months after the plan (June 1994–January 1995). Furthermore, the real income of poor Brazilians increased an estimated 50 percent during this period because of government efforts to secure the prices of subsistence goods.[45]

In sum, the mechanisms of political development within presidential institutions—direct popular appeals and alliances with patronage machines—do indeed appear to describe the ability of Cardoso to win the presidency in first-round voting on November 15 (his votes exceeded the sum of votes for all other candidates). Both the electoral alliance and the governing coalition between Cardoso's social democratic PSDB and the conservative PFL have received significant criticism from partisans, journalists, and Brazilian intellectuals. Even Cardoso's campaign manager feared that core supporters from southeast urban areas would shift to the PT because of the traditional conservative character of the PFL if the campaign went into a second round. However, these concerns in late June soon gave way before the immense popularity of the real. Cardoso's initiatives had not only reduced inflation without imposing monetary and fiscal austerity or orthodox adjustment policies; real wages had actually increased during the eight months following the plan— 20 percent on average and an estimated 50 percent for the poorest Brazilians.

The velocity and range of fluctuations among voter's intentions during the 1989 and 1994 presidential campaigns suggest that the plebiscitarian character of direct popular appeals also drives political events in Brazil. During the 1989 contest, Collor's ratings in the polls rapidly rose to 45 percent, then fell to 28 percent in the first round. In 1994, PT candidate Luiz Inacio da Silva fell from a high point of 42 percent in polls, taken on May 1, to 22 percent in a poll on September 30, accurately reflecting his final share of the vote. Cardoso's trajectory in opinion polls from 16 percent on May 3 to 48 percent on September 30 is even greater. This velocity and range of change in voters' intentions are considerably greater than the glacial shifts that characterize the ideological voters and rigidly organized party systems of Europe.[46]

CONCLUSION

Presidential institutions have shaped political development in Brazil since the first republican constitution of 1891. From 1945 to 1964, the mechanisms of precocious political development within presidential and federal institutions, first identified by Max Weber and James Bryce, defined the course of democratization. During the transition from military rule, new issues, new parties, and new political leadership emerged because direct executive elections facilitated alliances between the broad plebiscitarian appeals of campaigns and the diverse patronage machines that controlled regional and local politics. The evidence from past and present suggests that Brazilian presidentialism will continue to present opportunities for political change and reform as the twenty-first century approaches.

Can these mechanisms of political development in presidential and federal systems—links between direct plebiscitarian appeals and patronage machines—properly be described as democratization? Different perspectives on Brazilian presidentialism should be expected. Positive and negative views still drive debates about nineteenth-century populism, patronage, and mass inclusion. Given this disagreement, Max Weber's description of the American trajectory as an example of passive democratization is attractive because the concept distinguishes the need to understand new trends in party-electoral politics from the equally important need to consider the normative implications of these patterns.[47] Furthermore, by forcefully juxtaposing passivity with democratization, and by stressing authoritarian elements among professional politicians, Weber's work challenges contemporary scholars to check their normative instincts to condone or endorse these mechanisms of political change.[48]

Weber also provides more sensible perspectives on the political reform of presidential institutions than those who would discard presidentialism for parliamentarism. After emphasizing the rapidity of political development in the United States, Weber notes the deleterious consequences of this trajectory, such as governance by dilettantes and the need for civil service reform.[49] These concerns are certainly relevant to the Brazilian case. A central task for political reform in Brazil is to professionalize politicians who emerge from careers with populist talents and patronage machines. Unlike recent arguments for wholesale institutional change, however, Weber's argument that the complexity of work in congressional committees and party-electoral organizations could routinize party careers, weed out demagogues, and avert problems of governance. This level of analysis appears more appropriate for political reform than generalizations about responsible party systems or assertions about the relative attributes of presidential and parliamentary institutions. The complex negotiations required to build alliances across the vast electoral territory of Brazil's federal system suggest that political careers within existing institutional arrangements may endow professional politicians with the balanced skills needed to govern.

The election of Fernando Henrique Cardoso to the presidency in 1994 confirms the importance of this level of analysis. The agenda of political reforms that Cardoso proposed during the campaign and pursued once in office can be described as understated. The Cardoso administration has sought to gradually deepen institutional reforms begun during the 1988 constitution, such as increasing congressional control over budgetary matters, reforming civil service laws, and redesigning the social security system. This process of muddling through, combined with the further dispersion and separation of powers among Brazil's congress, courts, state governments, and newly empowered independent organizations from civil society seems the most likely path for producing durable political change in Brazil. President Cardoso's goal is far from declaring a road to socialism, a phrase still influential for his generation, which lived as exiled Brazilians through Salvador Allende's demise.

The unprecedented impeachment of President Collor in 1992 also suggests that presidential systems may be less rigid than their critics argue. While the ability to remove executives through a vote of no confidence is considered unique to parliamentary systems, congressional proceedings in Brazil in fact impeached President Collor. The conflicts and cleavages that produced President Collor's downfall appear to have arisen within political elites and were caused by his centralization of authority and his unwillingness to negotiate legislative and political coalitions with elites from the developed southeast region. After his initial successes during 1990, Collor failed to transform the plebiscitarian appeals of his electoral camp into flexible legislative coalitions.

In conclusion, both the centrality of presidential institutions in Brazilian history and the opportunities for current political reform counsel strongly against adopting parliamentary institutions in Brazil. Given that the impact of plebiscitarian appeals can be ameliorated by scheduling legislative elections with direct executive elections, given that budgetary reforms have reduced patronage abuses and that civil service reform could further that goal, given that popular identification with government occurs more through presidential elections than through durable partisan affinities or European ideologies, and given the exclusive character of previous periods of parliamentary rule in Brazil (1822–89, 1962–63), abandoning direct presidential elections risks disenfranchising large portions of Brazilian society. Without direct presidential elections, the representation of popular sectors so critical in Latin American politics (which Guillermo O'Donnell describes as "lo popular") would decrease, the incentives for politicians to articulate alliances between broad popular appeals and patronage machines would also decrease, and patronage politics would instead prevail in the corridors of a parliament skewed toward traditional rural areas, reducing not only popular input but governability as well.

PART IV

The Eastern European Context
Presidential Institutions and the Dual Transition to Democratic Politics and Market Economies

CHAPTER 7

Presidents and the Transition in Eastern Europe

Valerie Bunce

The Gorbachev reforms, followed by the collapse of state socialism
in the eastern half of Europe, have together produced a most surprising possibility: the future of Eastern Europe might well be liberal democracy.[1] This is surprising on two counts. First, by the late
1980s most specialists in European politics assumed that state socialism would be a permanent feature of the Eastern European
landscape. After all, these regimes had survived a number of crises
and had been in existence for more than forty years. Moreover, the
largest and most powerful country on the European continent—the
Soviet Union—functioned as their patron. Second, even if state socialism fell, there was little reason to expect that liberal democracy
would take its place. Liberal politics does not have historical roots
in Eastern Europe. Even prior to the development of state socialism,
this region was dominated by dictators, not democrats.[2] Even
Czechoslovakia, the country with the strongest democratic tradition
in the region, could claim only twenty years' experience with democratic politics.

All of this suggests that the transition to liberal democracy in
Eastern Europe will be a long and difficult process. Indeed, there is
no reason to assume that what is going on in the region today is necessarily a transition to democracy. There are a number of other important issues on the agenda of postcommunist states—for example,
the creation of a capitalist economy, the construction in many cases
of new states, and a major reconfiguration of the relationship between the state and the international system.[3] These issues may very
well overshadow, if not undermine, the movement toward liberal
political orders in Eastern Europe. For this reason, the phrase "transition to democracy in Eastern Europe" should be followed by a
question mark.[4]

What, then, will be the key factors determining whether the liberalized regimes in Eastern Europe will become consolidated democracies?[5] Specialists in recent democratic transitions in Latin America and Southern Europe seem to concur that the design of democratic political institutions has a strong impact on democratic prospects.[6] As Scott Mainwaring explains:

> Choices of political institutions matter. Institutions create incentives and disincentives for political actors; they shape actors' identities; they establish the context in which policy-making occurs; they can help or hinder in the construction of democratic regimes. And among all choices regarding institutions, none is more important than the system of government: presidential, semi-presidential, parliamentary or some hybrid. . . . Choices of political institutions are especially important during transitions to democracy.[7]

With the "right" institutional choice, it is argued, desirable outcomes are enhanced. Good institutional design translates into democracy, which is more inclusive, more stable, and more long-lived. Indeed, type of democratic government has even been linked to variations in economic performance, another factor that seems crucial to the consolidation of democracy.[8]

This chapter enters this debate about the relationship between institutional arrangement and democratic consolidation by comparing institutional choices in postcommunist Eastern Europe. It makes the following arguments. First, very few of these regimes have opted for either a parliamentary or a presidential system. Instead, the great majority have adopted the French model; that is, a system that combines parliamentary government with a presidency that is directly elected and has significant policy-making powers. Second, while there is a variety of reasons that this system is preferred, the dominant reasons have to do with the specific constraints on—and the goals of—the transition from state socialism to a liberal order. Third, the preference for directly elected presidents with some (and sometimes a great deal of) power is not—Juan Linz to the contrary—a cause for concern insofar as the consolidation of a liberal order in Eastern Europe is concerned.[9] There are, in fact—in this context—real advantages to a system that tilts in the direction of presidentialism. Moreover, there are some disadvantages to a pure parliamentary system in the postcommunist context. Finally, a comparison of postcommunist developments in Eastern Europe brings to the fore a larger issue. It is debatable whether we can assume, as do many specialists on Southern Europe and Latin America, that institutional arrangements have powerful effects on the course of democratization. In the Eastern European context at least, institutions are best understood as dependent, not independent, variables. Institutions (political and otherwise, formal and informal) are in the process of formation in the postcommunist context. The shape they will take, like the prospects for democratic consolidation, will be determined by the dynamics of what is going to be a long process of economic, political, and social transformation.

THE CONTEXT OF INSTITUTIONAL CHOICE

Institutional choice, once made, is not written in stone. A number of Eastern European countries—most recently, Kyrgyzstan—have altered the structure of their government several times since the transition from authoritarian rule. In addition, many of these states are not yet operating on the basis of new constitutions. In fact, the democratic rules of the game are based on (1) agreements struck between the opposition and the communists during the last days of state socialism, (2) agreements struck between members of the ruling coalition following each election, and (3) amended state socialist constitutions. Thus, Hungary and Poland as of this writing do not yet have postcommunist constitutions fully in place.

This is important to keep in mind, because delaying the process of institutional construction can be quite costly insofar as the consolidation of democracy is concerned. Procrastination can undermine the prospects for constructing fair and durable institutions and can, at the same time, render the crafting of constitutions so conflictual that democratic breakdown becomes a real possibility. What is assumed here is that, the longer the transition, the more likely individuals will develop strong preferences for one outcome (and thus procedure) over another.[10] Two likely outcomes follow from a bargaining situation combining strong preferences with high stakes. If some individuals dominate the crafting of the constitution (as we have seen in Russia), the structure of the government will be biased in the direction of their interests. If no individual or group can dominate (as in Armenia), a political stalemate can develop. In either case, the cause of democracy is not served.

Another consequence of slow and partial institutional reform is that situations could arise where the formal rules of the game are in conflict.[11] A good example of this problem was the periodic jousting that went on from 1990 to 1993 between the president of Hungary, Arpad Goncz, and the Hungarian prime minister, Jozsef Antall. This was not simply the familiar situation within democracies where people from different parties occupying different political positions compete with one another and, in the process, try to expand the powers of their particular offices. It was also a situation where the laws defining the powers of these two offices (and the powers, as well, of parliament and the Constitutional Court) directly contradicted one another. This is most evident in the case of defining presidential versus prime ministerial powers in foreign affairs, a major problem in not just Hungary but also Poland and Russia.[12] Another area where these problems are legion is in defining political control over the media.[13]

These conflicts carry with them enormous costs. Conflicts between central laws and republic laws and among central laws were crucial, for example, in the disintegration of the Soviet state. But there are other less dramatic, albeit still significant, costs. One is the possibility of political crisis as the parliament, the government, and the president spend all their time fighting over the question of who has the power to do what through which procedure. Such a crisis renders government unable to deal with the issues of the transition and also contributes to public cynicism about politicians in the postcommunist order.[14] Another cost is the undermining of the process of creating a law-based state and a political culture appreciative of the rule of law by giving politicians and publics the sense that people and not laws define political positions, procedures, and (thus) power. That state socialism had a similar understanding of "bourgeois" law, of course, merely adds to the ease of such perceptions.[15]

Another contextual consideration is that the process of choosing institutions in Eastern Europe is far from rational. The rule has been that choices are made in an environment of limited information, little time, much political conflict, and unpredictable results. The battles throughout 1991 between President Lech Walesa and the legislature in Poland over the question of defining electoral structures provide a good example. The legislature consistently favored a purely proportional representation system, whereas Walesa supported a combined proportional representation/winner-take-all system with a very high threshold for party representation in parliament.[16] These positions, however, were contrary to the interests of these two players. The legislature was supporting a system that would weaken the legislature, whereas the president was supporting a system that could empower the legislature and thereby weaken the president!

Eastern Europeans generally look to the West for ideas on institutional design.[17] In practice, this has meant two models: France's mixed presidential-parliamentary model and Germany's parliamentary model. The American and British styles of government have been far less influential.[18] For example, the one attempt in the region to introduce an American-style presidential system—through a referendum held in Lithuania in May 1992—failed to win sufficient popular support. This was due in part to low voter turnout and in part to public concern that the real point of the constitutional changes was President Landsbergis's interest in expanding his base of political power.[19]

What has emerged in this process has not been wholesale importation of a single model but, rather, a combining of several Western models and a revision of particular models. Let me provide a few examples. The minimum votes needed to take a seat in parliament in Slovenia is 3 percent, whereas in Germany it is 5 percent. In Croatia, the French and the German models are combined; the parliamentary electoral system is German in origin (with a combined single-member and proportional representation system), whereas the definition of presidential powers and the mode of presidential election follow the French precedent. Finally, while the Polish and the Russian governments are based on the French model of a combined parliamentary and presidential system, they are in practice rather different from each other and rather different as well from the French case. The Russian president has a good deal more formal power than the French president, and the French president has a good deal more formal power than the Polish president.[20]

Institutional choice in Eastern Europe, therefore, is a very complex matter. Models are borrowed from the West but are substantially amended; constitutions are sometimes incomplete and often contradictory; choices are made on the basis of ad hoc considerations; and constitutions are repeatedly revised in very important ways. This seems to deviate from transitions to democracy in Southern Europe and Latin America, most notably the process of constitutional construction in post-Franco Spain. Thus, we must be careful in using such familiar phrases as "the crafting of political institutions," the "design of political institutions," or even "institutional choice" to summarize institutional developments in postcommunist Europe. With this in mind, let us turn to a comparison of institutional structures in Eastern Europe today.

VARIANCE IN SYSTEMS OF GOVERNMENT

For the sake of brevity, I categorize the political systems of Eastern Europe into four systems based on mode of presidential election and degree of formal presidential power. Of the four systems, the least common is the parliamentary system, in which presidents are elected by parliament and their powers are limited. Parliaments and governments are (in a constitutional sense) the dominant political players. Hungary, the Czech Republic, and Slovakia are prime examples of this system. Thus the great majority of presidents in Eastern Europe are directly elected for a fixed term in office. What distinguishes these cases from each other are the powers allocated to the president (versus those allocated to the government and the parliament). By presidential powers, I refer to the constitutionally defined rights of the president to (1) conduct foreign policy, (2) form and dissolve the government, (3) appoint public officials (with varying degrees of parliamentary scrutiny), (4) introduce and veto legislation, and (5) declare a national emergency and rule (and for how long without parliamentary approval) by executive decree.

These distinctions produce three types of presidential system: a strong one, a mixed one, and a ceremonial one. In a strong presidential system, presidents are in a formal position to dominate (albeit not fully control) the government, the parliament, and policy making. Examples include Macedonia, Uzbekistan, Russia, Kazakhstan, and Croatia. In the Croatian case, the president has the constitutional right to bypass parliament in appointing the prime minister. Indeed, this is precisely what President Franjo Tudjman did following his reelection in August, 1992.[21] In mixed presidential-parliamentary system, there is a separation of powers among the president, the government, and the parliament. Presidents, as a result, are significantly constrained in their capacity to dominate appointments, government formation, parliamentary dissolution, and policy making. Recent constitutional changes in Poland, Romania, Bulgaria, Ukraine, Armenia, and Belarus place these regimes in this category.[22] cases where presidents are directly elected but where their role is a ceremonial one are few; only two clear examples, Estonia and Slovenia, exist. Cases that come close are those of Hungary, Slovakia, and the Czech Republic. Thus twenty-two of the twenty-seven postcommunist states in Eastern Europe embrace a mixed presidential-parliamentary system. The question is, Why this preference for presidents?

PREFERRING PRESIDENTS

There are four important reasons that most postcommunist states opted for semipresidential systems.[23] One reason is the extent to which such a system is the logical outcome of the bargaining situation. The bargaining situation that applied to much of the former Soviet Union is one of dramatic changes in the external environment enhancing the opposition and undermining the communists but domestic conditions weakening the opposition and strengthening the communists. That is, the opposition was poor but upwardly mobile, and the communists were rich but downwardly mobile. In this bargaining situation, a liberalized political system with a strong presidency was a perfect compromise: the opposition gained a more liberalized environment, while the communists (now ex-communists, in most cases) maintained through the presidency at least some of their considerable political powers.

In the other bargaining situations, the communists were weak but were buttressed by strong external support, and the opposition was strong but was uncertain about the costs and the limits of political liberalization. In this situation, a semipresidential system emerged as halfway between state socialism and a liberalized political order. A good example of this bargaining situation is the early 1989 Roundtable between Solidarity and the Polish United Workers Party.[24] The mixed presidential-parliamentary system of government that emerged reflects a perfect compromise between the concerns and the uncertainties of the two players. The communists traded semicompetitive elections, semirepresentative government, and promises of further political liberalization in the future for a relatively strong presidency and the promise that "their" candidate would occupy that post.[25] The consequences of this deal, however, were far different from what anyone imagined. General Jaruzelski, the communist candidate for president—and the man who had declared martial law against Solidarity in December 1981—almost lost his vote in parliament during the summer of 1989. What allowed him to be elected president was the support of his erstwhile enemies, the Solidarity members of the parliament!

But bargaining games are not the only reason behind the preference for semipresidential government in postcommunist countries. The second reason is that institutional selection often represents the intersection of the interests of those making the decision, the perceived need to act quickly, and the limited knowledge that decision makers have of alternative institutional arrangements. In virtually all of the republics of the former Soviet Union, the 1991 disintegration of state socialism and the Soviet Union led to the adoption of governments where presidents were given important powers, and this can be explained by the fact that independence in many cases came suddenly and that the one model of government easily and quickly emulated was the presidential model developed by Gorbachev. That Gorbachev developed this model to preserve his powers and enhance his capacity to direct the reform process facilitated, of course, his decision to follow the Soviet model. To this was added another innovation, this one from the Russian case: to give the president a national mandate through a popular election.[26]

A third reason for the choice of semipresidentialism was the desire to counteract divided, and therefore weak, parliaments and weak governments. The following logic seems to have operated in Poland, Russia, Ukraine, Croatia, Belarus, Tajikistan, and Macedonia. Presidents were assumed to derive significant powers from a national mandate and to make decisions alone or in small groups, in contrast to parliaments, with their circumscribed mandates and large size. Furthermore, it was assumed that these new parliaments and governments would be divided and fractious and, therefore, weak, an assumption based on certain givens in the Eastern European postcommunist context (that these societies are divided along ethnic, religious, and regional lines). Moreover, other important cleavages—generational, urban-rural, and communist-noncommunist—would, it was thought, produce a large number of political parties, especially when an electoral system of proportional representation was put in place.[27] There were reasons to expect that these parties would have an unusually hard time cooperating with each other and maintaining stable public and even parliamentary memberships. The parties had narrow and antagonistic political, social, and economic bases, and they often functioned as, in effect, fickle fan clubs for individual leaders.

According to this logic, in such circumstances, governments would be difficult to form, would turn over frequently, and could be paralyzed, thus jeopardizing the transition to democracy—and capitalism. Presidents (as long as they operated under certain constraints) were deemed necessary to counteract these problems. What influenced this logic, of course, was not just where politics might be heading but also where it had been in the interwar period in Eastern and Central Europe.

This leads us to the fourth reason behind the preference for presidential power: the agenda of transition. (I deal with this issue in some detail below and, therefore, will be brief here.) The transition was to be not only to democracy but also to a capitalist order, and the latter process would, it was thought, be very difficult, very painful, and quite long. Thus a successful transition to capitalism required a strong presidency, to ensure political and policy continuity. A strong presidency would also create an official who could claim a national mandate and who could unite the nation on divisive issues. These considerations seemed to have been important in discussions about the presidency in Ukraine and Macedonia, and they surfaced as well in the extended debates about presidential power in Belarus.[28] Whether this analysis is correct, of course, is open to question, especially if the presidential system is combined with a multiparty system.[29]

One could argue, then, that the distribution of political powers between communists and the opposition, knowledge about institutional arrangements, government stability, and the agenda of transition favored semipresidential government over either purely parliamentary or purely presidential systems. Was this choice a good one insofar as the consolidation of a democratic order is concerned?

THE COSTS AND BENEFITS OF PRESIDENTIALISM

The three major objections to presidential government in new and uncertain democracies are as follows.[30] First, presidential elections can be divisive, because the office is all-important, the term is fixed, and the results are winner take all. Too much, in short, is at stake—a serious problem for democracies that are fragile and societies that are extremely divided. Second, there is no way in such a system to ascertain who really speaks for "the people." Moreover, the system lends itself to deadlock and not to stability, supposedly the hallmark of presidential systems. Deadlock can lead, in turn, to presidential dictatorship, an outcome made more likely by the personalized character of presidential power.[31] Deadlock can also lead to a military coup d'état, especially when civilian control over the military is weak and the country is facing a perceived crisis. In either case (and they often are the same case), the result is identical. Democracy falls to the wayside. The third objection has to do with the costs of a fixed term in office, the argument being that it undermines rational policy making by forcing it into a cycle. Not only are policies unusually sensitive to the electoral cycle, but relations between the legislature and the president also follow an electoral rhythm. The cycle disallows the possibility of rational decision making, particularly with respect to foreign affairs and economic policy, two areas where public opinion is particularly sensitive.

These arguments were developed in the context of democratic transitions and presidential government in Latin America and Southern Europe, but they are relevant to semipresidential government because of that system's direct election and fixed presidential term. Presidential and semipresidential systems are also similar in terms of presidential powers and the propensity for deadlock. Does it then follow that semipresidentialism in Eastern Europe is a major problem for democratic consolidation? There can be no definitive answer to that question, in part because the transitions now under way in Eastern Europe are at their earliest stage, and we do not yet have the data to measure, for example, the cyclical character of policy making. However, some tentative observations can be made.

It is evident from developments in Eastern Europe thus far that presidential elections do render stakes too high and therefore work to divide the public. This seems particularly true of the Polish presidential election of 1991 and the Belarussian election of 1994. Further, the separation of powers system confuses both public and elites about the distribution of political powers among institutions. This confusion is behind the continuing and heated debates over presidential versus legislative powers in Romania, Bulgaria, Poland, and Lithuania. Furthermore, the separation of powers system concentrates powers in the presidency as to undermine the democratic processes of government. This issue has divided the "in" parties from the "out" parties in, for instance, Croatia, Serbia, Ukraine, Lithuania, Russia, Romania, and much of central Asia. Indeed, in Bulgaria, this issue has divided the president and the government even when they belonged to the same (albeit repeatedly fissured) political party. Making this issue even more of a concern is the fact that presidents easily compensate for weak governments. This is of special concern when the president is an ex-communist (as in Romania, Ukraine and Kazakhstan).

However, these caveats do not lead to the conclusion that semi-presidential systems in Eastern Europe, like presidential systems in the "southern transitions," will undermine the transition to a liberal order. Many of these concerns about presidential government are concerns that could be voiced about parliamentary government, as well.

PRESIDENTIAL VERSUS PARLIAMENTARY SYSTEMS

At least some of the concerns about presidential systems apply equally, if not more so, to parliamentary systems. Let us take the issue of immobilized government, or what has been called, for the American case, the problem of gridlock. During the interwar period in Eastern Europe, parliamentary systems were quite unsatisfactory precisely because they produced immobilized, unstable, and therefore weak governments, thus paving the way for dictatorial regimes. Parliamentary and not presidential government, in short, was widely viewed as *the* reason democracy failed. There is every reason to assume that these costs could materialize again if a "pure" parliamentary system were reinstituted.

As in the interwar period, elections in postcommunist Eastern Europe are based on a proportional representation system.[32] This system has, of course, created certain incentives with respect to the multiplication of political parties competing for office. For example, in the Estonian elections of September 1992, sixteen parties contested 101 parliamentary seats; and in the Bulgarian elections of October 1991, forty-two parties nominated candidates for 240 parliamentary seats.[33] Other factors fragmenting the party system and the electorate, splintering the parliament, and weakening governments patched together by "overpartied" parliaments are the great social, economic, political, and cultural diversity of most of these countries and their legacy of state socialism. The diversity is why a system of proportional representation is preferred, if not necessary.[34] But this diversity is important in and of itself, for it helps shape the nature of the party system—and therefore parliament—and in the process produces immobilized and weak governments. It is not accidental, for example, that a major problem in most of these countries is the proliferation of parties based on regional, ethnic, or religious identities and the absence of parties based on, say, class. As for the legacy of state socialism, the system did not encourage the development of those experiences and skills that enhance the capacity of individuals and groups to engage in cooperative behavior and to mold compromises. Instead, the irony of the "collective" experience was that it generated individualistic and privatized behaviors.

Given these considerations, parliaments in Eastern Europe are likely to be divided and, therefore, weak. This reflects the fact that political parties have proliferated, divided (even in parliament), and refused to cooperate to form stable governments.[35] The recent collapse of the Bulgarian government and the revolving door of Polish government since 1990 are two cases in point.

It could be countered that there are two mechanisms whereby parliaments and governments can be strengthened. One is to introduce voting thresholds (which most of the countries have done), and the other is to make it difficult for a government to fall. Voting thresholds have reduced the number of parties, but they are still numerous. Moreover, voting thresholds have no impact whatsoever on the "nonbargaining" culture of these parties. Making it difficult for a government to fall generates its own costs: Hungary, for example, has a system that encourages the durability of governments; however, this has led to concern about the prime minister having too much power (whether during the Democratic Forum, 1990–94, or during the socialist regime, 1994 to the present). A prime minister functioning as a president (in the sense of having, in effect, a fixed term) but without a president's national mandate introduces another problem. One of the purported strengths of a parliamentary system is its capacity to change governments in response to changes in public support, a strength that works against the immobilism of presidential government when presidents have lost their mandate.[36] But giving prime ministers and their governments considerable security means introducing the same problem, as the Hungarian case again reminds us.

I do not argue that adding presidents to the equation necessarily helps defray these costs. Moreover, we cannot be sure that the weak governments in Eastern Europe will produce the interwar outcome of weak democracies giving way to dictatorships. Many of the factors that worked against liberal democracy in the interwar period are not in evidence today, when there is much greater international support for democracy, a domestic class structure that supports a democratic outcome, and a process of transition that was itself an exercise of democratic politics (as opposed to democracy in the interwar period, which was a product of decisions forced on the region by the victors of World War I). I do argue, though, that one can hardly trust a pure parliamentary system: if parliaments are weak, governments will be weak, and there is every reason to assume that the first condition is being met in most cases.

On the presidential side of the equation, there are reasons to defend semipresidential government in the Eastern European context. One has already been noted—the extent to which presidents (operating under formal political constraints) might help offset weak parliaments. This has certainly been the case in Bulgaria and, to some degree, in Russia.[37] Another reason to look favorably on presidential government is that presidents represent the entire nation, a distinct advantage in plural societies, certainly in plural societies that developed the political or social wherewithal for consociational governance.

Furthermore, the economic agenda of these transitions (unlike transitions in Latin America and Southern Europe) makes a presidential or a semipresidential system attractive. There are enormous stresses associated with the transition from a state socialist to a capitalist economy. With a fixed term and a nationwide mandate, presidents are in a far better position than a parliament or a government to spearhead a painful economic transition—particularly when they have a large national mandate or are granted considerable emergency powers. A case in point is Boris Yeltsin, president of Russia, who had both a mandate and emergency powers prior to the December 1993 elections.[38]

Finally, the international context of these transitions is very different from the context of the recent transitions to democracy in Southern Europe and Latin America. For Eastern Europe, so much more is in flux: national identities, state boundaries, political-military alliances, and the relationship of the state to the international economy. Political leaders in these new regimes thus face enormous

international responsibilities. A nation that speaks with one voice—
through a president—is crucial, as is speedy decision making. The
presidential system was in fact created in many of these countries
precisely because of the international context.[39]

I do not argue, of course, that semipresidential systems are inherently superior to parliamentary systems. The specifics of the
Eastern European transitions are my central consideration. Moreover, presidential systems are not without flaws: they can lead to divided government, they can produce divisive elections, they represent an unstable combination with a multiparty system, and they
tempt occupants to flirt with dictatorial government.[40] Then, too, we
must not exaggerate the importance of the formal design of political
institutions.

HOW IMPORTANT IS TYPE OF POLITICAL SYSTEM?

Political institutions have been thought to considerably influence the process and outcome of democratization. I am not convinced of this, if only because institutions are always flexible and
always rooted in the larger political, economic, and social environment. Moreover, I agree with Adam Przeworksi that the "best" institutions depend heavily not on objective characteristics but, rather,
on national context.[41]

If there are questions about the power of institutions in shaping
the prospects for democratic consolidation in general, there are
even more questions when we focus on the Eastern European transition, whose major characteristic is its extraordinary fluidity and,
thus, uncertainty.[42] Although all transitions from dictatorship to
democracy are uncertain, postcommunist transitions are unusually
uncertain.[43] Perhaps the best way to drive this point home is to compare Eastern European transitions with recent transitions in Southern Europe and Latin America, many of which are cases of redemocratization.[44] While Czechoslovakia might fit into this category,
the rest of our cases would not. In addition, the earlier transitions
were within an established, cold war, international order; the transitions in Eastern Europe, by contrast, are taking place in an international order also in transition. Indeed, that is one reason why war
broke out in the former Yugoslavia.

But one might ask, What exactly is in transition? In Southern
Europe and Latin America, political institutions and procedures

changed following the weakening of authoritarian rule; these were, in short, regime—and not state—transitions.[45] In Eastern Europe, by contrast, regime transition is just one of many aspects of leaving state socialism. The other aspects include reformulating national identity; redefining state boundaries, structures, and roles (especially where there are new states); restructuring the operating principles of the economy and society; and redefining the relationship of the state to the international economy and the international system of power. Virtually everything that can be in transition is in transition in Eastern Europe. Nor is this surprising. Not only are capitalist liberal democracy and state socialism polar opposites, since the former combines certain procedures with uncertain results, while the latter combines uncertain procedures with certain results.[46] The transitions to liberal politics and economics in Eastern Europe are taking place within an international system that is in transition. All of these transitions complicate one another. For instance, how can the building blocks of liberal politics—interests, interest groups, political parties, and the like—be constructed with an economic and social system in transition?

What all of this suggests is that, while transitional situations are always fluid, the transitional situations in Eastern Europe are unusually fluid. This has important implications for the impact of institutional arrangements on the consolidation of democracy in Eastern Europe. One is that extremely fluid situations favor idiosyncratic factors over structural factors: for example, what offices exist matters perhaps less than who occupies these offices. Another implication is that it is premature to speak to questions of the impact of political arrangements on the consolidation of democracy, because political institutions as we know them are not yet in place and because, if that is the case, then the issue cannot be one of consolidation of democracy but, rather, the construction of democracy. The final implication follows from this. What is happening in Eastern Europe is not a matter of specific political institutions affecting the future of democracy. Rather, the issue is one of institutional formation, not only in the formal and political sense but also in the informal and social and economic sense.

The point, then, is that institutions are dependent variables; they are not independent variables. In this sense, political systems in Eastern Europe, like economic and social systems, are still very much in the making. Indeed, this is one reason we do not see in

Eastern Europe the pattern of institutional "freezing" one finds in other recent transitions to democracy. What we see, instead, is either substantial delays in the selection of institutions (as in Poland and Belarus) or substantial revision of institutional arrangements in cases where institutional selection came relatively early in the transitional process (as in Kyrgyzstan). What is less common is early and durable selection of governmental institutions.

For a number of reasons, then, the structure of postcommunist governments is not a major factor in the prospects for democratic development. If there is any one factor with explanatory power, it is whether the democratic opposition won the first competitive election. Where it did (as in the Baltic states, Hungary, Czechoslovakia, and Poland), the future of democratic governance seems to be secure. That these countries represent the full gamut of institutional possibilities, moreover, reminds us once again of the limits of institutional design as a factor shaping democratic consolidation.

CHAPTER 8

Semipresidentialism, Charisma, and Democratic Institutions in Poland

Michael Bernhard

POLAND'S NEW INSTITUTIONS

Poland's extrication from Soviet-type authoritarianism began with the Roundtable Agreement of 1989. This pact provided for semicompetitive elections later that year and led to the formation of a noncommunist government. This was followed by competitive elections for the presidency in 1990 and for the National Assembly (Zgromadzenie Narodowe) in 1991. Since that time, Poland has continued to make strides toward democratic government and a market economy.[1]

Still, Poland's emerging democracy is often unwieldy, with over-lapping lines of power, changing and ill-defined rules, and institutional arrangements that leading scholars in comparative politics deem problematic. First, Poland has, in every sense of Duverger's definition, a semipresidential system.[2] The president is directly elected by universal suffrage, and the office has considerable powers (e.g., constitutionally mandated responsibility for national defense, foreign policy, and national security, as well as veto power over all legislation). Yet, there is executive dyarchy: the president shares power with a prime minister, who is responsible to the legislature. Thus, the Polish executive is composed of a parliamentary-based prime minister and a directly elected president who is more than a figurehead but less than a chief executive in the American sense. While their powers have supposedly been demarcated constitutionally, they still overlap to some degree, and this has led to almost incessant interbranch conflict.[3]

Second, the Polish National Assembly is bicameral. One house, the Sejm, is composed of 460 deputies elected from multiple-candidate electoral districts. The second house, the Senat, is composed of 100 senators, who represent Poland's forty-nine voivodships (*województwa*).[4] These provinces were somewhat artificially created by one of Poland's communist leaders in the 1970s to break up thirteen larger provinces that served as convenient local power bases for ambitious pretenders to the post of first secretary. The voivodships do not have a substantial history of local self-government (the Polish People's Republic was a centralized state). Although there are some exceptions, there seems to be little pressing justification for these provinces to be represented in a separate house of parliament. The chief function of that house, the Senat, has evolved into amending or rejecting the legislation approved by the Sejm, which can then choose to accept or reject the Senat's actions.[5] Thus, the Sejm does the lion's share of legislative work, while the less representative Senat makes the legislative process more cumbersome.

Third, the rules of the electoral system have changed with each new election. Initially, the president was elected by joint vote of both houses of the National Assembly. Now, the president is directly elected and must secure a mandate of 50 percent of participating voters. If no candidate wins 50 percent, a runoff is held between the two most popular candidates.

With respect to parliamentary elections, the situation is even more complex. Poland's three postcommunist National Assemblies have been elected under three different sets of the rules. The first was elected in a semicompetitive fashion (more on this later). The first democratically elected Assembly and its successor were chosen by two radically different sets of rules. The first set produced an Assembly that was so representative that it had governability problems, and the second produced an Assembly whose representativeness (and thus legitimacy) is subject to question. As a result of the highly proportional electoral rules of the first free election (October 27, 1991), twenty-nine parties reached the National Assembly. Several parties received a seat for only 0.2 percent of the vote, and one received a seat for fewer than 2,000 votes—in a nation of over thirty-eight million people.[6]

Under the much more restrictive rules of the second election (September 19, 1993), two parties who won 36 percent of the popular vote received almost two-thirds of the seats in the Assembly. The votes of over a third of the voters did not result in anybody winning a seat in the Sejm.[7]

Having examined the central legislative and executive structures of Poland's emerging democracy, I question whether anyone would purposefully try to create such a unwieldy system of government. I begin to answer this question by examining some of the recent literature in comparative politics on institutional choice.

ARE THE POLES WILLFULLY PERVERSE?

Much of the recent literature on choosing democratic institutions focuses on whether parliamentary democracy or presidential democracy is more likely to result in stable consolidated democracy. After reading it, it is tempting to answer yes to the rude question I pose above. Fred Riggs, for example, notes that there are few examples of stable presidential democracy (the United States, France, Chile, Uruguay, and Costa Rica).[8] He further argues that the stability of presidentialism in America is a product of exceptionalism, that it works not so much because of the constitutional arrangements but because of unique paraconstitutional practices. In a followup study, Riggs provides even more evidence on the instability of presidential regimes and contrasts it with the more satisfactory record compiled by parliamentary regimes.[9] Of the thirty-three Third World countries that had adopted presidential constitutions at the time of Riggs's study, not one avoided a serious disruption (coup). In contrast, thirty of forty-three parliamentary regimes (69 percent) survived without any serious disruption.[10] Although it is possible to take issue with some of Riggs's data, the fact remains that parliamentary regimes have a better record of democratic stability than presidential ones.[11]

An all-out assault on the viability of presidential democracy has been waged by Juan Linz and Arturo Valenzuela, who in their most recent effort declare the failure of presidential democracy.[12] In a series of related articles, Linz raises a number of serious concerns about presidential democracy.[13] These include the following drawbacks:

— winner-take-all elections
— divided government and conflict between branches because of separation of powers and the dual legitimacy created by separate elections of president and legislature
— rigidity in the executive term of office, which can turn a governmental crisis into a systemic crisis
— unpredictable or weak governments
— electoral competition that gives undue influence to extremists

— plebiscitary presidential elections, which may give presidents
an inflated sense of mandate[14]

What is striking about the reservations that Linz notes is that they
are cast as tendencies and arrangements that "can foster" failure.
These are not lawlike generalizations that inexorably lead to the failure of presidential regimes.

Both Linz's and Riggs's critiques of presidentialism lack a subtle
understanding of how the elements for the selection and exercise of
executive and legislative power work together. Donald Horowitz ad-
dresses this limitation in a rejoinder to Linz, in which he questions
how it is possible to criticize presidential systems for both being
"winner take all" and weakened by "divided government."[15] The
winner-take-all aspect of the presidential systems that Linz criticizes
are, to Horowitz, an aspect of their electoral laws.[16]

Similarly, the literature on Latin American cases shows that the
problem is not presidentialism as such but problems of overall institutional design, which include presidentialism as an element.
Both Scott Mainwaring and Valenzuela attribute the fragility of
presidentialism in Latin America to complex institutional arrangements rather than to presidentialism itself.[17] The problem is the
combination of a plurality system for electing the president and a
proportional representation system for electing the legislature. This
often leads to fragmented parliaments that cannot form stable ruling coalitions to cooperate with presidents. As a result, many Latin
American presidents, both past and present, have been beset by political paralysis because they lack consistent support in the legislature and fail to secure a majoritarian mandate in their own election.

YOU CAN'T GET THERE FROM HERE

Having surveyed the recent debate on the relative advantages
and disadvantages of presidential and parliamentary democracy, I,
like Riggs, concede that parliamentary regimes have a more successful historical record and, like Linz, I find the political advantages of parliamentarism outweigh its disadvantages and the advantages of presidentialism.[18] Still, I am not prepared to believe that the
Poles made the wrong choices or that their fledgling democracy is
doomed because of these choices.

There is a larger problem with the debate over institutions, which is attributable to the mistaken idea of "crafting" institutions. This term, coined by Alfred Stepan and Juan Linz and most recently taken up with enthusiasm by Guiseppe Di Palma, attributes a high level of autonomy to actors in the democratization process in selecting and installing institutions.[19] On the contrary, democratization is fraught with political constraints on actors, which make their control of institutional selection far smaller than the term *crafting* implies. The problem with the debate then, is not that its conclusions concerning the long-term viability or relative merits of regimes is wrong. The problem is that, given the circumstances at the moment of transition and beyond, it may not be possible to opt for parliamentary institutions or it may be that opting for them is far more risky for the democracy (e.g., there may be more obstacles to installing a parliamentary regime) than opting for presidentialism. Thus, even if parliamentary institutions are preferable, perhaps they are not feasible with a given constellation of political actors and constraints. Quite literally, you may not be able to get there from here. As David Stark reminds us, institutional choice does not occur on a tabula rasa. Theories of crafting view institution building as a process in which actors choose some correct, best, or ideal set of democratic institutions. Stark criticizes its counterpart in economics as "cookbook capitalism."[20] The reality of institutional choice in the polity is much more complex than "designer democracy." Institutional choices are constrained by the political realities of moments of decision making—specifically, who is empowered to decide what and whether other actors will stand for it.

The purpose of this chapter is to provide an account of the process by which democratic institutions emerged in Poland. While their institutions do not look crafted, the Poles already have more than five years' experience of near-democratic and democratic rule. They have these institutions for good reasons, based on the relative strengths of political actors and the conditions that they faced. It is not a question of whether they made "correct" choices, as the crafters would have it, but rather of understanding why the Poles have chosen this specific set of institutions.

To date, other accounts of the process of institutional choice in Eastern Europe have been rare or have fallen short.[21] My account explains why the Poles created their particular variant of democracy despite what the experts in the burgeoning democratization industry tell us. In filling this gap in the literature, I hope to turn the debate away from a consideration of which institutions are best to a consideration of how real institutions come into being. It is only on the basis of such an understanding that we can then discuss whether democratic institutions will be viable.

Building on the earlier work of David Stark and Terry Lynn Karl, I treat the process of institutional choice as path dependent.[22] In particular, I pay attention to how institutional choices were shaped by the conditions and rules that political actors faced. Three elements are critical in explaining why the Poles have the constellation of executive and legislative power described above. The first of these is the terms of extrication from the previous authoritarian regime.[23] The second crucial element is the presence of a charismatic leader. The third element is the weakness of all political forces in the wake of the transition. I begin with a discussion of the Roundtable Agreement, Poland's extrication pact from authoritarianism.

POLAND'S EXTRICATION PACT
FROM AUTHORITARIANISM

The Roundtable Agreement of April 1989, while it provided for open contestation of a number of seats in the new National Assembly, was not designed to immediately inaugurate democracy in Poland.[24] In fact, it was designed only to give Solidarity a weak say in the exercise of power (as well as a share of responsibility for policy outcomes). In this sense, in its original form it was intended to install what Przeworski calls broadened dictatorship, not democracy. Because of the unforeseen results of the elections of June 1989, it produced a transitional political system that approximated Przeworski's "democracy with guarantees" prior to the holding of fully contested elections for president (1990) and parliament (1991).

The Roundtable Agreement, and the basket of six bills passed by the Sejm on April 6 implementing it, changed the fundamental structure of state institutions in Poland. The old unicameral Sejm, with its 460 deputies, became one house of the National Assembly. A second house, the Senat, was created.[25] Thus the bicameral structure of parliament that exists today was established at this point.

New elections to both houses of the Assembly were set for June 4, 1989, with a second round planned for two weeks later to decide contests where no candidate took 50 percent in the first round. These elections were only partially contested. A full 65 percent (299

Table 8.1 Composition of the Sejm Following the Semicontested Elections of 1989

| | Seats | |
Party	Number	Percentage
Communist-led Coalition	299	65.0
Polish United Workers' Party (PZPR)	173	37.5
United Peasant Party (ZSL)	76	16.5
Democratic Party (SD)	27	6.0
Proregime christian groups	23	5.0
(PAX)	(10)	(2.2)
(Christian-Social Union)	(8)	(1.7)
(Polish Catholic Social Union)	(5)	(1.1)
Solidarity	161	35.0
Total	460	100.0

Source: Polish Television News Coverage, 1989.

mandates) of the Sejm was reserved for the ruling communists: the Polish United Workers' Party (PZPR) and its electoral allies (the satellite parties it had preserved as transmission belt organizations and proregime Catholic groups). Of these, 37.5 percent (173 mandates) were later reserved for the PZPR itself, a percentage that would give the communists enough strength on their own to prevent the overriding of presidential vetoes or the rewriting of the constitution (see table 8.1 for details on how the 65 percent was apportioned). The remaining 35 percent (161 mandates) in the Sejm and the 100 Senat seats were open to full contestation.

This arrangement clearly was aimed at creating a broadened dictatorship, incorporating Solidarity into the structures of the party-state but keeping real power in the hands of the communists and their allies. The agreement gave the ruling coalition control of the Sejm and thus, under the terms of the Polish constitution, the legislative agenda. If Solidarity could win control of the Senat, it would have the ability to block or amend legislation passed by the Sejm. However, Solidarity control of this body did not seem realistic before the June elections. In any case, the Sejm could overturn the Senat's reservations by a two-thirds majority, and the ruling coalition had already been guaranteed 65 percent of the seats in the lower house. Thus, if they won only a handful of openly contested Sejm mandates, the communist coalition would have enough votes to override a Solidarity majority in the Senat. All parties to the agreement fully expected the communists and their allies to form the first government after the elections.

The Roundtable Agreement also created a new head of state. The old collective Council of State (Rada Państwa) was replaced by a president with significant powers. This included a veto over legislation, which could be overturned by a two-thirds majority in the Sejm. The presidency was also endowed with special powers in the areas of foreign policy and national security: he was commander in chief of the armed forces and the chair of the Committee for National Defense; he had the power to ratify or renounce international agreements; and he had the power to declare martial law and states of emergency for up to three months without the consent of the National Assembly. The president was to be elected by a majority vote of the combined houses of the National Assembly, with a quorum of two-thirds. Again, it was expected that the communists and their allies would easily elect their candidate as president. After all, they were guaranteed 299 seats in the Sejm, of a total of 560 in both houses combined.

Even though Solidarity and other opposition groups were legalized and the National Assembly was opened to partial contestation, the Roundtable Agreement was essentially a conservative agreement. It gave exceptionally strong guarantees to both the PZPR and the Soviet Union. It was designed to prolong, not to end, the rule of the communists and their allies through a modified system, relying to a greater extent on rule of law through state structures. The almost guaranteed election of Wojciech Jaruzelski to the new and powerful presidency was expected to protect Soviet interests and assuage their fears. If Solidarity could win control of the Senat and prevent the communists and their allies from gaining those few mandates that would give them a two-thirds majority in the Sejm, the union would gain the power to block or to slow government initiatives. Prior to the elections of June 1989, this was the best result that Solidarity leaders had reasonably expected. It would have forced some sort of power-sharing, dual-responsibility arrangement between Solidarity and the old ruling elite, perhaps through some sort of government of national unity.

Despite its conservative logic, the ultimate result of the Roundtable Agreement exceeded all expectations. It turned into an extrication pact that brought "democracy with guarantees" rather than broader dictatorship. This is because the results of the June elections were a disaster for the PZPR, and its coalition partners defected to improve their future political prospects. In the Senat elections, Solidarity took ninety-nine of a hundred seats. The final results of the elections to the Sejm are presented in table 8.1. Here, Solidarity took every mandate of the 35 percent open to contestation.

The defeat and humiliation of candidates associated with the old regime went beyond the trouncing they received in competitive elections. Another guarantee that the communists and their allies had negotiated under the Roundtable Agreement was the right to place a small number of candidates on a national list (*lista krajowa*). These candidates did not face direct electoral competition (other candidates from the coalition faced competitors from within their own parties; e.g., two communists ran against each other in a district). However, their election was not guaranteed. If 50 percent of the voters struck a candidate from this list off their ballot, they were not elected. This happened in thirty-three of thirty-five cases.[26] This was a profound embarrassment to the communists and their electoral allies because the national list was loaded with their most senior and most prominent politicians.

Additionally, many of the contested races for seats guaranteed for the ruling coalition were not decided in the first round. In the second round, Solidarity endorsed candidates that it felt were more sympathetic to it, and these candidates tended to win. The defeat of the PZPR and its allies at the polls was near total. In its aftermath, the leaders of the United Peasant Party (ZSL) and the Democratic Party (SD) began to question their alliance with the PZPR, and this finished off the Roundtable Agreement in its original form.

After the elections, the ruling coalition began to disintegrate when the ZSL and the SD did not enthusiastically call for Wojciech Jaruzelski to stand for president. At the time of the signing of the Roundtable Agreement, all had assumed that the communist leader would be the first president. Although their defection from the coalition was not outright, it was clear that the leaders of the ZSL and the SD were concerned about being too closely linked to the PZPR in anticipation of the next scheduled election (1993), which would be fully contested.

On July 19, Jaruzelski was barely elected president. Election required a candidate to receive the endorsement of more than 50 percent of the members of both houses of the National Assembly with a quorum of two-thirds present. The final vote was 270 for and 233 against Jaruzelski, with 34 abstentions. A significant number of deputies from the SD and the ZSL voted against Jaruzelski or abstained, whereas Solidarity deputies and senators, in order to avoid scuttling the Roundtable Agreement and provoking a crisis, either did not attend the joint session, abstained, or cast invalid ballots in order to lower the number of votes Jaruzelski needed.

Attempts by the PZPR to form a government came to naught, and Solidarity explored the possibility of putting together a coalition government under its leadership. The leaders of the ZSL and the SD overtly defected from their former communist allies and happily entered into the Mazowiecki government, allowing them to distance themselves from the PZPR. Several communist ministers were also brought into the cabinet, including Jaruzelski's nominees for the ministers of defense and internal affairs. In this way, the Roundtable Agreement was transformed from a pact that envisioned only broadened dictatorship to one that resulted in democracy with guarantees for the communists (the presidency, 37.5 % of the lower house, and key national security portfolios in the cabinet).

When we look at Poland's institutions today, much of that architecture is composed of remnants from the Roundtable Agreement. The most significant institutional legacies are the bicameral nature of the National Assembly (which exists because the Roundtable was designed to limit Solidarity's power in the legislature) and the presidential/prime ministerial dyarchy of executive power. The president continues to hold the veto power assigned to the office under the Roundtable Agreement, and while the presidency does not have as extensive special powers in national security and foreign policy as it did under Jaruzelski, it still has special responsibilities in these areas under the terms of the Little Constitution.[27] Even though the Roundtable Agreement rapidly fell apart, its terms proved to be critical in determining the structure of Poland's new democratic institutions. The Roundtable Agreement accounts for the dyarchical nature of executive power and the bicameral structure of the legislature.

A CHARISMATIC LEADER

The plebiscitary election of the president and the creation of the rules for fully contested parliamentary elections entailed the removal of guarantees that had remained in place for the communists despite their disastrous showing at the polls. This removal became feasible with the collapse of communist power in the neighboring states in late 1989 and Soviet acceptance of this fait accompli. If a parliament could be freely elected in Budapest, and if Václav Havel could sit in the presidential palace in Prague, the Poles did not have to respect guarantees that were put in place to assuage Soviet fears about rapid democratization and the political fate of local communists.

New elections also became possible because the PZPR disbanded itself at its Eleventh Party Congress in January 1990 and its activists split into two successor parties—the Social Democracy of the Republic of Poland (SdRP) and the short-lived Polish Social-Democratic Union (PUS). Additionally, the ZSL tried to shed its past by frantically remaking itself as the Polish Peasant Party "Renewal" (PSL "Odrodzenie"). After incorporating elements from Rural Solidarity and remnants of the old populist movement, it renamed itself the Polish Peasant Party in an attempt to co-opt the legacy of the popular postwar opposition party it had helped destroy. Neither the external constraints that favored maintenance of the Roundtable Agreement nor the major political forces that had negotiated the terms of the pact with Solidarity existed any longer. The door was open to the full democratization of the Polish system.

The presence of a charismatic leader, Lech Wałęsa, had a definitive influence on how the institutions left over from the Roundtable were democratized. First, he ensured that the presidency was preserved rather than abolished. Second, his attempt to secure the office turned it from a position selected by the Assembly into one that was directly and democratically elected. Third, to pursue the presidency, Wałęsa accelerated the disintegration of the Solidarity movement, which in turn contributed to the weakness of political forces, explaining the changing electoral rules for the Sejm.

Prior to the election of Lech Wałęsa in 1990, Poland had never had a directly, and popularly, elected president. In the interwar republic, the president had little tangible power and was selected by the parliament; the selection of Gabriel Narutowicz to that office was controversial, however, and his assassination soon after being sworn in was a disaster from which interwar Polish democracy never recovered.[28] Without a charismatic leader like Wałęsa, it is debatable whether the Poles would have preserved a powerful presidency after the collapse of the Roundtable Agreement. No other

party leader aspiring to presidential power was capable of mobiliz-
ing the kind of support Wałęsa could mobilize.[29] Furthermore,
Wałęsa's position at the time of the demise of the Roundtable Agreement also worked to preserve the presidential office. Although his
charisma was a major factor in Solidarity's electoral victory in 1989,
he did not stand for office.[30] While he remained Solidarity chairman
and continued to assert his control over the union's political apparatus, the Citizen's Committees, he had stayed out of the government to allay the fears of the communists and the Soviets and perhaps to ensure that he and his power were not compromised if
Solidarity's foray into government was not successful.

In this situation, a campaign to unseat Wojciech Jaruzelski as
president became the path by which Poland moved beyond the
Roundtable toward full democratization. Jaruzelski, while legally
entitled to the office he held, was vulnerable because of his past role
and because he had been elected by a "contract" parliament. Wałęsa,
who was beginning to chafe at being on the sidelines of the unfold-
ing political game, clearly aspired to replace him.[31] Furthermore,
numerous Solidarity activists were prepared to support Wałęsa's
presidential ambitions as a way to advance their own positions, at
the expense of the activists concentrated around Prime Minister
Mazowiecki. By late February–early March 1990, talk of replacing
Jaruzelski with Wałęsa began in earnest in certain Solidarity circles.[32] The problem was that Jaruzelski's term did not expire until
1995.

In April 1990, when Wałęsa announced that he was running for
president, a range of political forces supported him: the newly
formed Center Alliance (PC), the Christian-National Union (ZChN),
the Congress of Liberal Democrats (KLD), the newspaper *Tygodnik
Solidarność* (Solidarity Weekly), elements from Rural Solidarity, activists in many local citizens' committees, and other small right-of-
center groups. These forces, through a publicity campaign that
stressed Jaruzelski's role in the imposition of martial law in 1981,
kept pressure on him to resign. They also argued that Poland was
falling behind other former bloc countries in building democracy
because it continued to honor the guarantees made to the communists under the Roundtable Agreement.[33]

The reticence of the Solidarity elite around Mazowiecki to break
the Roundtable Agreement led to an outright split within Solidarity
between the prime minister's and Wałęsa's supporters. Polemical ex-

changes between the two sides led to a struggle over Solidarity's Citizens' Committees in the spring of 1990. After declaring a "war at the top" (*wojna na gore*), Wałęsa continued to push for rapid change and expanded his criticism to include the pace of the Mazowiecki government's reforms. Because of the massive economic dislocation caused by Finance Minister Balcerowicz's shock therapy, these attacks found a ready-made audience. These attacks on the government placed the prime minister in the uncomfortable position of being Wałęsa's major antagonist and, thus, his probable opponent in any future contest for the presidency.

For his part, President Jaruzelski established a constructive relationship with the Mazowiecki government, particularly on the issue of depoliticizing the ministries of national defense and interior. He did make some political missteps though. He seemingly played into the hands of his detractors when, in May, he pleaded for retaining July 22 as a national holiday (this was the date the pro-Soviet Polish Committee of National Liberation issued a manifesto unilaterally declaring itself Poland's provisional government in 1944). On July 19, 1990, Jarulzelski finally decided he had enough and, one year after taking office, announced his willingness to resign.[34] Important questions of procedure had to be resolved if Jaruzelski's resignation was to lead to a fully democratic system. How would his replacement be selected? Leaving the selection to the old "contract" parliament was not acceptable to many. Thus, new and fully democratic elections needed to be held. Logically, two options were possible: a new National Assembly could be elected, which, in turn, would select the new president; or a new president could be directly elected, with new legislative elections following later.

While pro-Wałęsa forces like the Center Alliance initially supported the idea of parliamentary selection of a new president because they felt that their man would triumph over Prime Minister Mazowiecki even in the "contract" Sejm, most other political groups supported the idea of direct presidential elections.[35] The latter groups included Citizens' Movement–Democratic Action (ROAD), which was a bulwark of the pro-Mazowiecki wing of the Solidarity camp, as well as parties descended from the old ruling coalition. For Mazowiecki and his supporters, direct elections seemed like the only viable option.[36] The deputies from the old ruling coalition were happier to see early presidential rather than parliamentary elections. Furthermore, they were content to see Solidarity's leader bash the government in his quest for power: the prospect of an inexorable split between Solidarity factions and a dilution of the union's electoral strength was attractive. Wałęsa decided the issue when he supported the direct election option.[37] Thus, early and direct presidential elections became the first step in a second political pact, which resolved the question of how to proceed further with political reform.

On September 18, 1990, a meeting of Primate Glemp, President Jaruzelski, Lech Wałęsa, Prime Minister Mazowiecki, the marshals of the Sejm and the Senat, and the leaders of the largest parliamentary caucuses led to an agreement on the timing and procedures that would fully democratize the Polish system. Direct presidential elections were to be held no later than December 1990, whereas the National Assembly would set a date for its own dismissal no later than the first quarter of 1991.[38]

In the first round of the presidential elections that followed on November 25, 1990, Lech Wałęsa placed first, over five other candidates. In a major surprise, Stanisław Tyminski, an émigré businessman with a obscure past, bumped Prime Minister Mazowiecki from second place.[39] In the second round, which followed two weeks later, Wałęsa decisively defeated Tyminski.[40]

WEAK POLITICAL FORCES

The last element in the institutional choice made by the Poles is the changing rules for election to the National Assembly. Under the terms of the September agreement, the contract National Assembly elected in June 1989 was allowed to set the rules for the election of its successor, subject to the veto of the newly elected president. All political forces within the National Assembly were weak and thus had good reason to doubt their prospects in new elections.

The postcommunist forces, who controlled 65 percent of the Sejm, were nervous about their chances for success in fully contested elections. Certainly, the poor showing of the communist coalition in the elections of 1989 did not give them great confidence. Attempts to reconfigure and repackage individual parties had led to splits in a number of political clubs. The political strengths of the political actors represented in the Sejm as of November 1990, after much of the political reorganization in postcommunist circles had taken place, is presented in table 8.2. By this time, the Solidarity

Table 8.2 Composition of the Sejm, November 1990

	Seats	
Party or Parliamentary Club	Number	Percentage
Parliamentary Club of the Democratic Left		
(including SdRP)[a]	104	22.7
Polish Social-Democratic Union	41	8.9
Club of Independent Deputies	9	2.0
Club of Military Deputies	7	1.5
Polish Peasant Party (1)[b]	75	16.3
Democratic Party	21	4.6
PAX Association	10	2.2
Christian-Social Union	8	1.7
Polish Catholic Social Union	5	1.1
Polish Peasant Party (2)	4	0.9
Citizen's Parliamentary Club (Solidarity)	155	33.8
Unaffiliated Deputies	20	4.4
Total[c]	459	100.1

Source: Stanisław Gebethner, "Geneza i tło polityczno ustrojowe wyborów prezydenckich 1990 r." (The genesis and politico-systemic background of the presidential elections of 1990), in Dlaczego tak głosowano, Wybory prezydenckie '90 (Why did they vote that way? The presidential elections of 1990), ed. Stanisław Gebethner and Krzysztof Jasiewicz (Warsaw: Instytut Studiów Politycznych, 1993), 31.

a. Only twenty deputies were officially part of the Social-democracy of the Republic of Poland party caucus.

b. There were two competing Polish Peasant Parties. This one was formed largely from the ZSL caucus, which in turn became the PSL Odrodzenie and then merged with a small number of rural Solidarity deputies led by Roman Bartoszcze. The second Polish Peasant Party, below, was composed of three deputies elected on the Solidarity ticket and one from the ZSL.

c. The total is 459 instead of 460 because of a seat left vacant by a death. Percentage does not equal 100 due to rounding.

caucus (the Citizen's Parliamentary Club) had become the largest caucus. Furthermore, legislation passed by the Mazowiecki government allowed a part of the vast fortune of the PZPR to be expropriated, denying the postcommunists the advantage in resources they had enjoyed in 1989.

At this juncture, the size of the Citizen's Parliamentary Club (OKP) is somewhat deceiving due to Wałęsa's declaration of a "war at the top." The split between supporters of Mazowiecki and supporters of Wałęsa fractionalized the Solidarity caucus and weakened the government's base of support. The factions within the OKP, circa November 1990, are listed in table 8.3. Thus, while Solidarity had

**Table 8.3 Factional Groupings within Solidarity's Citizens'
Parliamentary Club, November 1990**

	Number of Mandates	
Group	Sejm	Senate
Christian-National Union	3	3
Christian Democrats	29	7
Rural Solidarity and the		
Polish Peasant Party, Solidarity	19	8
Center Alliance	25	11
Liberal Democrats	3	6
Forum of the Democratic Right	4	2
Citizens' Movement—Democratic Action	30	24
Independents[a]	31	21
Belonging to no group	11	17
Total	155	99

Source: See table 8.2, 32.

a. The Independents (Niezrzeszonych) were organized as an official circle within the OKP, while those "belonging to no group" (bez przynależności do żadnego koła) had no affiliation within the OKP.

done exceptionally well in June 1989 and emerged as the largest organized group in the local elections of May 1990, the fractionalization meant that most parties (or protoparties) stemming from Solidarity were highly unsure of their potential electoral strength.[41]

The splintering of political forces in both the postcommunist and Solidarity camps had an important impact on the shape of the Polish electoral system. Unsure of their political strength or fearful that their support was not sufficient to keep their parties in parliament, most politicians favored a highly proportional electoral system. In this way, any support they could muster would preserve at least some representation in parliament and thus keep them in the political game.

No important political forces supported a majoritarian political system, but the two most important parties from the Solidarity camp, the Democratic Union (UD) and the Center Alliance (PC), supported a more restrictive electoral law, mixing majoritarian and proportional elements.[42] President Wałęsa also favored a system of this sort. The UD, composed of former Prime Minister Mazowiecki's supporters, was fairly sure that its level of support (15–20 %) would stand up well under a mixed system, because Wałęsa's supporters were spread across a number of parties and because most likely none of the postcommunist parties could muster a similar level of support. At the time of the debate on the electoral law, the PC, whose leaders were among the president's closest advisers, aspired to become the presidential party and had reason to hope that the president would endorse it. However, between them, these two parties did not have the political strength to push through a more restrictive statute.

When it came time to write the new electoral statute, the version the Sejm passed was highly proportional; when Wałęsa, fearing a fragmented parliament, rejected this bill, the Sejm overrode his veto. Under the terms of this statute, 391 Sejm deputies were elected from thirty-seven election districts. Depending on the size of its population, each district elected between seven and sixteen deputies. Voters cast their ballot for a single party by putting an X next to the name of one of the candidates on that party's district list. Within these districts, seats were allocated to the parties by the Hare-Niemeyer method.[43] The remaining sixty-nine seats were awarded proportionally to national lists of parties that surpassed a 5 percent national threshold or that won seats in five or more electoral districts. The rules for Senat elections were also made less restrictive: seats were no longer individually contested on a majoritarian basis; instead, they were awarded on the basis of the first two or three past the post in the voivodship as a whole.

The election that replaced the contract Sejm did not take place in the spring, as many of Wałęsa's supporters desired, but was put off until October 27, 1991, because the majority of Sejm deputies preferred to postpone their reelection campaigns as long as possible. Under the terms of the new electoral law, the result was a highly fragmented Assembly, with twenty-nine parties represented. The results for the Sejm are summarized in table 8.4. The electoral system almost perfectly reflected the fragmented results that the voters provided. As figure 8.1 shows, the electoral result was very close to perfectly proportional; it translated the percentage of votes into the percentage of seats at a rate of close to 1:1. With these results, the minimum number of parties needed to form a majority coalition was five, but no party from the post-Solidarity camp was prepared to form a coalition with the SLD (Alliance of the Democratic Left, which had the second highest total of seats—sixty). A potential existed for a coalition within the post-Solidarity camp, uniting five of

Table 8.4 Elections to the Sejm, October 27, 1991

	Seats		
Party	Number	Percentage	Votes (%)
Democratic Union (UD)	62	13.5	12.3
Alliance of the Democratic Left (SLD)	60	13.0	12.0
Catholic Electoral Action (WAK)	49	10.7	8.7
Polish Peasant Party (PSL)	48	10.4	8.7
Confederation for an Independent Poland (KPN)	46	10.0	7.5
Civic Alliance Center (POC)	44	9.6	8.7
Liberal Democratic Congress (KLD)	37	8.0	7.5
Agrarian Alliance (PL)	28	6.1	5.5
Independent and Self-governing Trade Union Solidarity (NSZZ)	27	5.9	5.1
Polish Beer-Lovers' Party (PPPP)	16	3.5	3.3
German Minority (MN)	7	1.5	1.2
Christian Democracy (ChN)	5	1.1	2.4
Solidarity of Labor (SP)	4	0.9	2.1
Party of Christian Democrats (PChD)	4	0.9	1.1
Polish Western Union (PZZ)	4	0.9	0.2
Union of Real Politics (UPR)	3	0.6	2.3
Party X (X)	3	0.6	0.5
Movement for the Autonomy of Silesia (RAS)	2	0.4	0.4
Democratic Party (SD)	1	0.2	1.4
Democratic Social Movement (RDS)	1	0.2	0.5
Agrarian Electoral Alliance Piast (LPWP)	1	0.2	0.4
Cracow Coalition in Solidarity with the President (KKSzP)	1	0.2	0.2
Union of Podhalans (UPod)	1	0.2	0.2
For Great Poland and Poland (WP)	1	0.2	0.2
Agrarian Unity (JL)	1	0.2	0.2
Electoral Committee of the Eastern Orthodox (KWP)	1	0.2	0.1
Solidarity '80 (S'80)	1	0.2	0.1
Union of Great Poles (UWie)	1	0.2	0.1
Alliance of Women Against the Hardships of Life (SKpTŻ)	1	0.2	0.0

Source: Krzysztof Jasiewicz, "Poland," *European Journal of Political Research 22* (1992), 489.

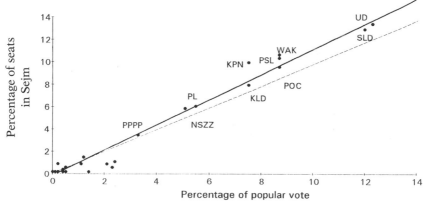

Fig. 8.1. Translation of Popular Votes into Sejm Mandates, Election of October 27, 1991. See table 8.4 for party abbreviations. Only the top ten parties are displayed. This figure was prepared following the format used by John R. Hibbing and Samuel C. Patterson, "A Democratic Legislature in the Making: The Historic Hungarian Elections of 1990," *Comparative Political Studies* 24 (1992): 430–54.

the six parties (UD, WAK, POC, KLD, PL, and Solidarity), but many of these parties were still hostile to the UD in the wake of the Wałęsa/Mazowiecki split.

This electoral result did not produce stable and long-lasting governments. In the period between October 27, 1991, and September 19, 1993, the date of the second free election to the National Assembly, two governments (Olszewski's PC-led coalition and Suchocka's UD-led coalition) fell. They did, however, manage to conduct some significant legislative business, such as proceeding with the privatization of state industry and promulgating the Little Constitution, which better specified the relationship between the president and the National Assembly.

On May 28, 1993, the Suchocka government fell after failing by one vote in a vote of confidence. Following the fall of the government, forces in the Assembly from both governing and opposition parties moved to enact a new, more restrictive electoral law in case President Wałęsa decided to call for early elections rather than designate a new prime minister. This new law, which had been in preparation since 1992, was supported by five of the larger parties (UD, SLD, KLD, KPN, PSL). This left Wałęsa the option of signing or vetoing the new ordinance and thus choosing between the highly proportional electoral statute of 1991 or the new one. He opted for both new elections and the more restrictive statute. The new elections for the Senat were conducted under the rules established in 1991.

The new electoral procedures for the Sejm were much more restrictive than those of the statute used in 1991. To win seats in the Sejm, parties had to win at least 5 percent of the vote nationally; coalitions needed 8 percent.[44] Three hundred and ninety-one deputies were still elected from multiple-candidate electoral districts (which had three to seventeen mandates, depending on population). However, the 1991 district lines were redrawn to coincide with individual voivodship boundaries (there were actually fifty-two districts, because the highly populated voivodships of Warsaw and Katowice needed more than one district to be fairly represented). Sixty-nine deputies continued to be elected on national party lists. However, this time parties needed to clear a 7 percent threshold to be eligible. Finally, the new statute also rewarded the larger parties by replacing the less restrictive Hare-Niemeyer system of distribution with the more restrictive d'Hondt method.[45]

The results of the general election of September 19, 1993, came as a shock to the post-Solidarity elite. Postcommunist forces (SLD and PSL) took first and second place in the voting (see table 8.5). A large number of parties from the post-Solidarity right failed to clear the thresholds established under the new electoral law (8 percent for electoral coalitions and 5 percent for individual parties). The two postcommunist parties took a combined 35 percent of the vote, while three post-Solidarity formations that got past the threshold (UD, UP, and BBWR) took a little more than 23 percent of the vote.

The big losers in this election were the parties of the post-Solidarity right and center-right. Parties or groups with a Solidarity pedigree took close to half of the popular vote, but the right was so fractionalized that the 24.8 percent of the vote it captured did not translate into any seats in the Sejm. For the larger parties, including the postcommunist formations, this meant that they were assigned seats well in excess of their share of the popular vote (see figure 8.2). Thus the two postcommunist front-runners received almost double the percentage of seats in parliament than their share of the popular vote. The parties of the post-Solidarity center and left—the Democratic Union (UD) and Union of Labor (UP), which placed third and

Table 8.5 Elections to the Sejm, September 19, 1993

	Seats		
Party	Number	Percentage	Votes %
Parties elected to the Sejm	460	100.1[a]	65.6
Alliance of the Democratic Left (SLD)	171	37.2	20.4
Polish Peasant Party (PSL)	132	28.7	15.4
Democratic Union (UD)	74	16.1	10.6
Union of Labor (UP)	41	8.9	7.3
Confederation for an Independent Poland (KPN)	22	4.8	5.8
Nonparty Bloc in Support of Reforms (BBWR)	16	3.5	5.4
German Minority (MN)	4	0.9	0.7
Parties not elected to the Sejm (5% and below for individual parties, 8% and below for coalitions)			34.4
Catholic Electoral Committee "Fatherland" (members: ZChN, PK, SLCh, PChD)			6.4
Independent and Self-governing Trade Union Solidarity (NSZZ)			4.9
Center Alliance (PC)			4.4
Liberal Democratic Congress (KLD)			4.0
Coalition for the Republic (KdR)			2.7
Agrarian Alliance (PL)			2.4
Polish Beer-Lovers Party (PPPP)			0.1
Others			9.5

Source: Krzysztof Jasiewicz, "Polish Politics on the Eve of the 1993 Elections: Toward Fragmentation or Pluralism?" Communist and Post-Communist Studies 26 (1993), 411.
a. Does not equal 100 due to rounding.

fourth—also received seats in percentages that outstripped their popular votes. The Confederation for an Independent Poland (KPN), a nationalist party that predates Solidarity, and the Nonparty Bloc for the Support of Reform, an organization of President Wałęsa's dwindling number of enthusiastic supporters, were the only parties of the right to surpass the threshold. Both of these parties received a smaller percentage of seats in the Sejm than their share of popular vote, because they did not clear the 7 percent threshold that would have entitled them to a share of the sixty-nine mandates for national party lists.

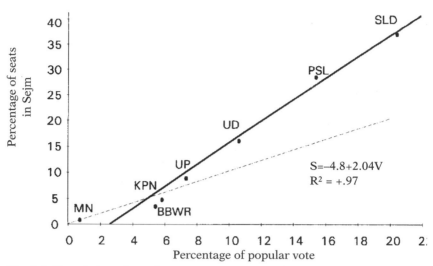

Fig. 8.2. Translation of Popular Votes into Sejm Mandates: Election of September 19, 1993. See table 8.5 for party abbreviations.

The adoption of the new, more restrictive electoral statute that produced these results, curiously enough, is also attributable to the weakness of political forces in the Assembly. However, the decision on electoral rules was taken this time with the knowledge of how parties had fared in 1991; that is, actors had some rough notion of their strengths relative to each other. In 1993 a coalition of the larger parties forced the new law through at the last instant in the hope of eliminating some of the small parties and of gaining seats in the Sejm.

This is a good example of how new knowledge changes the behavior of actors facing similar situations (a fractionalized polity with weak political forces). The critical factor in the framing of the electoral laws of 1991 and 1993 was the weakness of the political parties. What differed was that they had some rough idea of their potential electoral strengths. This allowed the larger parties to cooperate in formulating a more restrictive electoral law in pursuit of the rational goal of increasing their representation in the Sejm. While the new law essentially had its intended effect, it was for some, like the liberals (KLD), a gross miscalculation. Other forces like the PSL and the SLD gained even more than they expected due to the shortsightedness of the post-Solidarity right in disregarding the effect that its fractionalization would have under a more restrictive electoral system.

CONCLUSIONS

The findings in this chapter concerning the way Poland's new democratic institutions came into being are summarized in table 8.6. Poland's present institutions were laid down in four fairly discrete steps. The first step, the establishment of the basic institutional framework—that is, a bicameral legislature and a semipresidential executive arrangement—was accomplished by the Roundtable Agreement of April 1989. It was not until the second step that these newly constructed institutions were subjected to universal electoral contestation—that is, fully democratized. This was accomplished through Lech Wałęsa's push to capture the presidency in 1990. It resulted in the negotiation of a second pact in September 1990, which led to the direct election of a new president later that year, followed by fully contested parliamentary elections in 1991.

Steps three and four concern the establishment of the rules of electoral competition for the Sejm. In both 1991 and 1993, one can explain the rules selected by the fact that all political forces were weak. In both cases, the actors empowered to make the rules for the next election, the deputies of the Sejm, acted in pursuit of their self-interest as politicians (to maintain their power). In 1991, the highly proportional electoral system was a product of both the contract parliament created by the Roundtable and the splitting up of Solidarity into competing parties and factions. All actors were uncertain about their electoral strength. Solidarity-based parties were unsure about how much of the Solidarity constituency they could capture. Those parties descended from the old authoritarian system were scared that after the elections of 1989 their association with the old regime would continue to hurt them electorally. Under these circumstances the contract Sejm enacted a hyperproportional electoral law. The new system largely avoided restrictive measures like single-member districts and high-threshold clauses to minimize the prospects for parliamentary extinction of existing parties (this nevertheless happened to the SD). The results of the election produced a highly fractionalized National Assembly, with no simple solutions to the problem of maintaining a stable ruling coalition.

In the final evolutionary step, the framing of the current election

Table 8.6 The Evolution of the Polish Political System, 1989–1993

Branch of Government	Old Structures	Roundtable Agreement (Pact I, April 1989)	Wałęsa's Push to Become President (Pact II, September 1990)	Weakness of Political Forces	Final Result (1993)
Executive	Council of State (collective head of state, largely symbolic)	Creation of executive presidency with substantial powers (elected by parliament)	Direct popular election of president		Semipresidential system with a bicameral parliament and a more restrictive set of electoral rules for the Sejm
	Prime minister and Council of Ministers (high degree of independence from weak legislature; highly subservient to PZPR leadership)	Prime minister and Council of Ministers made dependent on parliament			
		Executive dyarchy established			
Legislative	Sejm (460 members; no substantial contestation of mandates)	Sejm retained (only 35% of seats contested)	Fully contested elections to both houses of National Assembly, to follow the above	Iteration 1: 1991 election (highly proportional electoral rules)	
		Creation of Senat (second chamber, with 100 members, fully contested)		Iteration 2: 1993 election (more restrictive electoral rules to Sejm)	

law in 1993, though the parties remained weak, one critical factor changed: the parties in the Sejm had some sense of their relative political strength. In this situation, when the fall of the Suchocka government presented the opportunity to write a new electoral law, a coalition of the stronger parties teamed up to force through a more restrictive statute to eliminate the numerous, minute "couch" parties. This turned out to be a major miscalculation for the fractionalized Solidarity Right and a major gain for the two largest postcommunist groupings, the SLD and the PSL.

These findings are congruent with the criticism above of a "crafting" approach to political institutions. The Polish case shows that the abstract consideration of what constellation of institutions is best for democracy is an elusive business. It is not always possible to "found" institutions on the basis of the well-intentioned suggestions of political analysts. On the contrary, Poland has put together working democratic institutions through a piecemeal process that was driven by the pursuit of power by the political forces that survived the collapse of the old system.

Such a result points out the advantages of an approach like path dependence, which pays close attention to local conditions and political struggles to explain institutional outcomes. The complex of legislative and political institutions chosen in Poland can be explained through consideration of the motives of the actors who were empowered to make decisions and political compromises at critical junctures in the process of institution building. This is both a question of the balance of political forces of the moment and of how legacies live on in institutional arrangement and norms. The best example of such a legacy provided by this account is the lasting impact of the Roundtable on the shape of Poland's institutions.

This insight in turn has ramifications for how we should approach the problem of stability in new democracies. It would be premature to dismiss one form of democracy as being doomed to failure in any particular case, despite parliamentarism's superior record. Like institutional choice, the stability of new democracies is best explained through careful consideration of organized political forces and the conditions and legacies they confront. What is key is the willingness of the major political actors to continue to play the political game by the rules established during democratization.[46] The prospects for the consolidation of stable democracy in Poland or any other new democracy can best be foretold by understanding the evolution of political forces, their strengths, and whether the interests they represent stand a fair chance of being realized under the new institutional framework. In this regard, the new democracies of Eastern Europe are difficult cases to gauge because the structure of interests in these countries have been subject to rapid change due to the transformation of their economic systems. Critical economic interests are still in a state of flux.

I close with some reflections on charisma and presidentialism. In the Polish case, the existence of a charismatic leader like Lech Wałęsa provided the opportunity to fully democratize the political system when the constraints built into the Roundtable Agreement no longer corresponded to the political reality in Poland. Despite the fact that Wałęsa's personal ambition played a part in his decision to challenge the system, this decision provided the opportunity to hold fully contested elections for executive and legislative power. In this sense Wałęsa's charisma served as a vehicle to democratize a system that had become politically obsolete during its short existence.

In his introduction to this volume, Kurt von Mettenheim points out how presidentialism may better reconcile the difficulties of maintaining liberal representative government in an era of mass politics subject to plebiscitarian pressures. A related and important consideration from the perspective of the process of democratization is the emergence of charismatic leaders in the period of crisis that precedes the end of authoritarianism and during the extrication phase itself. Presidentialism may offer the best chance to institutionally harness the revolutionary and democratizing power of charisma and subject it to the formal rules that are essential to the survival of a democratic system.

The examples provided by interwar and contemporary Poland are interesting in this respect. There was no position in the newly created interwar political system that fit the charismatic status of Piłsudski. He instead took a leading role in the military, and when the fractionalized parliament had difficulty in providing effective rule, he established his own dictatorship in 1926. Lech Wałęsa, on the other hand, has seen his popularity steadily erode under the pressures of office in the last few years. While some might argue, given his history of playing fast and loose with the rules, that his diminished prospects for success in a reelection campaign make him a greater potential threat to democracy, the diminution of his ability to charismatically mobilize a large constituency probably reduces the likelihood he could lead a successful assault against democracy. While these two examples suggest that presidentialism offers the better prospect for seeing charismatic authority evolve in a democratic rather than a dictatorial direction, the question still requires systematic study.

CHAPTER 9

President and Parliament in the Russian Federation

Jonathan Harris

In the summer of 1991, Boris Yeltsin was elected the first president of the Russian Republic (RSFSR) of the USSR. With the collapse of the USSR and the emergence of the Russian Republic as an independent state, Yeltsin sought to establish a "presidential republic" based on a constitutionally defined separation of powers between a popularly elected parliament and the chief executive. At the same time, the president (who served as his own prime minister for the first six months of 1992) introduced economic reforms designed to dismantle the state socialist system inherited from the USSR and to establish a "market economy" in its stead. In the process, he clashed repeatedly and with ever greater intensity with those members of the Congress of People's Deputies (the parliament, which had been elected in the spring of 1990) who sought to establish a "parliamentary republic" and who resisted or challenged the proposed economic transformation.

The growing conflicts over the distribution of political authority and economic policy became increasingly intertwined with conflict over the constitution. While the parliament attempted to limit Yeltsin's authority by amendments to the constitution, he sought to use referendums on constitutional and other issues to outflank his opponents. By spring and summer of 1993, an impasse seemed to have been reached. President Yeltsin began work on a totally new constitution and declared that only new parliamentary elections could resolve the conflict between the executive and legislative bodies. In September 1993, President Yeltsin dissolved the parliament and announced that a referendum on his draft constitution and new parliamentary elections would be held in December 1993. Yeltsin's leading opponents refused to abide by the president's decision and, in October, launched an abortive effort to overthrow the regime by force. The president ordered the army to crush the rebellion.

The referendum and parliamentary elections in December 1993

had an unexpected impact on the relationship between president and parliament. While the voters endorsed the constitution creating a presidential republic, they also gave massive electoral support to those political leaders and parties—including the nationalist Vladimir Zhirinovsky—who had assailed the president's economic program. As a consequence, the president's political opponents became a powerful force in the new bicameral Federal Assembly established by the constitution. The electoral success of Yeltsin's opponents seemed to have a dramatic impact on the president's behavior. He initially proved unwilling to confront the parliamentary opposition, despite the broad powers granted to the president by the constitution, and sought to find a common ground with the Assembly in the first months of 1994. But in the spring and summer of 1994 he reasserted his constitutional prerogatives once it had become clear that the State Duma was too deeply divided to challenge his authority. This chapter attempts to demonstrate how President Yeltsin's determined efforts to establish a presidential republic collided with the parliamentary institutions established in the last years of perestroika.

During the last two years of the USSR's existence, the Gorbachev leadership had attempted to democratize the political system by transforming the moribund Soviets into popularly elected legislative bodies. This effort to return "all power to the Soviets" gave immense authority to the new parliaments established in 1989 for the entire USSR and in 1990 in the RSFSR and the other member republics. When Yeltsin was elected president of the RSFSR in the summer of 1991, this new presidency was simply grafted onto a political system dominated by the Congress of People's Deputies and the Supreme Soviet.

The president's effort to overcome parliamentary dominance of the political system was complicated by his efforts to destroy the state socialist economic system established under the USSR. In early 1992, the Yeltsin regime abandoned state control of most prices and wages and began to dismantle most of the state structure that had administered the five-year plans, to transform state property into private property, and to encourage entrepreneurial activity. The leadership realized that this transition would not be easy for the society, but the extraordinary inflation and the disruption of production and employment caused by the reforms proved far more painful than expected. While the range and intensity of economic and personal hardship are intensely disputed and highly politicized, there is no question that the economic changes divided the society. When citizens expressed their views on the Yeltsin regime in a nationwide referendum in April 1993, 53 percent of the voters approved its social-economic policy while 45 percent expressed disapproval.

Social discontent with economic policy helped to transform the parliamentary bodies (which included many deputies long opposed to a market economy) into the major locus of opposition to President Yeltsin's program of political and economic reform. The conflict between parliament and president remained within certain limits during the first year of Yeltsin's reign; during that time he not only was prime minister of his own government (the Council of Ministers) but also enjoyed extraordinary decree powers granted by the Congress of People's Deputies in the wake of the abortive coup against the president of the USSR, Mikhail Gorbachev. While there were serious disputes over distribution of powers among president, government, and parliament and over the nature and scope of economic reforms, neither president nor parliament challenged each other's legitimacy as expressions of the people's will.

But in the second half of 1992, the conflict over separation of powers and economic policy became increasingly intense, and each side began to challenge the other's legitimacy. President Yeltsin resigned as prime minister, and on December 1 his extraordinary decree power expired. The major leader of the parliamentary bodies, Chairman of the Supreme Soviet Ruslan Khasbulatov, worked vigorously to retain the parliamentary republic established in 1990, to restrain President Yeltsin's authority, to challenge many elements of the economic reform, and to ensure that the state retained a large role in the economy. Khasbulatov and other parliamentary leaders began to claim that parliamentary decisions were far more accurate expressions of the people's will than the president's decisions and that President Yeltsin sought to establish dictatorial control behind a facade of democratic terminology. Yeltsin's most virulent opponents claimed that the president did not represent the citizens of the Russian Federation but the interests of Western imperalism.

President Yeltsin, for his part, worked assiduously to establish a presidential republic and to overcome the parliament's resistance to his economic and political reforms. As the conflict intensified, Yeltsin increasingly charged that the parliamentary leadership and its allies did not really support democratic institutions but sought instead to restore the "old Bolshevik order." In the summer of 1993, he declared that the parliament was "incompatible" with democracy—that it was so dominated by holdovers from the CPSU apparatus that it had degenerated into a hostile bureaucratic structure.

The conflict between the president and parliament not only dominated the entire legislative process but also has shaped the entire effort to develop a new constitution for the Russian Federation. Unfortunately for President Yeltsin, the existing constitution gave the Federal Assembly full control over the process of constitutional amendment. Since its election in 1990, the Assembly used this authority to prevent the writing of a draft acceptable to the president and to pass a series of constitutional amendments to limit his authority. The president has sought to counter the Assembly's prerogatives by calling for national referendums on constitutional issues, but these efforts were successfully thwarted by the Assembly. In the summer of 1993, after his impressive victory in a nationwide referendum in April, President Yeltsin convoked a constitutional assembly, which produced a new version of the country's constitution in July 1993. But parliamentary leaders did not regard this document as legitimate, continued to work out the details of its own version, and consistently sought to undermine the president's economic policy. Yeltsin sought to resolve the conflict by the dissolution of the Federal Assembly in September 1993.

THE LEGACY OF PERESTROIKA

The parliamentary structures of the Russian Federation are the direct outgrowth of the political reforms begun by Gorbachev at the Nineteenth CPSU Party Conference in the summer of 1988. The general secretary did not attempt to create new parliamentary institutions but to transform the institutions created by his predecessors. While parliaments had existed since the Bolshevik Revolution, in the 1930s Stalin transformed them into large bodies that ostensibly provided for popular control over the immense bureaucratic state structure established during the first five-year plan. Widely heralded as legislative and representative bodies with vast oversight responsibilities, these parliaments were in fact bogus institutions, which failed to fulfill any of these functions. They were rarely convened (for example, the Supreme Soviet of the USSR convened for forty-eight hours a year), and the thousands of elected deputies were essentially the instruments of the local party officials who nominated them and ensured their election by not permitting other names on the ballot. As a consequence, the parliaments had no coherent control over the vast centralized structure that employed the overwhelming majority of Soviet citizens and administered the series of five-year plans.

It is generally argued that this vast state structure was controlled by the Communist Party of the Soviet Union (CPSU), whose members staffed the most important administrative positions in the executive branch. In fact, it was not the immense CPSU (nearly twenty million members) that ruled the state, but the party's elite of full-time party officials who attempted to rule the state in the name of the CPSU by controlling all important personnel decisions and by imposing its party discipline on the rank and file members who staffed the state.

In 1988, General Secretary Gorbachev sought to limit party officials' authority and to increase the parliaments' control over the executive branch by transforming them into representative institutions with genuine legislative power and responsibility for oversight. Multicandidate elections were introduced at all levels of the political system in the late 1980s and early 1990s to achieve that end. But Gorbachev's political reforms were only partial. He remained unwilling to transform the CPSU into a purely parliamentary party—to break completely with the concept of a "vanguard party"—and he proved unwilling or unable to fully dislodge local party officials from their positions of authority. As a result, many local party officials (who often shifted to positions in the local executive structure) used their own authority to ensure their own election or the election of their favored candidates as deputies to the new parliaments.

Despite the incomplete nature of the political reforms, the introduction of standing legislatures on the basis of multicandidate elections provided the institutional framework for the destruction of the USSR. The gigantic Congress of People's Deputies of the USSR elected in 1989 included a vigorous parliamentary opposition, which engaged in a frontal assault on the CPSU's position and pressed vigorously for further democratization. At the same time, nationalist, separatist, and anticommunist movements and groups gained control of both legislative and executive bodies in a number of non-Russian republics in the late 1980s and made significant inroads in the federal and local parliaments throughout the Russian Republic (RSFSR) in 1990.

General Secretary Gorbachev, who had been elected as chairman of the Supreme Soviet of the USSR by the Congress of People's Deputies in 1989, and who sought to create some executive counterweight to cope with growing separatist activities in the borderlands, managed to persuade the Congress to elect him as the USSR's first president in March 1990. During his short reign Gorbachev desperately sought a political strategy to prevent the USSR from breaking apart. In the summer and fall of 1990 he cooperated with Boris Yeltsin, who had been elected chairman of the RSFSR Supreme Soviet by the RSFSR Congress of People's Deputies in the spring of 1990, but this coalition collapsed over questions of economic reform and the nature of the USSR's federal structure. In the fall of 1990, in the face of the USSR Congress's demands to extend executive authority, Gorbachev tightened control over the government, assumed broad emergency powers, and found new allies among the USSR's ministers for defense, security, and industry, who supported a powerful central government. Boris Yeltsin and leaders from other republics not only clashed increasingly with this central government but also called upon President Gorbachev to resign.

In the spring of 1991, President Gorbachev reversed field dramatically and turned to the elected parliamentary leaders of the republics in order to create a federal structure that would seriously reduce, but not eliminate, the central government's authority. This shift, coupled with a growing sense of economic chaos and polarization within the CPSU, led the leading ministers of the USSR, who were tacitly supported by many local party officials, to oust President Gorbachev in August 1991. While the junta (which named itself the State Emergency Committee) was able to seize the president, it was unable to arrest Boris Yeltsin, who had been popularly elected as the first president of the RSFSR in June 1991. Yeltsin used his new presidential powers to mobilize an effective resistance to the Emergency Committee and to restore Gorbachev to the presidency of the USSR.

PARLIAMENTARY ELECTIONS IN THE RSFSR, SPRING 1990

The relationship between President Yeltsin and parliament was shaped by the elections for the RSFSR Congress of People's Deputies in the spring of 1990. The elections of more than one thousand deputies were far more democratic than the elections of deputies to the USSR Congress of People's Deputies the previous year. In the 1989 elections, the CPSU leadership had reserved one-third of the seats in the Congress for the CPSU and various "public organizations" under its control, but in the 1990 elections in the RSFSR all deputies were elected on a geographic basis. While local party officials sometimes managed to ensure their own election as deputies, many deputies were nominal members of the CPSU and were deeply divided on social, economic, and national issues.

Two blocs of deputies emerged from the election—an alliance of reformist communists and noncommunists, known as Democratic Russia, and the Communists of Russia, a coalition of various types of orthodox communists. Democratic Russia was deeply committed to the defense of the RSFSR's sovereignty against the central government, the creation of a multiparty system, the reduction of the CPSU's influence, and the election of the independent-minded Boris Yeltsin (who was still a member of the CPSU at this juncture) as chairman of the Supreme Soviet. The Communists of Russia were generally hostile to the introduction of market reforms and the dismantling of the state socialist economic system favored by Yeltsin and his allies. While they represented themselves as the only true defenders of Russia's national interests and of those Russians who lived in the non-Russian republics of the USSR, they simultaneously opposed any action that might weaken the USSR as a state. Their opposition to the "renegade" Yeltsin was supported by President Gorbachev at this juncture. Yeltsin's very narrow victory on the third ballot was a striking victory for Democratic Russia, but the Communists of Russia remained a powerful center of opposition to Yeltsin and his program.

The federal parliamentary structures created by the 1990 elections were based on the USSR model. The directly elected Congress of People's Deputies was given the right to "decide" on the country's "most important constitutional, political, and economic issues" and to select from within its midst a standing bicameral legislature (the Supreme Soviet) of approximately 240 deputies. Unfortunately, the division of authority between the Congress and the Supreme Soviet was clear only at the margin. While the constitution could be adopted or amended only by a two-thirds vote of the Congress of People's Deputies, and the Supreme Soviet had to approve the government's budget, the division of authority on virtually all other questions remained obscure. Most important, the Supreme Soviet did not regard itself as bound by the resolutions of the Congress on "important" matters, and the Congress regarded its decisions as legislative acts binding on the government.

The very first sessions of the huge Congress of People's Deputies revealed it to be an extraordinarily free and open forum for the expression of deputies' opinions and orientations but badly equipped to produce coherent decisions on the RSFSR's problems. While Democratic Russia had formed a powerful coalition to elect Yeltsin, it splintered on virtually all other issues. And while the Communists of Russia remained relatively disciplined, particularly after the formation of the autonomous Communist Party for the RSFSR in June 1990, they did not form a majority; they later divided over the proper approach to Chairman Yeltsin.

These divisions and the very size of the Congress made it extremely difficult to develop coherent legislation. The failure to clearly delimit the authority of the Congress and the Supreme Soviet and the absence of any meaningful party discipline encouraged deputies to introduce their own draft legislation and allowed the Congress to modify these drafts in often bewildering and contradictory fashion. Chairman Yeltsin, who directed these discussions with extraordinary skill, was often unable to impose realistic decisions on important issues. Discussions and debates were prolonged for hours, and the agenda was often reworked on the basis of deputies' recommendations from the floor. After the initial burst of public-spirited enthusiasm, all activities became increasingly hampered by absentecism—and the related difficulty of obtaining the necessary quorum.

Televison transmission of the Congress's proceedings had an important impact on Russian citizens' orientation toward these new institutions. While citizens were initially clearly encouraged and impressed by the open and direct debate and by the almost complete disappearance of euphemism in the discussion of public policy, they were naturally distressed by the prolonged debate over the agenda, the wrangling over procedural questions, and the failure of these proceedings to provide instant solutions to pressing economic and social problems. Negative public perceptions were often reinforced by both print and TV journalists, who described Congress's sessions in derisive terms.

In contrast, the compact Supreme Soviet, selected from the

Congress of People's Deputies, proved to be a relatively efficient legislative body. Its functional commissions and committees prepared draft legislation often with the cooperation of their opposite number in the executive branch, debate was focused and businesslike, and inappropriate amendments by individual deputies from the floor were relatively rare. However, the bicameral nature of the Supreme Soviet produced serious difficulties. One house was designed to represent the non-Russian populations who lived in the so-called autonomous republics within the RSFSR and was designated the sole source of legislation dealing with the "nationality question" in the RSFSR. During the first year of the Supreme Soviet's activity, when attention was focused on the defense of the RSFSR's "sovereignty" against the central government, there was little discord between the two houses. But with the collapse of the USSR and the emergence of the Russian Federation as an independent state, the authority of the governments in the non-Russian territories, now known as "republics," became a divisive issue.

BORIS YELTSIN AS CHAIRMAN OF THE RSFSR SUPREME SOVIET, 1990–1991

In the spring of 1990, Boris Yeltsin was elected chairman of the Supreme Soviet by the Congress of People's Deputies by a very narrow margin. During the following year, Yeltsin transformed this position, which had been of marginal political significance before the 1990 elections, into a major instrument for the broadening of the RSFSR's "sovereignty" against the central government headed by President Gorbachev. It must be stressed that Yeltsin had no formal executive authority—he was merely the elected chairman of the Supreme Soviet—but he acted during the following year as if he were the RSFSR's chief executive officer, even though it did not yet exist! In his inaugural address, Yeltsin made it clear that he hoped to strengthen the power of the RSFSR, to extend authority to local parliaments, to ensure the introduction of a multiparty system, to limit the CPSU's political authority, to dismantle the state-managed economic system, and to move rapidly toward some form of mixed economy.

As chairman of the Supreme Soviet, he not only presided over sessions of the Congress of People's Deputies and the Supreme Soviet (which was sometimes chaired by his deputy, Ruslan Khasbulatov) but also dominated the formation of the new Council of Ministers for the RSFSR. He handpicked its chairman and, through a combination of bullying and cajolery, subordinated it to the decisions of the Supreme Soviet. Under his auspices, the Council of Ministers of the RSFSR became increasingly engaged in an argument with the central government of the USSR over the control of state economic agencies. Within this incredibly confusing context, the Council of Ministers sought to accelerate the transition to a market economy and to overcome the resistance to these efforts by the communist deputies in the Supreme Soviet, who had developed a more effective internal organization after the formation of the Communist Party of the RSFSR in June 1990.

Yeltsin's relationship with President Gorbachev changed dramatically and frequently during the 1990–91 period. During the first months of his reign, Yeltsin cooperated with President Gorbachev in attempting to develop a coherent program to accelerate the shift to a market economy and to create a federal structure that would grant greater autonomy to the member republics (without, however, destroying the USSR). But in the fall of 1990 this cooperation collapsed in a wave of acrimony, and Yeltsin evidently decided (the exact timing is not clear) that the RSFSR needed its own elected chief executive to protect itself and to serve as a counterweight to Gorbachev's presidential authority.

But this was not an easy task. As chairman of the Supreme Soviet, Yeltsin had worked to subordinate the government to the parliament's wishes, and many leaders of the parliament favored this arrangement. As a consequence, there was considerable conflict within this leadership over the proper distribution of authority between the elected parliament and the proposed elected president. The Constitutional Commission named by the Congress of People's Deputies was unable to resolve this issue. When it published a draft constitution in November 1990, the text contained two alternative definitions of the president's authority.

The first variation, which was supported by Chairman Yeltsin and his closest supporters, defined the president as the RSFSR's chief executive and gave him the right to name the Council of Ministers without the Supreme Soviet's participation and a limited right to veto its legislation. The president was given vast authority in the field of foreign affairs, broad appointment power, the right to impose a state of emergency (with only expost facto approval from the parliament), and the right to issue binding decrees without any apparent limitation.[1]

The second variant, which reflected the views of many parliamentary leaders, defined the president as a head of state rather than as chief executive and obliged him to consult with the leaders of the major political parties in the Supreme Soviet in selecting a chairman of the Council of Ministers for the Supreme Soviet's approval. The government was declared responsible to the parliament rather than to the president, his authority over local officials and the range of his decrees were limited, and provisions for his impeachment were included in the text. The Supreme Soviet was to be the country's only legislative and representative body (which seemed to imply that the president did not have such a function). It was given the right to interpret legislation and to supervise the executive, and its committees were granted the right to issue binding orders (under certain conditions). Political parties represented in the Supreme Soviet were assured proportional representation in its commissions and in the ordering of parliamentary debate.[2]

The draft constitution was never approved, and in the first months of 1991, with the intensification of personal conflict between Yeltsin and Gorbachev and the outbreak of a bitter "war of laws" between the USSR and RSFSR governments over control of governmental agencies and public policy, Yeltsin evidently pressed hard for a powerful presidency. In March 1991, the USSR leadership sponsored a nationwide referendum on the future of the USSR, and Yeltsin managed to tack on an additional referendum calling for the popular election of the president for the RSFSR. Massive popular support for an elected president evidently convinced the Congress of People's Deputies to follow suit.

During the first months of 1991, Yeltsin pressed at every turn for a broadening of the RSFSR's "sovereignty," but he did not endorse full independence for the RSFSR. In fact, in April 1991, soon after the populace voted to continue the USSR by referendum, Yeltsin joined with President Gorbachev and the leaders of the majority of republics to sign a new federal treaty broadening the republics' autonomy within the USSR. Yeltsin's commitment to a "new federalism" alienated some members of Democratic Russia, who favored full independence for the non-Russian republics, but evidently they helped Yeltsin win support in the Congress of People's Deputies for the concept of a strong president. In May 1991 the Congress ap-

proved constitutional amendments that provided the legal basis for
the relationship between the president and parliament.[3] The president was defined as the chief executive and given the right to "lead
the activity" of the government and to appoint and dismiss its members—with the approval of its chairman, who was named by the
president. But the Supreme Soviet was granted considerable authority as well. The amendments mandated Supreme Soviet "approval" of the president's nomination for chairman of the government and of his dismissal of the government. They also prohibited
the president from disbanding parliament under any circumstances,
outlined a procedure for his impeachment, made it easy to override
his objections to legislation, and seemed to confine his decree power
to the implementation of existing legislation.

A few days after the Congress's approval of these constitutional
amendments, the official campaign for the presidency began.[4]
Yeltsin enjoyed an extraordinary advantage. As chairman of the RS-
FSR Supreme Soviet he had been acting as if he were chief executive even though there was no such position in the RSFSR. During
the spring he had traveled throughout the country on "official business," promising aid and support to local officials and playing a significant role in the resolution of serious disputes, such as the min-
ers' strikes. During the brief campaign in May–June 1991, he did not
deign to debate with the other candidates but essentially ran on his
record as chairman of the Supreme Soviet.[5]

But in the last week of the campaign, Yeltsin did give a series of
interviews in which he outlined his own views on the role of the
president and his relationship to political parties. Most important,
Yeltsin clearly regarded the president as "above" political parties
and their programmatic concerns. He insisted that the president
should not belong to any political party or be subordinated to its decisions and that no political party should have a privileged or dominant position in the state. Yeltsin claimed to support the concept of
a political round table, where representatives of political parties and
movements could make suggestions to the president—who would
obviously make the final decisions himself.[6] At the same time,
Yeltsin adopted a conciliatory approach to the CPSU. While he im-
plicitly condemned the CPSU leadership for failing to fulfill its
promise to give up its "leading role" in the state, he called for a "mutual understanding" with the party's rank and file, whom he described in strikingly positive terms.[7] Yeltsin's stance may have been

linked with his decision to name Aleksandr Rutskoi, a reform communist who had helped Yeltsin in April 1991 to undermine the unity of the orthodox CP/RSFSR, as his candidate for vice president.[8]

YELTSIN AS PRESIDENT: FROM COUP TO ECONOMIC REFORM

Yeltsin clearly regarded his impressive electoral victory in June as a significant popular mandate. He described it as of immense historical significance for the Russian state and implied that it would overcome the age-old gap between the state and its citizens and that he was the personal embodiment of Russian state power.[9]

Immediately after the inaugural, Yeltsin seemed to act on the basis of this vision by using his decree powers to create the institutional base for the presidency and to undermine the authority of the CP/RSFSR.[10] He created new advisory bodies staffed by bright young journalists, economists, and politicians, established a new presidential apparatus headed by a veteran party official who had worked with Yeltsin when he had been first secretary in Sverdlovsk, and banned the formation of all political party units operating in state agencies. While this activity was ostensibly directed against all political parties, it was obviously designed to destroy the CPSU's primary party organizations, which had served for years as party officials' major instrument to control state agencies. The leadership of both the CPSU and the CP/RSFSR called on President Gorbachev to abrogate Yeltsin's decree, but Gorbachev did not want a direct confrontation with Yeltsin over the issue, and the Russian president did not budge.[11]

Yeltsin had been president of the RSFSR for approximately six weeks when President Gorbachev was temporarily overthrown by the State Emergency Committee formed by the leading members of his own Council of Ministers. President Yeltsin eluded arrest, established his headquarters in the RSFSR parliament building, and used his presidential authority to discredit and topple the Emergency Committee. On the first day of the coup, he denounced its actions as both illegal and unconstitutional, decreed that all local executives who accepted the committee's authority would be prosecuted, and called on servicemen to disobey its orders.[12] The following day he declared himself in command of all the activities of the USSR's ministries of defense, security, and internal affairs on RSFSR territory, created his own military defense committee to coordinate resistance, and announced that all disloyal local officials would be fired. It is obviously impossible to determine the impact of these decrees and other similar orders on the behavior of the military forces assigned to attack the parliament building, but it seems obvious that Yeltsin's use of presidential powers helped to undermine the Emergency Committee's will and to allow President Gorbachev to resume his position.

It is also clear that the failed coup provided Yeltsin with the opportunity to use his decree powers with virtual impunity. Within a week after the coup Yeltsin "suspended" the activities of the CP/RSFSR on the ground that it had supported the Emergency Committee and decreed the nationalization of its considerable property.[13] He also used his decree powers to bolster the power of the RSFSR government vis-à-vis both the USSR and local executive authority. In August 1991, Yeltsin decreed that all enterprises operated by USSR ministries on the territory of the RSFSR were henceforth subordinate to RSFSR ministries.[14] Yeltsin then gave himself the right to name his own personal "representatives" to supervise local state executives on the grounds than many of them had not supported him during the coup.[15]

During the coup and its immediate aftermath, the Supreme Soviet of the RSFSR, now chaired by Ruslan Khasbulatov (who had been Yeltsin's first deputy chairman) cooperated fully with the president. For example, the Supreme Soviet quickly acceded to President Yeltsin's request for authority to appoint the leaders of local state executive bodies to ensure the establishment of a coherent system of executive authority.[16] But this cooperation began to collapse within a month after the coup. The chairman of the Supreme Soviet and many deputies had no desire to reduce the authority the parliament had acquired under Yeltsin's effective leadership. By September, they began to criticize the Council of Ministers of the RSFSR for its ostensible failure to work out a program to stabilize the economy and move to a mixed economy, and they urged Yeltsin to fire the ministers responsible for these failures.[17] In October, there was a serious clash over the proper way to select local state executives. During his campaign for president, Yeltsin had repeatedly endorsed the election of these officials, but in the aftermath of the coup he had convinced the Supreme Soviet to permit him to appoint them. In October, the Supreme Soviet had second thoughts and rescinded its earlier decision. Yeltsin called on the legislature to stand by its earlier ban on the election of local officials on the grounds that he needed to ensure control over administration leaders who had proved unreliable during the coup. He promised new elections for local officials and parliaments by the end of 1992, and the Supreme Soviet acquiesced.[18]

In late October, the Congress of People's Deputies convened to hear the president outline his program for economic reform. Yeltsin announced that his government sought to create a "healthy mixed economy" and a powerful private sector by imposing a restrictive financial policy and by widespread privatization of state property.[19] He also announced that prices would be "liberalized" to stimulate lagging production and that, after six months of painful adjustment, the supply of goods and services would be improved. He also declared that those citizens whose standard of living was most vulnerable to inflation would be given higher wages or direct economic support.

Yeltsin reaffirmed his determination to eliminate the CPSU's remaining influence and to prevent any political party from assuming its leadership role. He called on supporters of his reform program to form a parliamentary coalition to ensure passage of appropriate legislation and urged the Congress to support his desire to serve as his own prime minister, to appoint his own government, to issue decrees on economic questions even if in violation of existing legislation until December 1, 1992, and to ban all local elections for a year.[20]

Despite complaints from some deputies, the Congress approved Yeltsin's request by a massive majority. He named himself prime minister, appointed a government of young, promarket reformers headed by Egor Gaidar, and banned both the CP/RSFSR and the CPSU on the grounds that the parent CPSU had never really been a political party but a "special mechanism for wielding power by fusing with the state."[21] He then issued a series of presidential decrees and signed governmental orders introducing a series of economic reforms and asserting the RSFSR government's control over the USSR's ministries.[22]

Despite the Congress's overwhelming support for an extension of President Yeltsin's authority, the Supreme Soviet, chaired by the increasingly independent Khasbulatov, asserted its own prerogatives in number of fields. For example, in late November it simply ignored a presidential decree extending the government's control over the supply of money, gold, and precious stones and passed its own legislation on the subject.[23] From this juncture onward, the conflict over the relative authority of president and parliament became entangled with conflict over the government's program of rapid transition toward a "market economy." To confuse the issue, moreover, the Yeltsin government came under attack from a totally unexpected quarter—Vice President Rutskoi. Rutskoi had allied with Yeltsin in the spring of 1991 against the orthodox leadership of the CP/RSFSR and had played a very important role in the defense of the Yeltsin regime from the Emergency Committee in August 1991. But the existing constitution provided no coherent definition of vice presidential powers, and Rutskoi evidently decided to make use of this ambiguity to carve out a totally independent position. In December 1991 he charged that the liberalization of prices proposed by the regime would impoverish the majority of the population, and he derided the leaders of the new government for their youth and inexperience.[24]

The vice president's extraordinary position may well have encouraged the Supreme Soviet to assert its own independence. Whatever the case, in December the Supreme Soviet clashed with President Yeltsin over his effort to create a single unified security ministry for the RSFSR. In asserting the RSFSR's control over former USSR ministries, Yeltsin had decreed the merger of the Committee for State Security, responsible for internal security, with the Ministry of Interior, responsible for normal police activity.[25] The Supreme Soviet had explicitly prohibited such a merger and appealed Yeltsin's decree to the newly formed Constitutional Court, which declared it to be unconstitutional. In early January 1992, Yeltsin rescinded his own decree.[26]

THE RUSSIAN PRESIDENCY, 1992–1994

With the resignation of President Gorbachev and the collapse of the USSR, the Russian Republic became a fully independent sovereign state.[27] In January 1992, the Yeltsin government began its economic reform with a dramatic "liberalization" of prices. The massive inflation that followed, and the failure of the price increases to stimulate the promised production of goods and services, led to sharp conflict between on the one hand, the leadership of the Supreme Soviet and many of its members and, on the other hand, the

Yeltsin government. In mid-January, the chairman of the Supreme
Soviet clearly implied that the government was so incompetent that
it should be replaced.[28] Yeltsin responded that a powerful executive
was essential to implement the radical economic reform. He told the
citizens of Saint Petersburg that "democratization is democratization, but in parallel there should be a strong executive power, and
this power should make itself felt."[29] He told the deputies of the
Supreme Soviet not to "panic" in the face of temporary difficulties
and blamed the country's economic problems on the alleged resistance by representatives of the old regime, on the control of distribution channels by criminal elements, and on the "monopolists" who
refused to lower the prices for their goods.[30]

Yeltsin came under attack from a variety of critics. Some criticized him for acquiring too much authority, others charged that he
was overly dependent on his old party colleagues, and others
claimed that he ignored deputies' opinions.[31] At the same time, Vice
President Rutskoi intensified his own attack. He expressed reservations about the government's enthusiasm for private property and
charged that the government had "cut off" President Yeltsin from
the people, that the government had created a new parasitic class of
brokers and middleman who did nothing to support the country's
productive capacity, and that its policies would transform Russia
into a source of raw materials for Western capitalism.[32] Rutskoi
called for the restoration of state control over prices and monopoly
producers, legislation against speculation, and government support
for the defense industry, which he represented as vital to Russia's
technological advance and national security.[33]

The Supreme Soviet demonstrated its own opposition to the
government's policy by refusing to approve its budgetary requests
for the first quarter of 1992 on the grounds that the government's estimates of both income and expenditure were totally unrealistic and
inadequate.[34] Parliamentary resistance to executive power was also
reflected in the ongoing process of preparing a new constitution for
the Russian Federation. The draft of November 1990 had never been
approved, and in March 1992 the Constitutional Commission of the
Congress of People's Deputies finally produced a new draft, which
limited presidential authority and extended parliament's powers.
The new draft prevented the president from naming the government
without parliamentary approval and limited his decree-making
powers to the implementation of existing legislation. Moreover, the

Supreme Soviet was given the right to override presidential efforts to return legislation by a simple majority, to demand the resignation of individual ministers and presidential appointees, and to force the president to do so by simple majority rule.[35]

Needless to say, when the Congress of People's Deputies convened in April 1992, President Yeltsin made no effort to persuade the Congress to adopt this draft. In fact, it was widely reported that his advisers were busy preparing their own version, which would provide the legal basis for the presidential republic that Yeltsin favored.[36] The Congress of People's Deputies adopted the draft "in principle," pending the discussion of contradictory amendments proposed by both parliament and president. The Congress's failure to resolve these differences led to immense confusion over the interpretation of the existing constitution and its large number of amendments.

In the midst of this confusion, Yeltsin's opponents continued their assaults. Chairman of the Supreme Soviet Khasbulatov accused the executive of attempting to override or ignore the Supreme Soviet, the vice president charged the government with indifference to the fate of Russians who were being threatened in the former non-Russian republics, and a new coalition of communists and "patriots" called for the return of price controls, the appointment of experienced enterprise directors to the government, and the establishment of a parliamentary republic.[37]

In his own report to the Congress, Yeltsin balanced his defense of the fundamentals of government policy with significant concessions to his critics. He pointedly reminded the Congress that it had approved his government's program by a huge majority the previous October, that the majority of the population supported it despite the evident economic hardship, that production of scarce goods and services was beginning to improve, and that privatization and demonopolization had begun in earnest. But he also agreed that it was necessary to provide additional credits to hard-pressed state enterprises and to appoint experienced enterprise directors to the government. Yeltsin seemed to adopt a similar position on crucial political questions. On the one hand, he noted that, in March 1991, it had approved the concept of a popularly elected president and, the previous October, had granted him extensive decree powers to implement reforms. He insisted that any efforts to curtail these powers and establish a parliamentary republic with "decorative" presidential powers would run counter to the system "chosen by the people" and would be dangerous for the society as a whole. On the other hand, he implied that the need for a strong executive would be obviated by the development of a genuine civil society, a multiparty system, and an independent judiciary.[38]

The deputies' response to Yeltsin's report reflected both the divisions over the government's economic policy and the lack of any coherent party discipline from the various parliamentary fractions. The leaders of the parliament were essentially as divided as the Congress as a whole. Some of them criticized the Yeltsin government in quite moderate terms and focused on the growing powers of his various advisory bodies, while others charged that the government was so fascinated by the "market" that it ignored the needs of the Russian people and the country's unique characteristics.[39] The deputies tended to adopt extreme positions; some, like Rutskoi, charged that the government's policy enriched only a tiny speculative elite, while Yeltsin's supporters assailed "patriotic forces" for opposing the foreign private investment necessary for the country's development.[40] In the end, the Congress adopted a resolution highly critical of the government's performance.

While the government was so annoyed by this resolution that it resigned (for a few days), President Yeltsin evidently sought to end the confrontation with the Congress by making important concessions to his opposition. In his closing remarks, Yeltsin admitted that the reforms needed to be "amended" and that experienced enterprise directors should be added to the government. He pledged to clarify the authority of his various advisory bodies. Most striking, in the face of demands that he give up his position as prime minister, Yeltsin promised to name a prime minister within three months, and he went out of his way to stress the Congress's political legitimacy.[41]

Three weeks later, however, the president created a furor by implying that the Congress should be disbanded by a referendum on a new constitution. Russian press commentary focused on the "unpredictability" of the president and ignored the possibility that Yeltsin simply might have sought to intimidate the Supreme Soviet, which convened in May.[42] Whatever Yeltsin's intent, the May session did focus on passing legislation rather than on confrontation with the president, and the following month, in an extensive interview marking the first anniversary of his election, Yeltsin casually announced that his threat to disband the Congress had no "official" significance.[43]

Yeltsin's interview also revealed that he remained extremely optimistic about his own authority despite the immense resistance to the government's policies from both parliament and the society as a whole. Yeltsin claimed that he enjoyed a unique mandate from the people, that he remained very much "in control" of the situation in Russia, and that he was blessed with an intuitive sense of the population's needs. As he told his interviewers, "Every politician needs to have intuition, especially the president of Russia. Yes, there are times that you intuitively sense the people's mood and realize what they can and cannot stand." He once again expressed his firm opposition to the formation of a "presidential party" on the ground that it would inevitably degenerate into a "second CPSU," insisting that the president was above partisan conflict and should need do no more than "consult" with various parties. Yeltsin's experience made it difficult for him to understand that political parties able to nominate deputies to parliament and candidates for the presidency might help to overcome the conflicts between the executive and legislative branches.

A few days after this optimistic interview, Yeltsin abruptly resigned as prime minister and named Egor Gaidar acting prime minister (June 15, 1992). Yeltsin's resignation was widely interpreted as an attempt to distance himself from his own government's increasingly controversial economic policy, and it encouraged his parliamentary opponents to intensify their attacks on the government's reforms. From this point onward, the leaders of the executive and legislative branches clashed almost continuously and with increasing bitterness over a wide range of issues.[44] In July, President Yeltsin and Chairman Khasbulatov collided over the status of the newspaper *Izvestiia*. Khasbulatov sought to restore the paper (which had become an outspoken independent daily) to its previous role as the house organ of the Supreme Soviet, while President Yeltsin vigorously defended the paper's independence and the principles of freedom of the press.[45] In August, Yeltsin introduced important economic changes during the Supreme Soviet's summer recess. He unilaterally introduced a new system of privatization based on the distribution of checks to all citizens and announced a 50 percent increase in wages for government workers in education, health, and other social services whose incomes had been seriously undermined by inflation.[46]

When the Supreme Soviet reconvened in September 1992, the parliamentary opposition to Yeltsin had become increasingly well organized. Orthodox communist and extreme nationalist deputies united to form a faction named Russian Unity, which launched a concerted effort to oust the Gaidar government and began to call for the impeachment of President Yeltsin, whom they regarded as personally responsible for the destruction of the USSR and the subsequent "ruination of Russia."[47]

Yeltsin sought to counter this assault by an open appeal to deputies associated with the Civic Alliance, a newly formed "centrist" coalition of political parties whose leaders claimed to support the basic direction of economic reform and to seek changes in the government's policy and personnel rather than its ouster. In his address to the Supreme Soviet, President Yeltsin not only praised the Civic Alliance's views on reform but also openly criticized the Gaidar government's policies. He now charged that it had been so absorbed with "macroeconomics" that it had ignored the financial problems faced by thousands of hard-pressed enterprises and had failed to develop an adequate social policy to help those hurt by inflation, and he subjected three ministers responsible for economic affairs to harsh and detailed criticism.[48]

President Yeltsin also attempted to postpone a showdown with his opponents in the forthcoming meeting of the Congress of People's Deputies, which had been scheduled to coincide with the end of his special decree powers. Yeltsin called for a postponement of the meeting on the grounds that the new draft constitution was not ready for discussion, but the parliamentary leadership refused to support his request. Chairman Khasbulatov, who described himself as the head of the legislative branch and the virtual coequal to the president,[49] refused to endorse the president's position and the Supreme Soviet followed suit. In the months before the convocation of the Congress, political life became increasingly polarized. The orthodox communists and their nationalist allies sought to create new organization to mobilize opposition to the president, while the president's most loyal supporters, now grouped in the coalition known as Democratic Choice, called for a prolonged period of presidential rule to solve the country's problems.[50]

Yeltsin's own remarks to the Seventh Congress reveal that the loss of his special decree powers had seriously undermined his relative authority vis-à-vis the parliament. While he assailed the "unbridled political hysteria" directed against his regime, he clearly sought to avoid confrontation with the Congress. He outlined a moderate program of reform, insisting that the country needed a prolonged period of political stability to write a new constitution, curtail inflation, revive industrial production, improve people's standard of living, accelerate the process of privatization, and end crime. At the same time, he attempted to avoid conflict over the delineation of authority until a new constitution could be written. He pledged to forgo any attempt to renew his extraordinary decree powers if the Congress would focus on the preparation of a new constitution and if the Supreme Soviet world focus on its pending legislative agenda—and allow him to deal with the "most important" economic issues by presidential decree.[51]

Chairman Khasbulatov brushed aside Yeltsin's effort at conciliation and argued that the conflict between the president and parliament was not merely a constitutional issue but a reflection of fundamental differences over the country's economic future. Khasbulatov charged that the president had used his special decree powers to impose a "liberal" market economy based on the American model on the Russian Federation, while the Supreme Soviet's legislation was designed to create a "socially oriented market economy." Khasbulatov insisted that the Congress's various factions reflected the political diversity of citizen opinion and that it had the obligation to choose between these two models of economic development and to prevent further "autocratic degeneration" of the system.[52] Khasbulatov then introduced five constitutional amendments to limit the president's authority. Although two of the amendments narrowly failed to win a two-thirds majority, Khasbulatov gleefully characterized the new limits on presidential power as a major victory for the Congress.[53] Most important, the parliamentary opposition, evidently buoyed by these decisions, rallied to defeat President Yeltsin's nomination of Egor Gaidar as prime minister by a margin of 467 for and 486 against.[54]

Yeltsin clearly bore some responsibility for Gaidar's defeat; his nomination speech was strikingly halfhearted and ambiguous. But Yeltsin was evidently enraged by the Congress's action. He now charged that the parliamentary opposition wanted to restore the "totalitarian Soviet communist system," and he called for a national referendum in early 1993 that would allow the populace to demonstrate whom it "trusted its fate" to—the president or the Congress. Furthermore, in an apparent effort to disrupt the proceedings, the president dramatically stormed from the hall and called upon his supporters to follow suit. Only 120 deputies left the hall.[55]

While the president and the parliamentary leadership engaged in mutual recriminations, the chairman of the Constitutional Court, Valery D. Zorkin, who was clearly distressed about the dangers of further confrontation, intervened to negotiate a compromise between Yeltsin and Khasbulatov. Under pressure from Zorkin, the Congress adopted a resolution that replaced Yeltsin's proposed referendum with one on the "basic principles of the constitution" to be held on April 11, 1993, suspended the constitutional amendments limiting presidential authority until that date, and established a unique role for the Congress in the selection of a new prime minister. All of the factions were to submit nominations to the Congress for a vote, and President Yeltsin would select one of the three leading candidates as prime minister.[56]

This process (which had not been outlined in the constitution) led to Yeltsin's selection of Viktor S. Chernomyrdin, who had served as the chairman of the Fuel and Power Complex in the Gaidar government. Chernomyrdin had been a member of the Central Committee of the CPSU, a veteran ministerial specialist on the gas industry, and was widely represented in the press as a "non-party specialist."[57] But the new prime minister almost immediately expressed serious reservations about the desirability of market reform, and he appointed several veteran state administrators who shared his views to the Council of Ministers. As a result, serious divisions over economic policy developed within the Council of Ministers between proponents and opponents of market reform.

While a deeply divided Council of Ministers struggled to develop a coherent economic policy, President Yeltsin and his supporters sought to mobilize popular support for the referendum on the "basic provisions" of the constitution, which they hoped would clear the way for the elimination of the Congress and its replacement with a presidential republic with a bicameral legislature.[58] But Chairman Khasbulatov worked hard to retain Congress's control over constitutional reform. At first he sought to modify the referendum by suggesting that it include questions on the simultaneous election of a new president and a new Congress, but an angry President Yeltsin rejected the proposal out of hand.[59] Khasbulatov then sought to block the referendum on the grounds that only the Congress could create a new constitution, and he traveled throughout the country to convince the leaders of local soviets to support this position. At the same time, President Yeltsin sought to mobilize support for the referendum among the local executive authorities.[60]

But the conflict over the referendum became so intense that all agreed to convoke an extraordinary meeting of the Congress of People's Deputies, in March 1993, to resolve the issue. President Yeltsin opened the Eighth Extraordinary Congress with a vigorous plea for a powerful president as essential to implement vital, if unpopular, reforms; he insisted that limitations on his own authority were infringements on the people's will and urged that the referendum be held as agreed in December 1992.[61] But the Congress, urged on by Chairman Khasbulatov and other critics of the president, brushed aside Yeltsin's plea, canceled the referendum, and restored the constitutional limits on presidential authority approved at the Seventh Congress.[62] The congressional action was a major setback for Yeltsin's efforts to wrest control of the process of constitutional amendment from the Congress. In a nationwide TV address on March 20, 1993, Yeltsin charged that the abrogation of the referendum was a "dress rehearsal" for those who wanted to restore the old Bolshevik order and announced that he had decreed a "special regime," which would allow him to rule by decree until April 25, 1993, to forestall any effort at restoration. On that date, the people would be able to express their views on his presidency, on the principles of a new constitution, and on new elections for parliament.[63]

The Council of Ministers supported the president,[64] but his major opponents were furious. Vice President Rutskoi and Chairman of the Constitutional Court Zorkin both denounced the president's actions as divisive and unconstitutional,[65] and Chairman Khasbulatov urged the Supreme Soviet to recall the Congress into another extraordinary session. On the eve of the Congress, acting on a complaint filed by the Supreme Soviet, the majority of the Constitutional Court concluded that Yeltsin's address was a violation of the "separation of powers" embodied in the constitution.[66] Khasbulatov denounced Yeltsin's actions in his opening address, and oppositional deputies resumed their call for his impeachment.[67]

Although Yeltsin never actually established a "special regime," the intensity of the opposition evidently persuaded him to negotiate with Khasbulatov, Zorkin, and various deputies to find some way to avoid a confrontation. The three leaders proposed a purely political solution—simultaneous new elections for president and parliament in November 1993.[68] This proposal, which simply brushed aside the constitutional issues in dispute and directly threatened the status of the deputies who had been elected for a five-year term in 1990, enraged many deputies. The Russian Unity faction not only denounced the proposal but convinced the majority of deputies to conduct secret ballots on the impeachment of President Yeltsin and the ouster of Chairman Khasbulatov. In the end, 617 deputies (72 short of the two-thirds majority) voted to impeach the president, and 389 voted to oust Khasbulatov.[69]

While the Congress failed to impeach the president, it did limit his authority in a number of ways.[70] It also eliminated the question on the constitution from the proposed referendum and added questions that would allow citizens to express their displeasure with the president and his program. After considerable wrangling over wording, four questions were approved by the Congress for the referendum on April 25: (1) Do you have trust in President Yeltsin? (2) Do you approve of the social-economic policy implemented by the president and government since 1992? (3) Do you consider early (preterm) elections for president necessary? (4) Do you consider early (preterm) elections for people's deputies necessary?[71]

President Yeltsin received far more popular support on all four questions than anticipated by both Russian and foreign observers.[72] While his parliamentary opponents denigrated the significance of the referendum, Yeltsin sought to use his victory to regain control over the process of constitutional reform. A few days after the referendum, Yeltsin's spokesmen claimed that the outcome of the referendum had empowered the president to prepare a new constitution and had deprived the Congress of any legitimate role in this process.[73] On April 30, 1993, a "presidential" draft of the new constitution was made public, and Yeltsin's allies began to organize a constitutional assembly to discuss and amend the draft.

Yeltsin's opponents failed to derail the assembly, and when the president opened the assembly in early June, he made a blistering assault on his parliamentary opponents.[74] He now charged that the federal parliamentary institutions were "incompatible with democracy" and that the Supreme Soviet had been transformed by its leadership into an "ordinary bureaucratic" organization with bosses and subordinates. He also declared that Congress's failure to produce an acceptable constitution obliged him to take up this task, and he called for new parliamentary elections for October 1993.[75]

After a month of intense deliberation and debate, the assembly published its version of a new constitution in mid-July 1993. While this version reduced the vast extension of presidential authority envisioned in Yeltsin's original draft, the assembly's constitution gave the president vast authority vis-à-vis both government and the new bicameral parliament.[76] But the new constitution did not resolve the basic conflict with the Congress of People's Deputies. Chairman Khasbulatov had stormed out of the assembly in a huff over procedure, and many other parliamentary leaders had refused to participate in the president's assembly (there were some exceptions), insisting that their own version of the constitution was the only really legitimate text. Equally important, the president's focus on the constitutional assembly seemed to provide his parliamentary opponents with new opportunities for assault on his programs. While the assembly worked on the new version of the basic law, the Supreme Soviet sought to discredit the government and its personnel,[77] and to subvert its policies by overriding presidential decrees, passing a budget far larger than suggested by the government, and attempting to subvert the program of privatization. By the summer of 1993, both the president and the Supreme Soviet were repeatedly challenging each other's legitimacy.

In September 1993, President Yeltsin attempted to break the deadlock by disbanding the Congress of People's Deputies and scheduling a referendum on his draft constitution and on new parliamentary elections for December 1993. In his enabling decree, Yeltsin declared that the parliamentary bodies had repeatedly obstructed "the will of the democratically elected president," had violated the referendum of April 1993, and had no legal standing in the Russian Federation because these bodies had been established under the USSR. Yeltsin's leading opponents, Chairman Khasbulatov and Vice President Rutskoi, ignored the ban and convened a special session of the Congress, which named Rutskoi president on the grounds that the dissolution of the parliament was unconstitutional.[78]

Moreover, Khasbulatov, Rutskoi, and many of Yeltsin's most "irreconcilable opponents" continued to occupy the parliament building (which was soon surrounded by a police cordon) until early October 1993. When their supporters in the city broke through the cordon, Khasbulatov and Rutskoi called for an armed assault on the central television station, for the seizure of other government buildings, and for the ouster of the president. After some hesitation, Yeltsin ordered the army to crush the rebellion, and its leaders were arrested and incarcerated.

With the apparent elimination of his most hostile opponents, President Yeltsin banned a number of militant communist and nationalist groupings that had spearheaded the rebellion and focused on winning popular support for the draft constitution. In keeping with his oft-repeated insistence that he was "above politics," the president made no concerted effort to campaign for those parliamentary candidates who had supported his programs of radical economic reform. Although Yeltsin never explained the reason for this position, he may have feared that his own public endorsement of an economic program clearly opposed by large segments of society may have endangered support for his constitution.[79]

Whatever Yeltsin's assessment, the results of the referendum and parliamentary elections had a totally unexpected impact on the relationship between the president and the new bicameral parliament. Although the public supported the constitution and thereby created the presidential republic that Yeltsin had sought since 1991, this victory was seriously undermined by the parliamentary elections. The voters not only defeated many candidates who had supported the president's economic reform program, but also gave considerable support to the communists and nationalists, who charged that the regime's economic policies had impoverished the society and subordinated the Russian Federation to the capitalist West. The most unexpected result was the broad electoral support for the populist nationalist Vladimir Zhirinovsky, whose Liberal Democratic Party won more than 23 percent of the votes cast for the political parties to be represented in the lower house of the parliament, the State Duma (half of the house was elected on the basis of geographic districts, half on the basis of party lists).

Zhirinovsky's extraordinary showing can be attributed in part to his unique orientation toward the new constitution. While Zhirinovsky joined with other opposition parties in their condemnation of the president's economic policies, he did not support their assault on the constitution for establishing a "dictatorial" presidency. In fact, Zhirinovsky vigorously endorsed a strong presidency as essential for strengthening the Russian state. Since he represented himself and his party as a "third force" between communists and democrats, he evidently won considerable support from those who favored a strong presidency to solve the country's problems but who had grave misgivings about the imposition of market reforms or a return to some form of state socialism.

Whatever the basis for Zhirinovsky's startling success, it had a dramatic impact on the distribution of seats in the new State Duma. While the supporters of the continued radical reform, led by Russia's Choice, could muster no more than a third of the new house, the combined opposition of Communists Agrarian and Liberal Democrats gained more than 40 percent. (A variety of "centrists" of various persuasions held the remaining seats.) As a result, the president was faced with the likelihood of a hostile majority on many issues to come before the parliament.[80] Moreover, while the new upper house, the Council of the Federation, which was composed of two deputies from each subject of the Federation, reportedly was more supportive of the president, it was probably insufficient to overcome the powerful opposition coalition in the lower house.[81]

Most significant, Yeltsin initially proved unwilling to use the vast authority granted to the president by the constitution to confront the political opposition. Although the new constitution sharply limited the parliament's capacity to impeach the president or to limit his authority by constitutional amendments, Yeltsin at least initially seemed to act as if the new Federal Assembly retained these powers. Yeltsin actually seemed fearful of parliamentary opposition in the State Duma, and he did not address its opening session. Furthermore, although the new constitution granted the president immense leeway in naming his own government, Yeltsin allowed Chernomyrdin to remain as its chairman rather than confront the Duma, and he made no more than pro forma efforts to retain the leading advocates of market reform in the government.

When the State Duma convened, the political opposition immediately demonstrated its strength by pressing for an amnesty for the leaders of the October 1993 insurrection and the leaders of the abortive coup against Gorbachev in August 1991. While the amnesty won the Duma's support as part of a general statement on political accord pledging all parties in parliament to purely constitutional means,[82] the amnesty for Yeltsin's most vigorous opponents did not augur well for the president.

Yeltsin was clearly perturbed by this challenge to his authority, but he now sought to avoid direct confrontation with the parliamentary opposition. In his first report to the Federal Assembly on the "main lines of foreign and domestic policy" (mandated by the constitution) in late February 1994, he explicitly called for cooperation between the president, the government, and the Federal Assembly in "strengthening the Russian state."[83] Moreover, Yeltsin gave far more attention to the establishment of a "law-based state," the creation of a coherent judicial system, and the legislative definition of governmental authority and protection of citizens' rights than to his own presidential powers.[84] He implied that he would use his constitutional authority not to confront the legislature but to fight inflation, improve the population's standard of living, and ensure that the regime acted as the "social state" provided in the constitution. He now sought to meet his opponents and critics more than halfway. Attacking crime and corruption (one of Zhirinovsky's most frequent targets), Yeltsin called for vigorous governmental efforts to ensure citizens' personal security. He also acknowledged that the political and social costs of the efforts to create a market economy had been very high. While he defended the initial steps to dismantle the state socialist system, he explicitly recognized that the conflict between the executive and the legislature over economic policy had been disastrous for the development of the Russian state. Yeltsin now balanced his references to further market reform with an endorsement of various types of state intervention in the economy. He insisted that the regulation of a market economy was "not a retreat but a major movement forward" in strengthening the Russian state, announced that the regime would soon establish "financial production groupings" to ensure support for various industrial sectors, and urged the creation of trilateral commissions of government, management, and labor representatives to deal with the country's problems.[85]

But in the spring and summer of 1994, once it had become clear that the State Duma was too deeply divided to challenge his authority on substantive matters, Yeltsin vigorously reasserted his constitutional prerogatives with a barrage of presidential decrees on economic reform and the struggle against crime and corruption. His long-sought presidential republic had become a reality.

CONCLUSIONS

In the late 1980s and early 1990s, both Gorbachev and Yeltsin worked assiduously to promote the process of "democratization" by revitalizing moribund parliamentary institutions. But the new representative and legislative bodies that they helped create presented significant obstacles to their subsequent efforts to wield presidential power. Gorbachev's radical reform of the political system, embodied in the resurrection of the Leninist slogan, All Power to the Soviets, seriously undermined the CPSU's political authority and helped to destroy the USSR. Gorbachev's acceptance of multicandidate elections to these new bodies as the basis for political authority made it difficult for the CPSU to retain legitimacy except as a purely parliamentary party. It also made it virtually impossible for him to counter the separatist, nationalist, and anticommunist movements and individuals who were elected to power in the 1989–91 period. While Gorbachev was clearly hostile to Boris Yeltsin and his increasingly anticommunist position, he was unable to prevent Yeltsin from being elected chairman of the RSFSR Supreme Soviet in 1990 and president of the RSFSR the following year.

Yeltsin faced analogous if less dramatic problems in Russia. As chairman of the Supreme Soviet of the RSFSR in 1990–91, he labored to bring the Council of Ministers of the RSFSR, which had been little more than an agent of the USSR governments in the past, under the control of the Congress of People's Deputies and the Supreme Soviet. But the parliament's power over the government evidently proved insufficient to counter the continued authority of President Gorbachev and the Council of Ministers of the USSR. Yeltsin therefore moved vigorously in the first months of 1991 to establish an elected president as the RSFSR's chief executive.

Once elected as president, Yeltsin was obliged to confront the parliamentary authority that he had helped to create as chairman of the Supreme Soviet in the 1990–91 period. Yeltsin was initially able to bypass the Congress and the Supreme Soviet by using the president's decree powers, which he wielded with great effect during the abortive coup against President Gorbachev in August 1991. Yeltsin's immense popular support in subsequent months helped him persuade the Congress to grant him additional decree powers to implement the economic reform throughout the following year. In retrospect, it seems clear that these extraordinary powers enabled him to preserve his authority and freedom of maneuver in the face of the growing congressional opposition, fueled by the consequences of economic reform.

In December 1992, when Yeltsin lost his special decree powers, he suddenly became extremely vulnerable to the Congress, and he was nearly impeached in March 1993. But the referendum held in the following month clearly indicated that the Congress did not enjoy the majority support enjoyed by the president and his policies. Yeltsin convoked a constitutional assembly in the hope that this victory could provide the basis for the development of a totally new constitution.

In his speech to the constitutional assembly, Yeltsin explicitly called for new elections for the Congress in the fall of 1993. Yeltsin correctly concluded that the fundamental source of the conflict between the president and the parliament was the body of deputies created by the elections of 1990. It is important to remember that nearly half of these deputies had opposed Yeltsin's election as chairman of the Supreme Soviet in May 1990. In fact, the Communists of Russia actually prevented Yeltsin's election in the first two ballots by voting for Ivan K. Polozkov, an orthodox regional party leader who was elected first secretary of the Communist Party of the RSFSR the following month. It was not the "former communists" who led the opposition to Yeltsin but the orthodox communists elected in May 1990 who provided the parliamentary support for the various assaults on the president. The deputies in the Communists of Russia faction were extremely dubious of Gorbachev's political and economic reforms, opposed his effort to grant greater political power to the republics, and generally combined their support for a large role for the state in the economy with nationalistic positions. These deputies muted their hostility to Yeltsin in the second half of 1991, when popular reaction against the communists was at its height throughout the USSR. But in 1992, when the heroic days of August gave way to the economic difficulties produced by the market reforms, and the limits of presidential authority became obvious, the various offspring of the Communists of Russia pressed their attack with growing vehemence. As a result, by the summer of 1993 the mutual hostility between the president and his opponents in the Congress of People's Deputies had created a system of dual power, which made it difficult to govern the Russian Federation.

In September 1993, Yeltsin decided to dissolve the Congress and hold both a referendum on a new constitution and elections for a new bicameral Federal Assembly to end this impasse. The president and his supporters initially seemed to have presumed (probably on the basis of their interpretation of the referendum of April 1993) that the majority of the electorate would support these dramatic steps, but they soon discovered that the public mood of the spring had shifted significantly by the middle of winter. In December 1993, the electorate delivered a clear verdict on Yeltsin's plan: it supported the constitution establishing a presidential republic to cope with the country's increasingly difficult problems but elected many deputies to the Federal Assembly who had assailed the Yeltsin regime's social and economic policies.

The electorate's support for both communists and nationalists such as Zhirinovsky prompted considerable alarm among both Russian and Western observers about the future of Russian democracy. But this legitimate concern should not overshadow the fact that the political system established by the constitutional referendum is far more democratic than its predecessor. While the new constitution granted the president extraordinarily broad powers, it also provided legal safeguards for a wide range of civil and political liberties totally ignored by previous constitutions. It is possible that these guarantees of free expression and association may prove mere formalities, but they do provide a liberal framework for the development of a wide range of citizen-based activities. Furthermore, the elections of 1993 were far more democratic than those held in 1990. At that time, local CPSU officials influenced the outcome of many electoral contests and ensured the establishment of the Communists of Russia (which included many who subsequently became the leaders of powerful nationalist factions) as a powerful parliamentary force. In 1993, although Yeltsin banned electoral activity by parties implicated in the abortive insurrection in October, more than a dozen major political organizations participated in the election and provided the electors with a wide range of social, economic, and political programs. Finally, the adoption of the new constitution may help to provide the political system with a greater sense of legitimacy.

In the first half of 1994, both the president and his opponents in the Federal Assembly muted their challenges to each other's right to rule. In 1992 and 1993, the president's opponents in the Congress of People's Deputies had repeatedly referred to their constitutional powers in their assault on the president's authority and programs.

The president in turn had insisted that he was the first democratically elected leader of the country and attacked both the existing constitution and the 1990 elections as products of communist rule. But in early 1994, while Yeltsin expressed his annoyance with the election of communists and nationalists to the Federal Assembly, he did not question the legitimacy of the first elections held under the constitution he had worked so hard to develop. Nor did most of his opponents challenge the presidential powers endorsed by the electorate in a nationwide referendum. While conflict between Yeltsin and his opponents in the Federal Assembly will continue, the new constitutional order will probably prevent a repeat of the destructive collisions of 1992 and 1993.

Presidential Institutions, Democracy, and Comparative Politics

Kurt von Mettenheim and Bert A. Rockman

We conclude this volume by attempting to synthesize the contributions of the authors and to draw implications from their analyses of national and regional experiences for broader concerns about political institutions and democratic development. Can presidential systems in which the institutional separation and the potential diffusion of powers loom large provide compelling institutional prospects for democratic development? What specific risks and opportunities do presidential institutions present for democratic politics across the diverse regional and national settings analyzed in the chapters of this volume? While sustained research by regional specialists and comparative analysts will continue to address these questions, the analyses presented in this book suggest that arguments that seek to inexorably link presidentialism to instability, polarization, and legislative gridlock may be considerably overstated.

On the contrary, perhaps the central conclusion to be extracted from this volume is that presidentialism and the separation of powers remain timely and viable doctrines for addressing critical problems of democratic politics. The central features of presidential systems are the direct election of executive leadership and the institutionalized dispersion of power. One helps provide legitimacy; the other helps limit arbitrary rule. None of the contributions to this volume conceals the risks inherent in the direct election of executives and the dispersion of power. Under the least satisfactory conditions, the risks of interbranch paralysis and executive capriciousness are invited: legislatures risk incurring derision and delegitimation, while executives can threaten the rule of law.

Critics of presidential institutions overemphasize precisely these least satisfactory conditions.[1] Furthermore, it is by no means clear that institutions cause or even exacerbate the social and political divisions that generate these conditions.[2] While the recent experiences with presidential institutions examined in this book suggest that the separate and direct election of legislatures and executives does indeed carry risks, this core feature of presidentialism also provides significant opportunities for both the expression of popular expectations and the sober conduct of government. In sum, outcomes arise less from the institutional frame per se than from the nature and context of political problems. The presidential system does, however, combine the potential for strong leadership from the center with representational diversity and competing legitimacies derived from independently elected leaders.

From this perspective, presidential institutions provide different opportunities and risks for democratic politics, depending on their regional and national contexts. For those concerned with legislative gridlock and other problems of governance in the United States, Charles Jones and Bert Rockman argue that the separation of powers provides diverse and often competing policy agendas and negotiating opportunities. While these differing agendas can lead to gridlock, they also can be the basis for reconciling broad presidential visions with the concerns of a variety of interests and actors in the legislature. Whether pluribus produces unum depends heavily on the mind-set of both executive and legislative leaders. Compromise is almost always required in the separated system but not always sought.

For those concerned with the complex tasks of governance on the European continent, both the de facto separation of powers in parliamentary systems and the debates about adopting presidential government to improve policy making and representation suggest that presidential institutions may be more important than normally considered in the region. A major task for governments has been to further European integration while reconciling domestic representational claims. Neither the French experience with cohabitation nor the de facto pivotal veto situation that exists in many parliamentary systems (multiparty coalition governments) has proved fatal nor even necessarily detrimental to these efforts.

For those seeking to build new democracies in Latin America, Eastern Europe, and Russia, the possibility that directly elected presidents may be able to sustain economic reform, to rise above internal divisions, and to deepen democracy may be especially critical. It is possible, as Margaret Thatcher's prime ministership in Britain reminds us, for a prime minister under extremely limited conditions to play a powerful and transforming leadership role, not merely acting as the agent of her party but also seeking to transform it. The fact that presidents are directly elected, however, makes it even more plausible for them to seek to play a transformative role. Yet, to be truly successful they also need to appeal to the political constituencies of the legislature if not to the legislature itself—a lesson that President Yeltsin of Russia appears to have not yet learned. Thus, the paradox of presidentialism is that, while it provides a forum for executive leadership to rise above the hurly-burly of particularistic interests, this form of government also normally requires that executives come to terms, at least partially, with the claims of these interests, which are often articulated in the legislative arena. Alternatively, in a separated system the legislature is not only a forum for representation but also an active partner in policy making and, thus, can provide a genuinely alternative set of policy options.

The contributions to this volume suggest the value of looking at presidential institutions and democratic politics within the context of regional and national concerns. Just as there is no single model of parliamentary system, there also is no single model of presidentialism. While scholars of comparative politics tend to overemphasize the direct and even plebiscitary election of executives as being central to presidential government, Jones argues that the core characteristic of American institutions is the establishment of separate, independently derived legitimacies in the presidency and in the Congress. Jones and Rockman suggest that the complexity, diversity, and diffusion of powers encouraged by American institutions provide opportunities for fitting the broad popular expectations of newly elected presidents into the sober realities of ongoing legislative work. Much depends, as Rockman asserts, on the role played by norms rather than on the causal impact of institutions, per se. The fact is that the separated system, as both Mayhew and Jones point out, can be quite effective even under divided government—a condition that speaks to the importance of norms of accommodation between institutions that are separately legitimized.[3] Core assumptions about the separated system vis-à-vis unified political forces as represented by strong party government may well need to be revisited by students of comparative politics.

Of course, the balance between the executive and the legislature differs across presidential systems. The hybrid French system gives day-to-day operating control to the prime minister and the cabinet. And while the power to form the government derives from the parliamentary elections, clearly the French system is a much more executive-centered one, whether that be in the cabinet or in the presidency. Unlike the American system, where the balance of forces typically is adjusted between the legislative power and the president, in the French system that balance is adjusted between the government (represented by the prime minister and cabinet members) and the president. However, as John Keeler and Martin Schain note in their chapter, the equilibrium of forces strongly favors the president in the Fifth Republic. Overall, therefore, the French president may live in the best of all possible worlds, possessing the capacity to dissolve parliament, change prime ministers, and control the political scene without having to directly suffer the burdens of political responsibility, as American presidents do. The government may take the blame for policy failures or politically unpopular actions, while the president is able to escape such political responsibilities even while holding ultimate political power. Still, the president's control is inhibited by the prospect of divided government, a phenomenon that has existed, however, for only four years in the history of the Fifth Republic.

Although criticism of presidential institutions often attempts to link this form of government to patterns of instability in the Third World, Guy Peters observes that in Western Europe the primary concern is the extent to which institutional design can increase governing capacity. Indeed, special commissions convened in France, Switzerland, and Italy examined the possibility for improving governance through the adoption of presidential institutions. In a related development, Israel has sought to strengthen governance by introducing the direct election of future prime ministers.

Peters also suggests that dividing European systems of government into two polar types—parliamentarist and presidentialist—forces a complex and diverse reality into a false dichotomy. Peters believes that the elements of European politics that produce a functional, or de facto, separation of powers within parliamentary government are more important and will require further analysis. For example, phenomena within parliamentary systems such as coalition governments, considerable autonomy of government agencies beyond both executive and legislative control, a tendency of prime ministers to serve their full term before calling elections (much like the fixed terms of presidents), and media-style campaigns often make for surprising similarities with the separated American system.

The analysis of presidentialism in France by Keeler and Schain supports several arguments running throughout this volume. First, far from providing a single model ready for export, the character of the French presidency changed dramatically after 1958. Their analysis demonstrates that institutions are constantly reshaped by shifting circumstances, statecraft, and historical context. Indeed, they suggest that significant aspects of presidential power and constitutional tradition emerged in France from the bold acts of Charles de Gaulle, which often exceeded the letter of constitutional law. Furthermore, from a perspective that recognizes separation of powers as central to presidential institutions, Keeler and Schain also note that the description of the French system as a hybrid of presidentialism and parliamentarism may be misleading, because the concept of hybrid conceals the extent to which the French system tilts heavily toward the president.[4] On the contrary, the capacity of French presidents to dissolve the national assembly and call new elections suggests that hyperpresidentialism is, at least in certain periods, a more accurate description.

The analyses of Brazil and Bolivia by Kurt von Mettenheim and Eduardo Gamarra suggest that recent critics of presidentialism in Latin America have underestimated the opportunities that can exist within presidential systems. Far from the trajectory of polarization, legislative paralysis, and democratic breakdown that Linz, Valenzuela, Mainwaring, and others fear, the recent transitions from military rule in Brazil and Bolivia suggest that presidents succeeded in crafting new political alliances and new agendas of reform within these systems.[5] Bolivian President Paz Estenssoro's pact for democracy spanned parties and sustained economic reform in terms that defy the negative scenarios sketched by the critics of presidentialism. Contrary also to the notion that only parliaments tend to remove executives, Brazil's first directly elected president after the transition from military rule was impeached on charges of corruption in late 1992. The 1994 presidential campaign also focused Brazilian politics on compelling and viable alternatives. Instead of polarization, the presidential contest brought two new candidates to the fore: Luis Inacio da Silva and Fernando Henrique Cardoso, who represent new forces and new parties in Brazilian and Latin American politics.

It is important not to overstate causal claims about institutions in Latin America—or anywhere else, for that matter. While institutions matter, there are no easy solutions for the structural problems of Latin American politics. Deeply entrenched social hierarchy remains. Citizenship is denuded by patronage and corruption. And social groups continue to bypass electoral politics to extract benefits directly from state agencies. Indeed, the lofty debate among observers of Latin American politics about the formal attributes of parliamentary and presidential government often seem particularly unsuited to both the dizzy pace of political change and the complex circuits of informal influence in the region. The central realities of the region, such as largely unexpected transitions from military to civilian rule, rapidly shifting pacts and alliances, inflation and hyperinflation, dramatic neoliberal reforms and economic adjustment policies, volatile financial markets, increasingly internationalized economies, and a rapidly shifting new world order in the wake of the cold war, suggest that analysts should temper claims about the formal attributes of institutional architecture. While institutions matter, they are deeply embedded in national and regional contexts and the subtexts of informal influence.

Political institutions in Latin America have been both taxed and regenerated by social change, new global pressures, and what appears to be a simultaneous turn toward constitutionalism to produce legitimate governance and neoliberalism to reduce inflation and modernize economies. The cumulative impact of these changes tends to encourage a leaner state—smaller, yet stronger in the sense of being more predictable. The need for formal mechanisms of influence and for more predictable state-society relations implies a declining role for informal mechanisms. That is what the rule of law means. However complex and incomplete, the rule of law has in fact developed within the presidential regimes that predominate in the region. And, of course, this suggests that the deep currents of social, economic, and political change temper the independent impact of institutions on political life.

The analyses of Valerie Bunce, Michael Bernhard, and Jonathan Harris also emphasize both the risks and the opportunities presented by presidential institutions during democratic transitions in the wake of state socialism. In a pathbreaking comparative review of contemporary Eastern Europe, Bunce argues that presidential institutions may provide several advantages over pure parliamentary systems in the region. Presidents can counteract the oversized parliaments and party machines left by communist systems. Presidents also seek to represent a national unity over and above ethnic and regional divisions. Finally, by virtue of their political independence, presidents may be better able to maintain a steadier course of economic policy and to provide leadership in foreign policy as national borders, military alliances, and economic linkages are renegotiated.

Indeed, Eastern Europeans have developed their own perspectives on presidential institutions. Rather than the starkly separated U.S. system or the starkly concentrated one of Great Britain, mixed institutions are seen in this region as the most successful models. The French system, with its powerful president hovering over but not necessarily engaging directly in the affairs of the government, and the German system, with its distant but moral and conciliatory presidential voice, seem to be commanding more attention. However, once imported from abroad, institutions tend to develop significantly different attributes, reflecting the domestic processes of political and economic transition. Eastern European presidencies have emerged through a series of bargains struck between communist state elites and opposition groups. And contrary to the American tradition, which celebrates the separation and diffusion of powers, presidents are often seen in Eastern Europe as the only actors capable of concentrating power, given the large size of the parliaments and their communist legacy.

Two strains of caution run through Bunce's analysis of the unprecedented transitions from state socialism to market economies and democratic politics. First, she shares the concern of Linz and others about the vices of presidentialism. For Bunce, presidential institutions may indeed contribute to polarization (because of high electoral stakes), produce gridlock (because of divided powers), and force presidents to pursue irrational policy cycles (because of fixed terms). Bunce's second ground for caution about the possibilities of presidential institutions in Eastern Europe is the sheer speed and complexity of political and economic change in the region. Bunce argues that the shape and success of institutions in Eastern Europe remain dependent on other political, economic, and cultural variables.

The analyses of Bernhard and Harris clarify the impact of direct plebiscitarian appeals by presidents during the transitions from state socialism in Poland and Russia. The two experiences clarify the risks and opportunities of deepening democracy and representation through the direct links between a president and the public. According to Harris, Presidents Gorbachev and Yeltsin have been the primary motors of political and economic reform in Russia. The

Russian presidency endowed both Gorbachev and Yeltsin with the broad legitimacy and executive authority that might engender the capacity to sustain economic policies of adjustment against the intransigent opposition of ex-communists in parliament.

Bernhard argues that, contrary to the role of Russian presidents as reformers, the direct popular appeals and excessive centralization of power by Lech Wałęsa in the Polish presidency have set poor precedents for democratic politics. Consequently, despite a decade of sustained opposition and mobilization by independent organizations in civil society, Poland still lacks political institutions capable of providing diverse venues for the articulation and representation of different social groups and policy agendas.

While each analysis of national and regional experiences with presidential institutions contained in this volume stands alone, a few general comments about their broader implications for research and theory in comparative politics are in order. The first implication is simple but largely overlooked: because presidential systems can be as diverse as parliamentary systems, comparisons between the two conceal too much variety. Indeed, the analyses in this volume reveal that broad generalizations based on these two generic types of government simply tend to conflate more powerful, noninstitutional factors with institutional ones. This lesson is not new. The difficulty of establishing causal direction between presidential institutions and other political, social, and cultural factors in complex national and regional settings mirrors Rose's review of causal claims about American presidentialism.[6]

The second implication is that both the separationist content of the American system and its particular trajectory of party development can provide new perspectives for those building democratic institutions in Latin America, Eastern Europe, and the new republics of the former Soviet Union. The analyses presented in this volume suggest that presidential systems do not, by themselves, paralyze direction. On the contrary, presidentialism appears able to provide enhanced opportunities for both leadership and legitimation. In broader terms, the competing legitimacies and separation of powers that are the core characteristic of American institutions strike a balance between a profound skepticism about decisive government and a recognition that it is sometimes necessary. In practice, of course, this balance is rarely stable and depends significantly on noninstitutional factors.

Third, shifting the focus of comparative analysis from Europe to the United States can also provide new perspectives on institutional reform and political change. In reaction to corruption, patronage, and the abuse of office by American parties nearly a century ago, the reforms of the Progressive era reshaped electoral mechanisms and professionalized governance. The somewhat contradictory character of these reforms reflects a tension between open access and technical expertise, which remains a central feature of the American system. In this era of democratic expectations, American institutions should be of interest abroad because, while they are remarkably open and accessible, they have also proved remarkably resistant to the populism that tends to well up in the United States. Because it is so open, American government rarely produces big decisions quickly. Yet, it is precisely these periodic and fundamental shifts in policy, accompanied by sudden institutional change and electoral realignment, that have decisively reshaped American politics.[7]

In conclusion, while there is no single model or easy solution for democratic political development, presidentialism and the separation of powers should not be rejected out of hand. Presidential government *can* produce strong leadership and popular support when it is most needed. Presidential institutions *can* provide a complex system of representation when bargaining, negotiation, and compromise are essential. The separation and diffusion of powers *can* make government more accessible. That these outcomes are possible but not predetermined may dismay both politicians involved in day-to-day political work and scholars seeking bold causal claims. In a word, institutions are but a solvent, not a salvation.

While recognizing that neither parliamentary nor presidential government provides a panacea, this volume provides significant evidence that the American system of separating powers is a complex institutional alternative that should no longer be ignored in comparative political analysis. The political problem faced by the framers of American institutions was, after all, the same one faced by democrats throughout the world today—namely, how to reconcile the need for innovative leadership within a framework that can sustain liberty. More than two hundred years later, the idea of Madison and Hamilton—to separate powers and establish competing legitimacies—still increases access, removes policy from the exclusive domain of elites, and tempers the excesses of majority rule. Such a system is very far from perfect, particularly when viewed in terms of the frustrations of the moment. But, in the long run, the separated system has provided routine accessibility, allowed for decisive leadership when most needed, and permitted the cooling of majoritarian passions through a complex system of representation.

Notes

Preface

1. Juan Linz and Arturo Valenzuela, eds., *The Failure of Presidential Democracy in Latin America* (Baltimore: Johns Hopkins University Press, 1994).
2. See Kurt von Mettenheim, *The Brazilian Voter: Mass Politics in Democratic Transition, 1974–1986* (Pittsburgh: University of Pittsburgh Press, 1995).

Introduction
von Mettenheim, Presidential Institutions and Democratic Politics

1. On views of American political institutions abroad during preceding eras of democratic transition, see Klaus von Beyme, *America as a Model* (New York: St. Martins, 1987); Carl Friedrich, *The Impact of American Constitutionalism Abroad* (Boston: Boston University Press, 1967).
2. Samuel Huntington argues that American political institutions are unique because they are based on premodern ideas from Tudor England about the dispersion and separation of powers. See his *Political Order in Changing Societies* (New Haven: Yale University Press, 1968), chap. 2.
3. Juan Linz began the recent round of criticism of presidential institutions in underground papers circulated during 1984 and later published as "The Perils of Presidentialism," *Journal of Democracy* 1 (1990): 51–69, and in *Parliamentary versus Presidential Government*, ed. Arend Lijphart (New York: Oxford University Press, 1992). See also Alfred Stepan and Cindy Skatch, "Constitutional Frameworks and Democratic Consolidation: Parliamentarism versus Presidentialism," *World Politics* 46 (1993): 1–22; Juan Linz and Arturo Valenzuela, eds. *The Failure of Presidential Democracy in Latin America* (Baltimore: Johns Hopkins University Press, 1994); and the selections in Lijphart, *Parliamentary versus Presidential Government*.
4. This definition is based on Charles Jones's "separationist" perspective on American institutions, which is presented in chapter 1 and which deeply influenced the contributors to this volume.
5. Giovanni Sartori discusses the role of minimal and descriptive definitions in linking complex problems to empirical research in his *Parties and Party Systems* (Cambridge: Cambridge University Press, 1976), 62–63.
6. In a notable exception, Matthew S. Shugart and John M. Carey analyze the prospects for balancing powers between executives and legislatures in

their *Presidents and Assemblies: Constitutional Design and Electoral Dynamics* (New York: Cambridge University Press, 1992).

7. Lijphart, *Parliamentary versus Presidential Government*, 2–6.

8. Linz, "Perils of Presidentialism," 53. Linz focuses on two additional characteristics of presidential systems that also tend to generate instability: that both presidents and legislatures are directly elected and endowed with significant powers and that both are elected for fixed terms in office.

9. On the importance of analyzing the specific risks and opportunities associated with different institutional arrangements, and specifically when analyzing presidential and parliamentary government, see R. Kent Weaver and Bert A. Rockman, eds., *Do Institutions Matter? Government Capabilities in the United States and Abroad* (Washington, D.C.: Brookings, 1993), chap. 1.

10. See Jones's contribution to this volume; David Mayhew, *Divided We Govern: Party Control, Lawmaking, and Investigations, 1946–1990* (New Haven: Yale University Press, 1991).

11. Plato, *Republic*, bk. 6.

12. For a review of Polybius's theory and comparison with Hobbes's notion of sovereignty, see Kurt von Fritz, *The Theory of the Mixed Constitution in Antiquity* (New York: Columbia University Press, 1954).

13. Machiavelli, Niccolò. *The Discourses*, bk. 1, chaps. 2 and 4.

14. In this respect, presidential institutions are a product of eighteenth-century revolutionary theory. Douglas Verney notes: "By abolishing the monarchy and substituting a president for the King and his government, the Americans showed themselves to be truly revolutionary in outlook." See his "Parliamentary Government and Presidential Government," in Lijphart, *Parliamentary versus Presidential Government*, 41.

15. John Locke, *Second Treatise of Government*, chap. 12, para. 143.

16. Charles-Louis Montesquieu, *The Spirit of the Laws* (Cambridge: Cambridge University Press, 1989), pt. 2, bk. 11, chap. 6.

17. The central focus of *Federalist Paper* 51 is the separation of executive and legislative powers.

18. On debates about minority representation in the American Constitution, see: *The Federalist Papers*, Alexander Hamilton, James Madison, John Jay. (New York: Signet Classics, 1961) (chs. 10 and 63); and *The Complete Federalist*, ed. Herbert Storing (Chicago: University of Chicago Press, 1981) (7 vols.).

19. John C. Calhoun. *A Disquisition on Government and Selections from the Discourses* (New York: Liberal Arts Press, 1953).

20. I thank James Malloy for noting the importance of Arendt's emphasis on the separation of powers in her analysis of the lost legacies of the revolutionary tradition and its applicability to contemporary concerns about governability. See Hannah Arendt, *On Revolution* (New York: Viking, 1963).

21. Louis Bergeron notes that "plebiscitary democracy simply passed over representative institutions and inhibited the development of public opinion." See his *France under Napoleon* (Princeton: Princeton University

Press, 1981), 9. On the history of plebiscitarianism in Europe, see Charles S. Maier, "Fictitious Bonds of Wealth and Law: On the Theory and Practice of Interest Representation," in Suzanne Berger, *Organizing Interests in Western Europe* (Cambridge: Cambridge University Press, 1983).

22. For a comparison of these analyses by Marx and Tocqueville, see Raymond Aron, "The Sociologists and the Revolution of 1848," in his *Main Currents in Sociological Thought,* vol. 1 (New York: Doubleday, 1968).

23. Alexis de Tocqueville, *Recollections* (Berkeley: University of California Press, 1977) 187.

24. Karl Marx, *The 18th Brumaire of Louis Bonaparte* (New York: International Publishers, 1964).

25. Verney also notes that "equally important for the proper operation of the presidential system is the election of the president at the time of the assembly elections. This associates the two branches of government, encourages party unity, and clarifies the issues." Verney, "Parliamentary Government and Presidential Government," 41.

26. Max Weber, "Politics as a Vocation," in *From Max Weber: Essays in Sociology,* ed. Hans Gerth, and C. Wright Mills (New York: Oxford University Press, 1946); James Bryce, *The American Commonwealth* (New York: Macmillan, 1907). For party electoral politics, see the debate between Phillip Converse, Walter D. Burnham, and Jerrold Rusk in *American Political Science Review* 68 (1974): 1002–57.

27. Linz, "Perils of Presidentialism," 56–57.

28. Weber, "Politics as a Vocation"; Friedrich, *Impact of American Constitutionalism Abroad.*

29. On critical elections and realignments in American politics, see V. O. Key, "A Theory of Critical Elections," *Journal of Politics* 17 (1950): 3–18; William N. Chambers and Walter D. Burnham, *The American Party Systems: Stages of Political Development* (New York: Oxford University Press, 1967); and James Sundquist, *Dynamics of the Party System: Alignment and Realignment of Political Parties in the United States,* 2d ed. (Washington, D.C.: Brookings, 1983).

30. Von Beyme, *America as a Model*; Friedrich, *Impact of the American Constitution Abroad.*

31. Linz, "Perils of Presidentialism"; James L. Sundquist, *Constitutional Reform and Effective Government* (Washington, D.C.: Brookings, 1986).

32. Woodrow Wilson, *Congressional Government: A Study in American Politics* (New York: Houghton Mifflin, 1900); Richard Hofstadter, *The Progressive Movement, 1900–1915* (Englewood Cliffs, N.J.: Prentice-Hall, 1963); "Toward a More Responsible Two-Party System," *American Political Science Review* 44, supp. (1950):1–96; and Sundquist, *Constitutional Reform and Effective Government.*

33. Weaver and Rockman, *Do Institutions Matter?* chap. 1.

34. On problems in comparing the performance of parliamentary and presidential government, see ibid.

35. James G. March and Johan P. Olsen, *Rediscovering Institutions: The Organizational Basis of Politics* (N.Y.: Free Press, 1989).

36. For example, Stephen Skowronek, *Building a New American State* (Cambridge: Cambridge University Press, 1982); Theda Skocpol, *Protecting Soldiers and Mothers: The Political Origins of Social Policy in the United States* (Cambridge: Cambridge University Press, 1992).

37. Lijphart, *Parliamentary and Presidential Government.*

38. Weaver and Rockman, *Do Institutions Matter?* chap. 1.

39. Ibid., 8 (emphasis added).

Chapter 1
Jones, The American Presidency

1. Anthony King, "Whoever Said the U.S. President Was Powerful?" paper prepared for Presidency Research Conference, University of Pittsburgh, Pittsburgh, Penna., November 11–14, 1990, 1. The essay is published under the more prosaic title, "Foundations of Power," in *Researching the Presidency: Vital Questions, New Approaches,* ed. George C. Edwards III, John H. Kessel, and Bert A. Rockman (Pittsburgh: University of Pittsburgh Press, 1993).

2. G. Bingham Powell Jr., *Contemporary Democracies: Participation, Stability, and Violence* (Cambridge: Harvard University Press, 1982), 218.

3. See, for example, Arend Lijphart, ed., *Parliamentary versus Presidential Government* (New York: Oxford University Press, 1992), in particular the introduction by Lijphart (1–27) and the chapters by Douglas Verney (31–47) and Juan Linz (118–27).

4. Richard E. Neustadt, *Presidential Power: The Politics of Leadership* (New York: John Wiley, 1960), passim. For other examples see George Edwards III, *At the Margins: Presidential Leadership of Congress* (New Haven: Yale University Press, 1989), esp. chaps. 1 and 11; Erwin Hargrove and Michael Nelson, *Presidents, Politics, and Policy* (Baltimore: Johns Hopkins University Press, 1984), chap. 4; Mark Peterson, *Legislating Together: The White House and Capitol Hill from Eisenhower to Reagan* (Cambridge: Harvard University Press, 1990), chap. 3; Bert A. Rockman, *The Leadership Question: The Presidency and the American System* (New York: Praeger, 1984), chap. 4 and passim.

5. Powell, *Contemporary Democracies,* 218–19.

6. Peterson, *Legislating Together,* 6. Peterson provides a summary of the characteristics of the presidency-centered perspective, 2–6.

7. Ibid., 7.

8. Ibid., 8.

9. David R. Mayhew, *Divided We Govern: Party Control, Lawmaking, and Investigations, 1946–1990* (New Haven: Yale University Press, 1991), 90. Mayhew points out that his second retrospective sweep added substantially to the first contemporary sweep in regard to these years. In other words, many important laws were not picked up by contemporary analysts who ex-

pected deadlock. Many years earlier, Lawrence Chamberlain studied major laws enacted between 1873 and 1940 and discovered that the president was preponderant in just over one-fifth of these law. See his *The President, Congress, and Legislation* (New York: Columbia University Press, 1946).

10. King, "Foundations of Power," 446.

11. Neustadt, *Presidential Power*, 33.

12. This conclusion will surprise those who view Neustadt as the father of modern presidential research, much of which is presidency centered to a fault. I justify it by pointing out that much contemporary research ignores Neustadt's model, which is perceptual in orientation. In fact, Neustadt himself did not employ his own model for collecting data on what he argues were the primary sources of power for a president: "his vantage points in government, together with his reputation in the Washington community and his prestige outside" (ibid., 179). To my knowledge, we still lack an empirical test of reputation and prestige as sources of power in regard to policy issues, as measured by their effects on other decision makers.

13. William H. Riker, *The Art of Political Manipulation* (New Haven: Yale University Press, 1986), chap. 4: and Riker, "The Heresthetic of Constitution-Making: The Presidency in 1787, with Comments on Determinism and Rational Choice," *American Political Science Review* 78 (1984): 1–16.

14. Riker, *Art of Political Manipulation*, 39.

15. Riker, "Heresthetic," 14.

16. I came to know about this letter through Arthur Schlesinger's reference to it in *The Imperial Presidency* (Boston: Houghton Mifflin, 1973), 377. The letter itself is in Thomas Jefferson Randolph, ed., *The Writings of Thomas Jefferson*, vol. 2 (Boston: Gray and Bowen, 1830), 441–45.

17. Ernest Barker, *Essays on Government*, 2d ed. (London: Oxford University Press, 1951), 71.

18. Woodrow Wilson, *Congressional Government: A Study in American Politics* (New York: Houghton Mifflin, 1900); James MacGregor Burns, *Presidential Government: The Crucible of Leadership* (Boston: Houghton Mifflin, 1965).

19. Burns, *Presidential Government*, 313.

20. Schlesinger, *Imperial Presidency*.

21. Ibid., 377.

22. James L. Sundquist, *The Decline and Resurgence of Congress* (Washington, D.C.: Brookings, 1981), 16.

23. Ibid., 461.

24. It is precisely this separated legitimacy that worries some critics of the American system. See, for example, Juan Linz, "The Perils of Presidentialism," *Journal of Democracy*, 1.1 (1990): 51–69 (a portion of which is reprinted in Lijphart, *Parliamentary versus Presidential Government*). See also ibid., 15, where Lijphart observes that "when disagreement between them [president and Congress] occurs, there is no institutional method of resolving it—unlike the factor of legislative confidence that keeps the legis-

lature and executive in tune with each other in parliamentary systems."

25. It can be argued that, had it not been for Watergate, the Republicans would have won the 1976 presidential election. As it was, they nearly did so. Had they won, it is unlikely they could have captured control of Congress. Others point out that the Carter presidency itself had many separationist characteristics in spite of the fact that the Democrats won both ends of Pennsylvania Avenue. See Charles O. Jones, "The Separated Presidency: Making It Work in Contemporary Politics," in *The New American Political System: Second Version*, ed. Anthony King (Washington, D.C.: American Enterprise Institute, 1990).

26. John B. Bader makes such a comparison, "The 86th and 100th Congresses: Changing Goals and a New Definition of Success in Presidential Relations," paper prepared for the 1992 Annual Meeting of the American Political Science Association, Chicago, Sept. 3–6, 1992. Bader concludes that the concept of lame duck is not useful for analyzing these Congresses. "If we look more carefully at the various goals of the many participants, we begin to see that the traditional models of decline and failure may be simplistic and based on a normative model of 'activity' that is not appropriate for all presidents or all congresses at all times" (14).

27. Most of that analysis is based on the coincidence of the results rather than on voters making an association between their votes for president and their votes for members of Congress. Thus the result only *appear* to form a mandate. For a discussion of various types of mandates, see Charles O. Jones, *The Presidency in a Separated System* (Washington, D.C.: Brookings, 1994), chap. 5.

28. "The Republican Tide," *New York Times*, Nov. 9, 1966.

29. Barbara Sinclair, *The Transformation of the U. S. Senate* (Baltimore: Johns Hopkins University Press, 1989), 213, 214, 216.

30. Steven S. Smith, *Call to Order: Floor Politics in the House and Senate* (Washington, D.C.: Brookings, 1989), 44.

31. Neustadt, *Presidential Power*, 6–7.

32. John W. Kingdon, *Agendas, Alternatives, and Public Policies* (Boston: Little, Brown, 1984), 25.

33. Paul C. Light, *The President's Agenda: Domestic Policy Choice from Kennedy to Carter* (Baltimore: Johns Hopkins University Press, 1982), 233.

34. Kingdon, *Agendas, Alternatives, and Public Policies*, 4.

35. Charles O. Jones, "Presidents and Agendas: Who Defines What for Whom?" in *The Managerial Presidency*, ed. James P. Pffifner (Pacific Grove, Calif.: Brooks-Cole, 1991), 198.

36. "The Pressure Is on to Salvage 102d Congress's Reputation," *Congressional Quarterly Weekly Report*, Sept. 5, 1992, 2600.

37. Jones, *Presidency in a Separated System*, chap. 7.

38. James David Barber, *The Presidential Character: Predicting Performance in the White House*, 4th ed. (Englewood Cliffs, N.J.: Prentice-Hall, 1992), chap. 1.

39. Richard Rose, *The Postmodern Presidency: George Bush Meets the World*, 2d ed. (Chatham, N.J.: Chatham House, 1991), 49.

40. Hargrove and Nelson, *Presidents, Politics, and Policy*, 196–99.

41. As calculated from Mayhew, *Divided We Govern*, 52–73, 118.

Chapter 2
Rockman, The Performance of Presidents and Prime Ministers

1. For a detailed discussion, see R. Kent Weaver and Bert A. Rockman, "Assessing the Effects of Institutions," in *Do Institutions Matter? Government Capabilities in the United States and Abroad*, ed. Weaver and Rockman (Washington, D.C.: Brookings, 1993).

2. Michael M. Atkinson refers to these different needs as aggregative and integrative, respectively. See his "What Kind of Democracy Do Canadians Want?" Paper prepared for the SOG/IPSA Conference on the Consolidation of Democracies, Ankara, Turkey, Oct. 1993.

3. See, for example, Kenji Hayao, *The Japanese Prime Minister and Public Policy* (Pittsburgh: University of Pittsburgh Press, 1993).

4. Anthony King, "Foundations of Power," in *Researching the Presidency: Vital Questions, New Approaches*, ed. George C. Edwards III, John H. Kessel, and Bert A. Rockman (Pittsburgh: University of Pittsburgh Press, 1993).

5. As I argue elsewhere, only one dimension of the state is its decision-making structure. Concentrated governmental authority does offer the prospect of accelerated decision making based on nonconsensual arrangements, yet to define the power of the state as emanating only from this spare feature is akin to inferring physiology from anatomy. See Bert A. Rockman, "Minding the State—Or a State of Mind? Issues in the Comparative Conceptualization of the State," *Comparative Political Studies* 23 (1990): 25–55.

6. For a critique of nonformalized norms as a substitute for formalized rules, see F. F. Ridley, "There Is No British Constitution: A Dangerous Case of the Emperor's Clothes," *Parliamentary Affairs* 41 (1988): 340–61.

7. E. E. Schattschneider, *The Semi-Sovereign People: A Realist's View of Democracy in America* (New York: Holt, Rinehart, and Winston, 1960).

8. As an example of the style of accommodation politics associated with the idea of a repetitive game, see Thomas J. Anton, *Administered Politics* (Boston: Martinus Nijhoff, 1980).

9. See Charles Tiefer, *The Semi-Sovereign Presidency: The Bush Administration's Strategy for Governing without Congress*. (Boulder, Colo.: Westview, 1994).

10. Terry M. Moe, "The Politicized Presidency," in *The New Direction in American Politics*, ed. John E. Chubb and Paul E. Peterson (Washington, D.C.: Brookings, 1985).

11. Terry M. Moe, "Presidents, Institutions, and Theory," in Edwards,

Kessel, and Rockman, *Researching the Presidency*. Moe asserts that the president can seek to gain more control over the bureaucracy via two institutional strategies: politicization and centralization. "Although dealing with agencies designed and overseen by Congress, he can implement these two strategies on his own authority" (370).

12. For further exploration of inter- and intra-systemic variability in leadership conditions, see Weaver and Rockman, *Do Institutions Matter?* esp. 1–41 and 445–61.

13. King, "Foundations of Power."

14. Nathan refers to the aggressive effort to use the executive apparatus to thwart congressional intent as "the administrative presidency." See Richard P. Nathan, *The Administrative Presidency* (New York: John Wiley, 1983). Moe describes the same phenomenon as "the politicized presidency," in "Politicized Presidency."

15. In particular, see Colin Campbell's comparison of the organizational structures to facilitate interagency agreements in the Reagan and Carter administrations. The Reagan administration was organized to reach agreements below the presidential level, whereas the Carter administration was designed to overload even a hardworking and detail-oriented president. See Colin Campbell, *Managing the Presidency: Carter, Reagan, and the Search for Executive Harmony* (Pittsburgh: University of Pittsburgh Press, 1986).

16. For example, see Committee on the Constitutional System, "A Bicentennial Analysis of the American Political Structure," in Arend Lijphart, *Parliamentary versus Presidential Government* (New York: Oxford University Press, 1992); see also Juan Linz, "the Perils of Presidentialism" in ibid.

17. See Adam Przeworski and Henry Teune, *The Logic of Comparative Social Inquiry* (New York: Wiley-Interscience, 1970).

18. See also Charles O. Jones, *The Presidency in a Separated System* (Washington, D.C.: Brookings, 1994).

19. For example, see James McGregor Burns, *The Deadlock of Democracy: Four Party Politics in America* (Englewood Cliffs, N. J.: Prentice-Hall, 1963); Lloyd N. Cutler, "To Form a Government," *Foreign Affairs* 59 (1980): 126–43; and James L. Sundquist, *Constitutional Reform and Effective Government*, rev. ed. (Washington, D.C.: Brookings, 1992). A somewhat more complicated rendition emphasizes the interaction of a populist culture with institutions that disperse power. See James A. Morone, *The Democratic Wish: Popular Participation and the Limits of American Government* (New York: Basic Books, 1990); and Bert A. Rockman, *The Leadership Question: The Presidency and the American System* (New York: Praeger, 1984).

20. Stephen Skowronek, *The Politics Presidents Make: Leadership from John Adams to George Bush* (Cambridge: Harvard University Press, 1993).

21. Harvey Feigenbaum, Richard Samuels, and R. Kent Weaver, "Innovation, Coordination, and Implementation in Energy Policy," in Weaver and Rockman, *Do Institutions Matter?*

22. See David R. Mayhew, *Divided We Govern: Party Control, Lawmaking, and Investigations, 1946–1990* (New Haven: Yale University Press, 1991); and Jones, *Presidency in a Separated System.*

23. David R. Mayhew, "U.S. Policy Waves in Comparative Context," in *New Perspectives on American Politics*, ed. Lawrence C. Dodd and Calvin Jillson (Washington, D.C.: CQ Press, 1994).

24. Paul D. Pierson and R. Kent Weaver, "Imposing Losses in Pension Policy," in Weaver and Rockman, *Do Institutions Matter?*

25. For example, see James G. March and Johan P. Olsen, *Rediscovering Institutions* (New York: Basic Books, 1989).

26. Richard F. Fenno Jr., "The House Appropriations Committee as a Political System: The Problem of Integration," *American Political Science Review* 56 (1962): 310–24.

27. Johan P. Olsen, *Organized Democracy: Political Institutions in a Welfare State—The Case of Norway* (Oslo: Universitetsforlaget, 1983).

28. For example, see Eric M. Uslaner, *The Decline of Comity in Congress* (Ann Arbor: University of Michigan Press, 1993). Also see Colin Campbell and Graham K. Wilson, *The End of Whitehall? Death of a Paradigm* (Oxford: Basil Blackwell, 1995).

29. Richard Rose, *The Postmodern Presidency: George Bush Meets the World*, 2d ed. (Chatham, N.J.: Chatham House, 1991).

30. See Robert A. Dahl, *A Preface to Democratic Theory* (Chicago: University of Chicago Press, 1956).

31. Weaver and Rockman, "Assessing the Effects of Institutions."

32. Arend Lijphart, *Democracies: Patterns of Majoritarian and Consensus Government in Twenty-One Countries* (New Haven: Yale University Press, 1984); and Lijphart, *Democracy in Plural Societies: A Comparative Exploration* (New Haven: Yale University Press, 1977).

33. Seymour Martin Lipset's classic exposition of the relationship between affluence and democracy, of course, begs the question of directionality and the extent, if any, to which governing institutions can help trigger social effectiveness. See his *Political Man: The Social Bases of Politics* (Baltimore: Johns Hopkins University Press, 1981). An institutionalist perspective, however, can be found in Chalmers Johnson, *MITI and the Japanese Miracle: The Growth of Industrial Policy, 1925–1975* (Stanford, Calif.: Stanford University Press, 1982). Here, Johnson argues that it was the Japanese state, particularly in developing its economic strategy as a producer in world markets, that was responsible in a major way for the Japanese economic miracle and the growth of an affluent society in the postwar years. The Mieji restoration in the nineteenth century also might be thought of as state-sponsored economic development, moving imperial Japan into the role of an industrial power.

34. This is the principal conclusion drawn in Weaver and Rockman, *Do Institutions Matter?*

35. For these general results, see ibid.

36. Richard Neustadt, *Presidential Power: The Politics of Leadership* (New York: John Wiley, 1960).

37. Olsen, *Organized Democracy*, 116.

38. Ibid., 117.

39. Weaver and Rockman, *Do Institutions Matter?*, 445–61.

Chapter 3
Peters, Separation of Powers in Parliamentary Systems

1. Horowitz, for example, argues that if Latin American countries are the focus of analysis then presidentialism appears to be the problem. If, however, other areas of the world are considered, then parliamentary government appears to be the culprit. The problem for all of these countries may be poverty, rather than form of government. See Donald J. Horowitz, "Comparing Democratic Systems," *Journal of Democracy* 1 (1990): 73–79.

2. Maurice Duverger, "A New Political System Model: Semipresidential Government, *European Journal of Political Science* 8 (1980): 165–87.

3. G. Jones, "Presidentialization in a Parliamentary System?" in *Executive Leadership in Anglo-American Systems*, ed. C. Campbell and M. J. Wyszomirski (Pittsburgh: University of Pittsburgh Press, 1991).

4. I. Jennings, *Cabinet Government*, 3d ed. (Cambridge: Cambridge University Press, 1960); Anthony King, *The British Prime Minister*, 2d ed. (London: Macmillan, 1985); T. Larsson, *Regeringen och dess kansli* (Lund: Studentlitteratur, 1986).

5. D. Kavanagh, *Thatcherism and British Politics* (Oxford: Oxford Unversity Press, 1987).

6. On select committees, see G. Drewry, *The New Select Committees* (Oxford: Clarendon, 1985).

7. The position of the chancellor may, however, be reverting to something more like that of the prime minister in other parliamentary systems. See P. Haungs, "Kanzlerdemokratie in der BRD: Von Adenauer fir Kohl," *Zeitschrift für Politik* 33 (1986): 47–88.

8. K. Strom, *Minority Government and Majority Rule* (Cambridge: Cambridge University Press, 1990); The Ullsten government in Sweden from October 1978 to October 1979 was composed of only the Folkspartiet and only 11 percent of the seats in the Riksdag. A subsequent Center Party Folkspartiet government (Falldin) had 299 percent of the seats. Similarly, the first Willoch government in Norway had only 34 percent of the seats, but it survived twenty months.

9. There are, of course, more than two parties in Great Britain, but in almost all elections one of the two leading parties has won a majority of seats and formed a single-party government. The single-member district electoral system is a major contributor to the absence of coalition governments in the United Kingdom.

10. M. Laver and N. Schofield, *Multiparty Government: The Politics of Coalition in Europe* (Oxford: Oxford University Press, 1990).

11. D. Mayhew, *Divided We Govern: Party Control, Lawmaking, and Investigations, 1946–1990* (New Haven: Yale University Press, 1991).

12. D. MacRae, *Parliament, Parties, and Societies in France, 1946–1956* (New York: St. Martin's, 1967).

13. M. O. Heisler and R. B. Kvavik., "Patterns of European Politics: The 'European Politics' Model," in *Politics in Europe*, ed. M. O. Heisler (New York: David McKay, 1974). There are, of course, instances in which being a part of a governing coalition will be very much a poisoned chalice, and rational political parties may seek to avoid complicity in difficult policy choices. Such situations may result in the formation of minority governments.

14. B. G. Peters, "Politicians and Bureaucrats in European Governments; Who Is Who, and Does It Matter?" paper prepared for the annual meeting of the American Political Science Association, Chicago, Sept. 1992.

15. Richard Rose, *The Problem of Party Government* (London: Macmillan, 1974).

16. F. Meyers, *La politisation de l'administration* (Brussels: IISA, 1985).

17. M. Fiorina, "Coalition Government, Divided Government, and Electoral Theory," *Governance* (1991): 236–49. But see Mayhew, *Divided We Govern*.

18. Rose, *Problem of Party Government*; R. S. Katz, "Party Government: A Rationalistic Concept," in *Visions and Realities of Party Government*, ed. F. G. Castles and R. Wildenmann (Berlin: de Gruyter, 1986).

19. Fiorina, "Coalition Government, Divided Government, and Electoral Theory"; James Sundquist, "Needed: A Political Theory for a New Era of Coalition Government in the United States" *Political Science Quarterly* 103 (1988): 613–35.

20. Jones, "Presidentialization in a Parliamentary System?"

21. W. L. Miller, *Media and Voters* (Oxford: Clarendon, 1991), 149

22. For example, Norman Tebbit and his bicycle received a great deal of media attention in each of the Thatcher elections.

23. See G. Sartori, "European Political Parties: Case of Polarized Pluralism," in *Political Parties and Political Development*, ed. Joseph LaPalombara and Myron Weiner (Princeton: Princeton University Press, 1966). This pattern often depends upon which party within the coalition does best in the election, especially when there is a marked shift in the fortunes of the parties. In Sweden, for example, the bourgeois coalition shifted the premiership between two parties when it held office from 1976 to 1982.

24. R. J. Dalton, S. C. Flanagan, and P. A. Beck *Electoral Change in Advanced Industrial Countries* (Princeton: Princeton University Press, 1984); S. Bartolini and P. Mair, *Identity, Competition, and Electoral Availability* (Cambridge: Cambridge University Press, 1990).

25. To some extent, the same has been said of the leader of the Progress Party in Norway, Carl I. Hagen, although he has not enjoyed the success that Wachtmeister has with New Democracy in Sweden. Interestingly, Green parties are the other often cited example of new parties, and they have a distinctly nonpresidential style of campaigning and of participation in the parliament.

26. C. Turpin, "Ministerial Responsibility: Myth or Reality," in *The Changing Constitution*, ed. J. Jowell and D. Oliver (Oxford: Blackwell, 1985).

27. Of course, as Presidents Nixon and Collor can testify, there is the possibility of removal by impeachment, although that is outside bounds of normal politics.

28. Countries with the most political parties in parliament and the greatest potential for government change, for example Belgium, Denmark, and the Netherlands, showed substantial decreases in turnover.

29. W. Plowden, *Advising the Rulers* (Oxford: Basil Blackwell, 1987).

30. D. Hine and R. Finocchi, "The Italian Prime Minister," in *West European Prime Ministers*, ed. G. W. Jones (London: Frank Cass, 1991).

31. F. W. Riggs, "Presidentialism: An Empirical Theory," in *Comparing Nations: The Pendulum between Theory and Practice*, ed. M. Dogan and A. Kazancigil (Oxford: Basil Blackwell, 1991).

32. J. Blondel, "Ministerial Careers and the Nature of Parliamentary Government: The Cases of Austria and Belgium," *European Journal of Political Research* 16 (1988): 51–71.

33. J. Blondel, *Government Ministers in the Contemporary World* (London: Sage, 1985), 63–66.

34. E. Damgaard, *The Strong Parliaments of Scandinavia* (Aarhus: University of Aarhus, Institute of Politics, 1990).

35. The Committee on the Constitution and the associated ombudsman system are extremely effective checks on potential abuse by the executive.

36. The select committees were formed as a mechanism for doing just that type of monitoring but have not yet achieved the expectations of their advocates. See Drewry, *New Select Committees*.

37. B. G. Peters, *European Politics Reconsidered* (New York: Holmes and Meier, 1991), 80.

38. Jones, "Presidentialization in a Parliamentary System?"; P. Dunleavy, G. W. Jones, and B. O'Leary, "Prime Ministers and the Commons: Patterns of Behaviour 1868 to 1987," *Public Administration* 68 (1990): 123–40.

39. Arbeitsgruppe Fuhrungsstrukturen des Bundes, *Notwendigkeit und Kriterien einer Regierungsreform* (Bern: Bundesrat der Schweiz, 1991).

40. This is, at best, a partial idea about the differences; but the possibility in the presidential system of a "strong man" with an independent mandate makes usurpation logically more probable.

41. M. Landau, "The Rationality of Redundancy," *Public Administration Review* 29 (1969): 346–58; M. Feldman, *Order without Design: Information Production and Policymaking* (Stanford: Stanford University Press, 1989);

Mark Peterson, "How Health Policy Information Is Used in Congress," in Thomas E. Mann and Norman J. Ornstein, eds., *Intensive Care: How Congress Shapes Health Policy* (Washington, D.C.: The American Enterprise Institute and the Brookings Institute, 1995), 79–125.

42. P. Bachrach and M. Baratz, *Power and Poverty* (New York: Oxford University Press, 1970), John W. Kingdon, *Agendas, Alternatives, and Public Policies* (Boston: Little, Brown, 1984).

43. A. Barker and B. G. Peters, *Advising West European Governments* (Edinburgh: University of Edinburgh Press, 1992).

44. D. F. Kettl, "Micromanagement: Congressional Control and Bureaucratic Risk," in *Agenda for Excellence*, ed. P. W. Ingraham and D. F. Kettl (Chatham, N.J.: Chatham House, 1992).

45. This term was, of course, invented by the first editors of the journal of the same name.

Chapter 4
Keeler and Schain, Institutions, Political Poker, and Regime Evolution in France

1. Jacques Godechot, ed., *Les Constitutions de la France depuis 1789* (Paris: Flammarion, 1970), 5.

2. Arend Lijphart, introduction, to *Parliamentary versus Presidential Government* ed. (New York: Oxford University Press, 1992), 26.

3. "Following the French," *Economist*, June 12, 1993, 58–59.

4. Juan Linz, "The Perils of Presidentialism," in Lijphart, *Parliamentary versus Presidential Government*; Juan Linz, "Presidential or Parliamentary Democracy: Does It Make a Difference?" in *The Failure of Presidential Democracy in Latin America*, ed. Juan Linz and Arturo Valenzuela (Baltimore: Johns Hopkins University Press, 1994); see also Alfred Stepan and Ezra Suleiman, "The French Fifth Republic: A Model for Import?—Reflections on Poland and Brazil," in *Politics, Society and Democracy*, ed. H. E. Chehabi and Alfred Stepan (Boulder: Westview, 1995).

5. Linz, "Presidential or Parliamentary Democracy," 50.

6. See Lijphart, introduction to *Parliamentary versus Presidential Government*, 15–21.

7. See Linz, "Presidential or Parliamentary Democracy," 48–55; Stepan and Suleiman, *French Fifth Republic*, 393–94, 410–14.

8. Lijphart, introduction to *Parliamentary versus Presidential Government*, 8.

9. Seymour Martin Lipset, "The Centrality of Political Culture," in Lijphart, *Parliamentary versus Presidential Government*, 211.

10. As we each discuss at length elsewhere, the strengthening of executive power vis-à-vis parliament virtually assures some improvement in governmental stability and governing capacity. See John T. S. Keeler, "Executive Power and Policymaking Patterns in France: Gauging the Impact of

Fifth Republic Institutions," *West European Politics* 16 (1993): 518–44; Henry W. Ehrmann and Martin A. Schain, *Politics in France*, 5th ed. (New York: HarperCollins, 1992), chap. 9.

11. De Gaulle actually spoke of playing political poker, noting that he was "the strongest" player in the game; see Jean Lacouture, *De Gaulle, vol. 3; Le souverain* (Paris: Seuil, 1986), 592. In the same vein, Guillermo O'Donnell and Philippe C. Schmitter refer to the "chess game" played in transitional regimes; see their edited work, *Transitions from Authoritarian Rule: Tentative Conclusions about Uncertain Democracies* (Baltimore: Johns Hopkins University Press, 1986), 66.

12. They could also benefit from reflecting on the way in which both the Third and Fourth Republics developed constitutional cultures at variance with early expectations. The first president of the Third Republic, General Patrice MacMahon, lost a bitter confrontation with parliament that left the right of dissolution a dead letter and the powers of the presidency generally weakened. The first president of the Fourth Republic, Vincent Auriol, infused his office with more status and influence than the constitution makers had intended. See Olivier Duhamel, *Le Pouvoir politique en France* (Paris: Presses Universitaires de France, 1991), 142–43; Gordon Wright, *France in Modern Times*, 3d ed. (New York: Norton, 1981), 135–39 (on MacMahon); and Philip M. Williams, *Crisis and Compromise: Politics in the Fourth Republic* (New York: Anchor, 1966), 203–10 (on Auriol).

13. See Nicholas Wahl, ed., *Naissance de la Cinquième Rèpublique* (Paris: Presses de la Fondation Nationale des Sciences Politiques, 1990).

14. William G. Andrews, *Presidential Government in Gaullist France* (Albany: SUNY Press, 1982), 3, 22, 32.

15. For a detailed discussion of the Fifth Republic's constitutional weapons, see Keeler, "Executive Power."

16. Ehrmann and Schain, *Politics in France*, 425.

17. See Vincent Wright, *The Government and Politics of France*, 3d ed. (New York: Holmes and Meier, 1989), 15–16.

18. André Hauriou, as cited in Marie-Anne Cohendet, *La Cohabitation: Leçons d'une expérience* (Paris: Presses Universitaires de France, 1993), 54.

19. Didier Maus, *Les Grands Textes de la pratique institutionelle de la Ve République* (Paris: La Documentation Française, 1992), 28.

20. Cited in Ehrmann and Schain, *Politics in France*, 290.

21. Andrews, *Presidential Government*, 18.

22. Ibid., 21.

23. Ibid., 28; see also Olivier Duhamel, *La Gauche et la Ve République* (Paris: Presses Universitaires de France, 1980), 154.

24. Andrews, *Presidential Government*, 26.

25. Philip M. Williams and Martin Harrison, *Politics and Society in de Gaulle's Republic* (New York: Anchor, 1980), 30.

26. Roland Sadoun, "De Gaulle et les sondages," in *De Gaulle en son siè-*

cle, vol. 1; Dans la mémoire des hommes et des peuples (Paris: La Documentation française/Plon, 1991), 321.

27. Maus, *Les Grands Texts*, 28.

28. Jérôme Jaffré, "L'enquête d'opinion de la SOFRES," in *De Gaulle en son siècle, vol.* 1:327.

29. Maurice Duverger, *La Ve République* (Paris: Presses Universitaires de France, 1963), 18.

30. For excellent examples drawn from the case of health care, see Ellen M. Immergut, *Health Politics: Interests and Institutions in Western Europe* (New York: Cambridge University Press, 1992), chap. 3.

31. Andrews, *Presidential Government*, 128–30.

32. See Jean-Louis Quermonne, *Le Gouvernement de la France sous la Ve Républicque*, 2d ed. (Paris: Dalloz, 1983), 182. The notion of a reserved domain seemed implicit in many of de Gaulle's statements and actions, and the concept has certainly continued to shape perceptions of presidential power. However, de Gaulle himself clearly felt that the primacy of the presidency legitimately extended to domestic affairs as well. See Ezra Suleiman, "Presidential Government in France," in *Presidents and Prime Ministers*, ed. Richard Rose and Ezra Suleiman (Washington, D.C.: American Enterprise Institute, 1980), 113.

33. François Mitterrand, *Le Coup d'etat permanent* (Paris: Juillard, 1984; 1964), 98.

34. Duhamel, *La Gauche*, 172–74.

35. Williams and Harrison, *Politics and Society*, 37; Duverger, *La Ve République*, 16.

36. See Duverger, *La Ve République*, 57–58; Andrews, *Presidential Government*, 135–38.

37. Williams and Harrison, *Politics and Society*, 42.

38. Lacouture, *De Gaulle*, 3:569.

39. Duhamel, *La Gauche*, 178.

40. Charles de Gaulle, *Memoirs of Hope* (New York: Simon and Schuster, 1971), 314–15. De Gaulle's conception of his special relationship with the regime's institutions is developed in detail in his memoirs. One chapter begins with the assertion: "The new institutions were in place. From the summit of the State, how was I to shape them? To a large extent it was incumbent upon me to do so. For the reasons which had led me to this position, and the conditions in which I exercised it, did not derive from written texts. . . . If I had now assumed the country's highest office, it was because . . . I had come to be accepted as its final refuge. This was a fact which, alongside the literal provisions of the Constitution, had inevitably to be taken into account. Whatever interpretation might be given to such and such an Article, it was in any case to de Gaulle that Frenchmen turned. It was from him that they expected the solution of their problems" (270–71).

41. See Alec Stone, *The Birth of Judicial Politics in France: The Constitu-*

tional Council in Comparative Perspective (New York: Oxford University Press, 1992), 60–66. See also Louis Favoreu and Loic Philip, eds., *Les Grandes décisions du conseil constitutionnel*, 4th ed. (Paris: Sirey, 1986), 172–83.

42. Duhamel, *La Gauche*, pt. 2.

43. See Stanley Hoffmann, "Paradoxes of the French Political Community," in Hoffmann et al., *In Search of France* (New York: Harper, 1963), 96–97.

44. See Jaroslaw Kurski, *Lech Walesa: Democrat or Dictator*, trans. Peter Obst (Boulder: Westview, 1993), 100.

45. De Gaulle was fully aware that opinion polls had long shown direct election of the president to be popular with the public, however much it was opposed by members of parliament. Furthermore, support has increased dramatically since it was put into effect: in 1990, 88 percent of the public approved it, including even 64 percent of communist voters. See Jaffré, "L'enquête d'opinion," 329.

46. Williams and Harrison, *Politics and Society*, 48; Frank L. Wilson, *French Political Parties under the Fifth Republic* (New York: Praeger, 1982), 171.

47. Wilson, *French Political Parties*, 170–71.

48. Françoise Dreyfus, "The Control of Governments," in *Developments in French Politics*, ed. Peter A. Hall, Jack Hayward, and Howard Machin (New York: St. Martin's, 1990), 138.

49. See Wilson, *French Political Parties*, 174.

50. Maurice Duverger, "A New Political System Model: Semipresidential Government," in Lijphart, *Parliamentary versus Presidential Government*; Matthew S. Shugart and John M. Carey, *Presidents and Assemblies: Constitutional Design and Electoral Dynamics* (New York: Cambridge University Press, 1992), 155. The Schugart and Carey ratings, based on an analysis of strictly formal powers, give the French president a total power score of only 4, compared to 11 for the U.S. president and 8 for Finland's president.

51. See Duhamel, *Le Pouvoir*, 71.

52. Duverger, "A New Political System Model," 145.

53. See Duhamel, *La Gauche*, pt. 2; see also R. W. Johnson, *The Long March of the French Left* (New York: St. Martin's, 1981).

54. See Olivier Duhamel and Jean-Luc Parodi, eds., *La Constitution de la Cinquième République* (Paris: Presses de la Fondation Nationale des Sciences Politiques, 1985), esp. chapters by Jean Baudouin (on the communists) and Serge Sur (on the centrists).

55. On the Austrian case, see Shugart and Carey, *Presidents and Assemblies*, 72.

56. Suleiman, "Presidential Government," 117.

57. Ibid., 110.

58. See Olivier Duhamel, "The Fifth Republic under François Mitterrand," in *The Mitterrand Experiment*, ed. George Ross, Stanley Hoffmann,

and Sylvia Malzacher (New York: Oxford University Press, 1987), 143.

59. In 1985, Mitterrand's government did replace the original Gaullist electoral system for the National Assembly with a variant of proportional representation, but that system was used only once (in 1986) before the old system was reinstituted by Chirac's cohabitation government.

60. See John T. S. Keeler and Alec Stone, "Judicial-Political Confrontation in Mitterrand's France," in Ross et al., *Mitterrand Experiment*.

61. Based on a scheme that breaks presidential "resources" into seven categories, Olivier Duhamel rates the power of Mitterrand in this period as 17, compared to de Gaulle's 20 and Giscard's 9. See "Président, premier ministre, gouvernement, les différent cas de figure," 12, paper prepared for the Conference on Presidential France, 1962–1992, New York University Institute of French Studies, Dec. 4–5, 1992.

62. Ehrmann and Schain, *Politics in France*, 242–43; Duhamel, *Le Pouvoir*, 41.

63. Maurice Duverger, *Bréviaire de la cohabitation* (Paris: Presses Universitaires de France, 1986), 36–38.

64. Françoise Giroud, *La Comédie du pouvoir* (Paris: Fayard, 1977), 234–35.

65. Duhamel, *Le Pouvoir*, 41.

66. See the citation of Claude Emeri in ibid., 42.

67. According to the constitution's original provisions, only the president of the republic, the prime minister, or the president of either assembly could send bills on appeal to the council.

68. See Stone, *Birth of Judicial Politics*; Louis Favoreu, *La Politique saisie par le droit: alternances, cohabitation et conseil constitutionnel* (Paris: Economica, 1988); Léo Hamon, *Les Juges de la loi, Naissance et rôle d'un contre-pouvoir: le Conseil Constitutionnel* (Paris: Fayard, 1987).

69. See Keeler, "Executive Power."

70. Using the rating system cited in note 61, Duhamel, "President, premier ministre, gouvernement," scores the power of "Mitterrand III" as 11, versus 9 for Giscard.

71. See Duhamel, *Le Pouvoir*, 166–67.

72. Ehrmann and Schain, *Politics in France*, 243.

73. Lijphart, introduction to *Parliamentary versus Presidential Government*, 8.

74. The term *premier-presidentialism* is taken from Shugart and Carey, *Presidents and Assemblies*, 23.

75. Cited in Wright, *Government and Politics of France*, 71.

76. See ibid., 70–74.

77. Ibid., 70.

78. Jacques Chirac stated after the March elections that this round of cohabitation should not be "a sharing of power with a declining socialism," but rather—even in the foreign policy and defense area—"the full exercise of responsibility by the new majority." See *Economist*, Apr. 3, 1993, 47.

79. See *Le Figaro*, Mar. 29, 1993. Meanwhile, Chirac apparently expected to exercise informally a great deal of influence over Balladur and his government. It has been reported, for example, that he is connected to the special interministerial telephone network, through which he can be in constant contact with those wielding formal power; see *Le Monde*, Apr. 24 and 28, 1993.

80. R. Kent Weaver and Bert A. Rockman, "When and How Do Institutions Matter?" in *Do Institutions Matter? Government Capabilities in the United States and Abroad*, ed. Weaver and Rockman (Washington, D.C.: Brookings, 1993), 446.

81. See A. Jeyaratnam Wilson, "The Gaullist System in Asia: The Constitution of Sri Lanka," in Lijphart, *Parliamentary versus Presidential Government*, 156. On the Polish case, see Stepan and Suleiman, "French Fifth Republic," 403. On the Ukraine case, see Article 27 of the president's proposed "Constitutional Law of Ukraine" (circulated in typescript in Kiev, Apr. 1995).

82. See Georges Vedel, "Rétrofictions: Si de Gaulle avait perdu en 1962 . . . Si Alain Poher avait gagné en 1969." in Duhamel and Parodi, *La Constitution*.

83. For an assessment of the impact of the electoral system, see Ehrmann and Schain, *Politics in France*, 209–10; see also de Gaulle's views on the electoral system in *Memoirs of Hope*, 34–35.

84. See Williams, *Crisis and Compromise*, 254; Wright, *Government and Politics of France*, 1–3.

85. Before 1962, as Hoffmann notes, "Paradoxes of the French Political Community," 94, the "executive stability" provided by de Gaulle's presidency was not "enough to bring back to the government all that sense of duration, that broad perspective of time for its operations and calculations, which so many critics of the Fourth Republic had looked forward to," and "the dizzying turnover of individual ministers" was "about as great as it was during the cabinet crises of the Fourth Republic."

86. Linz also makes this point in "Presidential or Parliamentary Democracy?" 51.

87. See Keeler, "Executive Power."

88. See Wright, *Government and Politics of France*, 70–74; and the comments of Chirac's chief foreign policy adviser, Pierre Lellouche, in *Economist*, Apr. 3, 1993.

Chapter 5
Gamarra, Hybrid Presidentialism in Bolivia

1. See Scott Mainwaring, "Presidentialism and Multipartism: The Difficult Combination," *Comparative Political Studies* 26 (1993): 198–228; Arturo Valenzuela, "Party Politics and the Crisis of Presidentialism in Chile: A Proposal for a Parliamentary Form of Government," in *The Failure of Presiden-*

tial Democracy, ed. Juan J. Linz and Arturo Valenzuela (Baltimore: Johns Hopkins University Press, 1994); Bolivar Lamonier and Dieter Nolen, *Presidencialismo ou Parlamentarismo* (São Paulo: Edicoes Loyola).

2. Alfonso Ferrufino, Jose Ortiz Mercado, and Juan Cristobal Urioster, *Parlamentarismo o Presidencialismo? Propuesta para el Debate* (La Paz, Bolivia: Fundacion Milenio, 1995).

3. In 1994, this provision was changed to a congressional runoff between the top two finishers.

4. See Juan J. Linz, "Democracy, Presidential or Parliamentary: Does It Make a Difference?" in Linz and Valenzuela, *Failure of Presidential Democracy.*

5. See Eduardo Gamarra, "Political Stability, Democratization, and the Bolivian National Congress," Ph.D. diss., University of Pittsburgh; James M. Malloy and Eduardo Gamarra, *Revolution and Reaction: Bolivia, 1964–1985* (New Brunswick, N.J.: Transaction, 1988).

6. The first "constitutional coup" came in November 1979, when a congressional-military plot overthrew the interim "transactional" government of Walter Guevara Arce, which had been elected by Congress in August of that same year. In brief, the plotters expected a military coup, headed by Colonel Alberto Natusch Busch, to be followed by a congressional vote of no confidence for President Guevara. The plotters then expected the legislature to "elect" Natusch as president. Similar plots and variations on the theme were common between 1982 and 1985 against the government of Hernán Siles Zuazo, which was elected by Congress in October 1982. For the details of constitutional coup plots, see Gamarra, "Political Stability, Democratization, and the Bolivian National Congress."

7. For a similar argument, see Malloy and Gamarra, *Revolution and Reaction*: and James M. Malloy, "Democracy, Economic Crisis, and the Problem of Governance: The Case of Bolivia," paper prepared for the Fifteenth Annual Congress of the Latin American Studies Association, Miami, December 4–6, 1989.

8. Elsewhere, I have made the argument that, by allowing the proliferation of political parties and alliances, electoral laws undermined and even directly contradicted the nature of Bolivia's presidential system as established by the 1967 constitution. See Gamarra, "Political Stability, Democratization, and the Bolivian National Congress."

9. See Rein Taagepera and Matthew Shugart, *Seats and Votes: The Effects and Determinants of Electoral Systems* (New Haven: Yale University Press, 1989).

10. The 1979 reforms produced some questionable results. To get elected in La Paz, for example, a deputy required approximately seventy thousand votes. In the remote department of Pando, a deputy required only sixty-five hundred votes. See Gamarra, "Political Stability, Democratization, and the Bolivian National Congress," 189, for a discussion of the 1979 electoral reforms.

11. Party undiscipline was exacerbated by the high stakes each time a president was elected. Individual members of minority parties cut deals with those alliances having the greatest possibility of emerging victorious. Such votes were often rewarded with prominent posts in the executive branch or high-ranking leadership positions in the National Congress. My interviews with several deputies and senators over the past several years confirm that key swing votes are often bought and sold.

12. For an expansion on this, see Gamarra, "Political Stability, Democratization, and the Bolivian National Congress"; Malloy and Gamarra, *Revolution and Reaction.*

13. The term *salida,* or "way out," comes from my interview with a member of the National Congress in November 1984. When asked what the solution was to an impasse between the opposition-controlled legislature and Siles Zuazo's executive, the answer was, "in Bolivia there are no solutions, only *salidas."* Mainwaring and Linz note that presidential systems lack the mechanisms to overcome crises such as the one faced by Siles in October and November 1984. See Scott Mainwaring, "Presidentialism in Latin America," *Latin American Research Review* 25 (1990): 157–79; Juan Linz, "The Perils of Presidentialism," *Journal of Democracy* 1 (1990): 51–69. The Bolivian National Congress could have impeached Siles; however, the system would not likely have survived. Ways out of these impasses were always innovative but, also, inevitably unconstitutional. See Herbert Muller and Flavio Machicado, eds., *El diálogo para la democracia* (La Paz: Quipus, 1987), for a transcript of the negotiations that led to the end of the Siles government.

14. Bánzer had to control his supporters in the ADN, however, who had mobilized to take over the legislative palace to prevent the swearing in of Paz Estenssoro.

15. Public employment reductions, however, came mainly from the firing of mine workers, not of middle-class bureaucrats. For an analysis of the privatization objectives of the NPE, see Eduardo Gamarra, "The Privatization Debate in Bolivia," in *Privatization and Deregulation in Global Perspective,* ed. Dennis Gayle and Jonathan Goodrich (New York: Quorum, 1990).

16. See Article 111 of the Bolivian constitution. This is the main reason that Siles Zuazo was unable to launch a state of siege to control unrest between 1982 and 1985.

17. Because the MNR had seized upon many of the elements of ADN's economic stabilization program, Bánzer was put into an untenable situation. He could either oppose the NPE for purely political reasons or support a program designed by members of his own economic team. For an extension of this analysis, see Catherine Conaghan, James M. Malloy, and Luis Abugattas, "Business and Boys: The Origins of Neo Liberalism in the Central Andes," *Latin American Research Review* 25 (1990): 3–30.

18. For a similar analysis, see ibid.

19. Throughout the three-year duration of the pact, members of the ADN

and the MNR complained about the alliance. MNR militants were upset by the loss of sources of patronage and the perceived loss of the party's traditional populist electorate. ADN members, in turn, did not trust MNR's promises of support for Bánzer's presidential bid in 1989. Weekly meetings of representatives from each party resolved many of these issues. But in the main, the role and presence of both Bánzer and Paz Estenssoro prevented party discipline from breaking down earlier.

20. See Malloy, "Democracy, Economic Crisis, and the Problem of Governance."

21. The situation was made worse by the fact that the MNR had surrendered government posts to the MIR in return for the MIR vote in Congress for Paz Estenssoro. After the signing of the pact, the government was forced to generate patronage to feed the demands of three party organizations.

22. For a similar analysis, see Malloy, "Democracy, Economic Crisis, and the Problem of Governance."

23. See René A. Mayorga, "Tendencias y problemas de la consolidación de la democracia en Bolivia," paper prepared for the Fifteenth Annual Congress of the Latin American Studies Association, Miami, December 4–6, 1989. Under the previous (1956) law, even a party that had not obtained a "simple quota" of votes (defined as total valid votes divided by district magnitude) could participate in the allocation of seats remaining after the allocation of quotas. Those seats were allocated by largest remainders, a procedure that tends to favor the smaller parties when the quota is the simple quota. The 1986 law requires that a party receive a quota in order to be eligible for remainder seats.

24. The MIR's votes were not necessary to impose a state of siege. The MIR did not, however, join any interpellation maneuvers, which could have threatened the government's attempt to defeat organized labor's strikes.

25. The role of Sawyer and Miller, a public relations firm based in Washington, D.C., was crucial in the decision to break the pact. It was also responsible for the tone of the campaign.

26. The fact that, together, the MIR and the ADN controlled the electoral court proved to be the key to the exclusion of the MRN. Charges and countercharges of fraud were rampant. In the end, the three parties pledged to the Catholic Church that the first priority of the new government would be to reform the electoral law.

27. This statement was mainly aimed at the MNR for its violation of the alternability addendum to the Pacto por la Democracia.

28. Instead, the congressional leadership dominated by the ADN-MIR coalition declared a recess, which lasted for most of the ninety-day state of siege. Because the recess was approved without a quorum, it correctly gave rise to charges of unconstitutionality.

29. Members were elected by the Chamber of Deputies from a list submitted by the Senate. Members of the Supreme Court are elected for ten-year terms.

30. Tensions with the Supreme Court began when Paz Zamora, despite the absence of an extradition treaty, turned over to the U.S. Drug Enforcement Administration two former officials of the García Meza government accused of drug trafficking—Colonel Luis Arce Gómez and Herlan Echevarría. For an analysis of this conflict, see Eduardo Gamarra, *The System of Justice in Bolivia: An Institutional Analysis* (Miami: Florida International University, Center for the Administration of Justice, 1991).

31. The government's bargaining leverage was undermined by the naming of retired Colonel Faustino Rico Toro, whom the DEA suspected of ties to the narcotics industry, to head the Fuerzas Especiales de Lucha Contra el Narcotráfico, Bolivia's principal counternarcotics force. In the scandal that followed, the MNR spearheaded efforts to reduce Paz Zamora's term by calling for early elections. In 1995, Rico Toro was extradited to the United States; in a deal for a reduced prison term, he pleaded guilty to charges of narcotics trafficking.

32. The only party that has shared in the patronage distribution is Conciencia de Patria (CONDEPA), led by the populist radio and television station owner Carlos Palenque. CONDEPA's share came because it carried the department of La Paz in the 1989 elections.

33. According to one report, the Acuerdo Patriótico government increased the public payroll by twenty thousand since August 1989. See comments delivered by Juan Cristóbal Soruco at the conference, "Democracia y Problemas de Governabilidad en Bolivia y América Latina," sponsored by CEBEM and ILDIS, La Paz, May 16–18, 1991.

34. The MNR proposed a second round between the two top candidates as an alternative to the congressional negotions. Because the ADN and the MIR controlled the electoral courts, the MNR also demanded the establishment of an "apolitical" electoral court.

35. See Linz, "Democracy, Presidential or Parliamentary"; Mainwaring, "Presidentialism and Multipartism."

36. See Eduardo Gamarra and James Malloy, "The Patrimonial Dynamics of Party Politics in Bolivia, in *Building Democratic Institutions: Party Systems in Latin America*, ed. Scott Mainwaring and Timothy Scully (Stanford: Stanford University Press, 1995).

37. For an excellent discussion of Carlos Palenque's rise to power and prominence, see Joaquín Saravia and Jach'a Uru Godofredo Sandóval, *¿La esperanza de un pueblo?* (La Paz: ILDIS-CEP, 1991).

38. This analysis draws heavily on a presentation delivered by Carlos Toranzo at the seminar, "The Future of the Bolivian Left," sponsored by ILDIS, La Paz, May 20, 1991. The U.S. embassy has been the most nervous critic of Max Fernández, accusing him of making his fortune from cocaine trafficking. In 1991, however, the United States lifted proscriptions on Fernández's beer entering American ports.

39. For an extension of this analysis, see Gamarra, "System of Justice in Bolivia."

40. Since 1989 at least three such groups have made their appearance in Bolivia. The first, Zárate Wilka, has all but disappeared, owing to the government's crackdown following the May 1989 assassination of two young U.S. Mormon missionaries. A second group, the Ejército de Liberación Nacional—Nestor Paz Zamora, which boasted links to Peru's Tupac Amaru group, was dismantled after the kidnapping and subsequent assassination of Jorge Londsdale, a prominent businessman. The third group, the Ejército Guerrillero Tupac Katari, has been more resilient; it has resorted only to occasional bombings of electric utility stations and the like.

41. Under the terms of the MNR-UCS pact, Fernandez's followers secured one ministry, two undersecretary posts, two embassies, the presidency of one regional development corporation, and the first vice presidencies of the Chamber of Deputies and the Senate.

42. The MBL was promised one ministry, key congressional posts, and at least one embassy. Aranibar and the MBL extracted a high price, considering that this party won only 5 percent of the vote. Subsequently, Aranibar was named minister of foreign affairs.

43. In theory, these shares would be handled by pension fund administrators on behalf of the estimated 3.2 million Bolivians, who would then apply their shares toward a retirement fund. An August 1994 constitutional reform lowered the voting age from twenty-one to eighteen.

44. The UCS performed extremely well in the 1995 municipal elections. Johnny Fernández, the beer baron's eldest son, won the Santa Cruz mayor's race.

45. Political parties were not the only ones facing charges of egregious corruption. Perhaps the most serious was the allegation of corruption against two members of the Supreme Court. This crisis began in mid-1993, when relatives of a member of the court solicited a bribe from Antonio Ibarra, a former official of the Nicaraguan government who was facing extradition procedures. With U.S. assistance, the Bolivian police recorded the solicitation conversation and indicted the Supreme Court justices. In June 1994, in a Senate trial, the two justices were found guilty, sentenced to two years in prison, and barred from ever again holding public office.

46. The accusations detailed by the FELCN are reported in Eduardo Gamarra, *Entre la Droga y la Democracia* (La Paz: ILDIS, 1994).

Chapter 6
von Mettenheim, Brazilian Presidentialism

1. Of course, differences matter. A more in-depth analysis of Brazilian and U.S. presidentialism would have to consider more carefully the legacies of military rule in Brazil, the lack of direct presidential elections until 1989, the interpenetrated character of Brazilian state and society, and the new role of mass media.

2. For recent criticism of presidential institutions in Latin America, see

Juan Linz and Arturo Valenzuela, eds., *The Failure of Presidential Democracy in Latin America* (Baltimore: Johns Hopkins University Press, 1994); Scott Mainwaring and Matthew Shugart, eds., *Presidentialism and Democracy in Latin America* (Cambridge: Cambridge University Press, forthcoming). The classic statement of the responsible party system model is "Toward a More Responsible Two-Party System," *American Political Science Review* 44, suppl. (1950): Appendix, 1–96.

3. The debate between Burnham and Converse contain the most important references; see Walter D. Burnham, *The Current Crisis in American Politics* (New York: Oxford University Press, 1982); Philip E. Converse, "Change in the American Universe," in *The Human Meaning of Social Change*, ed. Angus Campbell and Phillip E. Converse (New York: Russell Sage, 1973). Also see Paul Kleppner, *The Cross of Culture: A Social Analysis of Midwestern Politics, 1850–1900* (New York: Free Press, 1970). On differences between European and American political development, see Samuel Huntington, *Political Order in Changing Societies* (New Haven: Yale University Press, 1968), chap. 2.

4. Weber makes this argument in two essays: "Politics as a Vocation," in *From Max Weber, Essays in Sociology*, ed. Hans Gerth and C. Wright Mills (New York: Oxford University Press, 1946); and Weber, "Parliament and Government in a Reconstructed Germany," in Weber, *Economy and Society*, vol. 2 (Berkeley: University of California Press, 1978). See also M. I. Ostrogorski, *Democracy and the Organization of Political Parties in the United States and Great Britain*, abridged (Garden City, N.J.: Doubleday, 1964); and James Bryce, *The American Commonwealth* (New York: Macmillan, 1907).

5. William N. Chambers and Walter D. Burnham, *The American Party Systems: Stages of Political Development* (New York: Oxford University Press, 1967).

6. Burnham, *Current Crisis in American Politics*.

7. Theodore J. Lowi, "Party, Policy, and Constitution in America," in Chambers and Burnham, *American Party Systems*.

8. Samuel Hays, "Political Parties and the Community-Society Continuum," in Chambers and Burnham, *American Party Systems*.

9. Hans Daalder, "Parties, Elites, and Political Developments in Western Europe," in *Political Parties and Political Development*, ed. Joseph LaPalombara and Myron Weiner (Princeton: Princeton University Press, 1966). On party building after the establishment of modern state bureaucracies, see Martin Shefter, "Party and Patronage: Germany, England, and Italy," *Politics and Society* 7 (1977): 403–51.

10. Daalder, "Parties, Elites, and Political Development," 46, argues: "In France and Germany powerful bureaucracies were built up as social control mechanisms long before nonbureaucratic social groups had learned to use the weapons of political organization to secure influence. Ever since, parties have had difficulty in obtaining full control. . . . In Britain, on the other hand, the buildup of the modern civil service occurred after nonofficial so-

cial groups were securely in political control; ever since, the civil service has loyally accepted control by party ministers."

11. See Sartori's preface to the Brazilian edition of his *Parties and Party Systems:* Giovanni Sartori, *Partidos e Sistemas Partidarios* (Rio de Janeiro: Zahar, 1982). Maria Souza also argues that "one cannot speak of party system institutionalization when the power of party groups emerges or is exercised exclusively through interaction with bureaucratic agencies, without an institutional site for parties to acquire a broader collective reality." See her *Estado e Partidos Politicos no Brasil: 1930–1964* (São Paulo: Alfa Omega, 1976), 151.

12. Douglas Chalmers, "Parties and Society in Latin America," in *Friends, Followers, and Factions,* ed. Steffen W. Schmidt et al. (Berkeley: University of California Press, 1977), 418; emphasis added.

13. On the concept of realignment in American electoral history, see Walter D. Burnham, *Critical Elections and the Mainsprings of American Politics* (New York: Norton, 1970); James Sundquist, *Dynamics of the Party System: Alignment and Realignment of Political Parties in the United Sates,* 2d ed. (Washington, D.C.: Brookings, 1983).

14. Michael Connif, *Urban Politics in Brazil: The Rise of Populism, 1925–1945* (Pittsburgh: Pittsburgh University Press, 1982); Gino Germani, *Authoritarianism, Fascism, and National Populism* (New Brunswick, N.J.: Transaction, 1978).

15. The clearest statement of Latin American populism as a multiclass front against imperialism can be found in the works of Víctor R. Haya de la Torre. See his *El Anti-Imperialismo y el APRA,* 4th ed. (Lima: Amauta, 1972). It is cited and discussed in Fernando H. Cardoso, *Autoritarismo e Democratização* (São Paulo: Paz e Terra, 1975), 167–171.

16. Patronage is a classic theme in Brazilian political studies. See Richard Graham, *Patronage and Politics in Nineteenth-Century Brazil* (Stanford: Stanford University Press, 1990).

17. Their central works on this subject are Oliveira Vianna, *Instituicões Politicas Brasieiras* (Rio de Janeiro: Editora National, 1954); Paula Beiguelman, *Formação Politica do Brasil* (São Paulo: Pioneiro, 1973).

18. The current description of Old Republic politics as *politica dos governadores* (governor's politics) focuses on the emergence of specific electoral and party practices that linked local and regional political machines with national politics. On the concept of *politica dos governadores,* see Paula Beiguelman, "A Primeira Republica no Periodo de 1891 a 1909," appendix to *Pequenos Estudos de Ciencia Politica* (São Paulo: Pioneiro, 1967); Maria C. C. Souza, " O Processo Politico-Partidario na Primeira Republica," in *Brasil em Perspectiva,* ed. Carlos Mota (São Paulo: Difel, 1969).

19. On the influence of American federalism in the 1891 Brazilian consitution, see Souza, "O Processo Politico-Partidario na Primeira Republica."

20. On the spoils system from 1945 to 1964, see Barry Ames, "The Congressional Connection: The Structure of Politics and the Distribution of

Public Expenditures in Brazil's Competitive Period," *Comparative Politics* 19 (1987): 147–71.

21. See the following reviews of theories about democratic breakdown in 1964: Youssef Cohen, "Democracy from Above: The Political Origins of Military Dictatorship in Brazil," *World Politics* 40 (1987): 30–54; Bolivar Lamounier and Rachel Mendguello, *Partidos Politicos e Consolidação Democratica: O Caso Brasileiro* (São Paulo: Brasiliense, 1986); Fabio W. Reis, "O Economico, O Institucional, e o Politico na Literatura Brasileira Recente," appendix to *Politica e Racionalidade*, Special Edition 37 (Belo Horizonte: Revista Brasileira de Estudos Politicos, 1984).

22. Souza, *Estado e Partidos Politicos no Brasil*, 140.

23. Souza argues that, for much of the postwar period, party politicians were kept out of state policy making dealing with core questions of redistribution. Because Getulio Vargas's Estado Novo (1937–45) centralized power in ministries and secretaries responsible only to executives on the federal and state level, legislators and party politicians dealt primarily with policies of regulation and distribution. This isolation of core questions of redistribution among centralized ministries in the executive meant that party elites gained little experience in core policy areas. Instead, they developed irresponsible populist discourses and patronage practices. Souza, *Estado e Partidos Politicos no Brasil*.

24. Both Souza and Olavo Brasil Jr. agree that the critical pre-1964 trend in elections is a shift not to minor parties but to party alliances of the most diverse sort. See Souza, *Estado e Partidos Politicos no Brasil*, chap. 4; Olavo Brasil Jr., "the Brazilian Multi-Party System: A Case for Contextual Rationality" (Ph.D. diss., University of Michigan, 1980).

25. Souza, *Estado e Partidos Politicos no Brasil*, 144.

26. Ibid., 140.

27. Lamounier and Meneguello, *Partidos Politicos e Consolidação Democratica*.

28. On the impact of Progressive-era reforms on the organization of American parties, see Burnham, *Critical Elections and the Mainsprings of American Politics*, 74–90.

29. See Guillermo O'Donnell, Philippe Schmitter, and Laurence Whitehead, eds., *Transitions from Authoritarian Rule: Southern Europe and Latin America* (Baltimore: Johns Hopkins University Press, 1986), conclusion.

30. For a review of the transition from military to civilian rule, see Thomas Skidmore, *The Politics if Military Rule in Brazil, 1964–1985* (New York: Oxford University Press, 1988).

31. Note Weber's analysis of the organization of parties during the German transition from empire to democracy: "In the beginning there were new kinds of party apparatuses emerging. First, there were amateur apparatuses. They are especially often represented by students of various universities, who tell a man to whom they ascribe leadership qualities: we want to do the necessary work for you; carry it out. Secondly, there are the appa-

ratuses of businessmen. But, both apparatuses were fast-emerging bubbles, which swiftly vanished again." "Politics as a Vocation," 113.

32. Sociologist Fernando Henrique Cardoso became widely known for a work he coauthored in 1969 (English translation, *Dependency and Development in Latin America*, Berkeley: University of California Press, 1979). Cardoso subsequently founded the influential independent social science research institute CEBRAP (Centro Brasileiro de Analise e Planejamento) in São Paulo and entered politics through university associations and by forging alliances across new opposition groups in the 1978 senate race.

33. On debates in Brazilian electoral sociology, see Kurt von Mettenheim, *The Brazilian Voter: Mass Politics in Democratic Transition* (Pittsburgh: University of Pittsburgh Press, 1995).

34. Senator Fernando Henrique Cardoso, interviewed by author, Nov. 4, 1986.

35. On civil society empowerment, see Alfred Stepan, "State Power and the Strength of Civil Society in the Southern Cone of Latin America," in *Bringing the State Back In*, ed. Peter Evans et al. (Cambridge: Cambridge University Press, 1985).

36. See Eli Diniz, *Voto e Maquina Politica: Patronagem e Clientelismo no Rio de Janeiro* (Rio de Janeiro: Paz e Terra, 1982); Maria D. Kinzo, *An Opposition Party in an Authoritarian Regime: The Case of the MDB (Movimento Democratico Brasileiro) in Brazil, 1966–1979* (New York: St. Martins, 1989); Teresa Caldeira, "Electoral Struggles in a Neighborhood on the Periphery of São Paulo," *Politics and Society* 15 (1986): 43–66.

37. See Bolivar Lamounier, "Authoritarian Brazil Revisited: The Impact of Elections on the Abertura," in *Democratizing Brazil*, ed. Alfred Stepan (New York: Oxford University Press, 1989).

38. Juan Linz, "The Transition from an Authoritarian Regime to Democracy in Spain: Some Thoughts for Brazilians," unpublished manuscript, Yale University, 1983.

39. On the 1985 elections, see Bolivar Lamounier, ed., *1985: O Voto em São Paulo* (São Paulo: Idesp, 1986).

40. The 1932 electoral code was based on Assis Brasil, *Democracia Representativa* (Rio de Janeiro: Imprensa Nacional, 1931).

41. In comparison to this rapid realignment of party elites during the transition from military to civilian rule, the concept of realignment suggests that electoral change in the United States trickles down from presidential elections through state and local politics over decades. See Sundquist, *Dynamics of the Party System*, 11.

42. Senator Fernando Henrique Cardoso, interviewed by author, Nov. 4, 1986.

43. More than 85 percent of registered voters viewed four televised debates, while two hours of party campaign programs were broadcast every day on prime-time television and radio for two months prior to November 15 and for two for weeks preceding the December 15 runoff election.

44. For analyses of the impeachment process, see Kurt Weyland, "The Rise and Fall of President Collor and Its impact on Brazilian Democracy," *Journal of Interamerican Studies and World Affairs* 35, (1993): 1–37.

45. Estimates from the Fundação Instituto de Pesquisas Economicas da Universidade de São Paulo and DIEESE (Departamento Intersindical de Estatistica e Estudos Socioeconomicos) are reported in *Folha de S. Paulo*, Mar. 26, 1995.

46. On electoral stability and change in Europe, see S. Bartolini and P. Mair, *Identity, Competition, and Electoral Availability* (Cambridge: Cambridge University Press, 1990).

47. Weber discusses the passive element in the organization of American politics in "Politics as a Vocation," 113; Weber, Parliament and Government in a Reconstructed Germany," 1398–402.

48. Compare Weber's analysis with the exchange between Walter D. Burnham, Phillip Converse, and Jerold Rusk, *American Political Science Review* 68 (1974): 1002–57.

49. Weber, "Politics as a Vocation," 108.

Chapter 7
Bunce, Presidents and the Transition in Eastern Europe

1. In this chapter Eastern Europe refers to that part of Europe that, in the cold war period, was referred to as Eastern Europe and the Soviet Union. During the state socialist period there were nine countries in this region; today there are twenty-seven. Needless to say, this chapter does not deal with all of these cases. Instead, I focus primarily on major themes common to the postsocialist experience and, for illustration, on Poland, Hungary, Romania, Bulgaria, Croatia, and Russia.

2. For two insightful analyses of differences between Eastern and Western Europe in their historical development (economic, political, and social), see Robert Brenner, "Economic Backwardness in Eastern Europe in Light of Developments in the West"; Gale Stokes, "The Social Origins of East European Politics," both in *Origins of Backwardness in Eastern Europe*, ed. Daniel Chirot (Berkeley: University of California Press, 1989).

3. Valerie Bunce, "Leaving Socialism: A Transition to Democracy?" *Contention: Debates in Society, Culture, and Science* 3 (1993): 35–47; Bunce, "Comparing East and South" *Journal of Democracy* (1995): 87–100.

4. There is a certain irony in the similarities between this perspective and the perspectives of the communist period. A popular joke during the communist period was, We know where we will be in the future. We just don't know where we are now.

5. On the concept of democratic consolidation, see, for instance, John Higley and Richard Gunther, eds., *Elites and Democratic Consolidation in Latin America and Southern Europe* (New York: Cambridge University Press, 1992).

6. See, for instance, Guiseppe Di Palma, *To Craft Democracies: An Essay on Democratic Transitions* (Berkeley: University of California Press, 1990); Juan Linz, "The Perils of Presidentialism," *Journal of Democracy* 1 (1990): 51–69; Alfred Stepan and Cindy Skatch, "Constitutional Frameworks and Democratic Consolidation: Parliamentarism versus Presidentialism," *World Politics* 46 (1993): 1–22. This is not to argue, however, that institutional design is the central concern of all theorists of democratic transitions. For example, institutions play no role whatsoever in a recent book on the transition to democracy in Western Europe and Latin America. See Dietrich Rueschemeyer, Evelyne Huber Stephens, and John D. Stephens, *Capitalist Development and Democracy* (Chicago: University of Chicago Press, 1992).

7. Scott Mainwaring, "Presidentialism, Multiparty Systems, and Democracy: The Difficult Combination," paper prepared for the Hungarian-American Roundtable in Political Science, Budapest, Dec. 15–18, 1991, p. 1.

8. The literature on these issues is quite large. See, for instance, Arend Lijphart, ed., *Parliamentary versus Presidential Government* (New York: Oxford University Press, 1992); Mainwaring, "Presidentialism, Multiparty systems, and Democracy"; Ronald Rogowski, "Governmental Institutions and Economic Performance in the OECD Countries, 1960–1988," paper prepared for the Hungarian-American Roundtable in Political Science, Budapest, Dec. 15–18, 1991; Linz, "Perils of Presidentialism"; Arend Lijphart, "Constitutional Choices for New Democracies," *Journal of Democracy* 2 (1991): 72–84. For arguments questioning whether specific institutional designs have such consequent political and economic effects, see Adam Przeworski, *Democracy and the Market: Political and Economic Reforms in Eastern Europe and Latin America* (Cambridge: Cambridge University Press, 1991).

9. Linz, "Perils of Presidentialism." Also see Scott Mainwaring, "Presidentialism in Latin America"; Fred W. Riggs, "Presidentialism: A Problematic Regime-Type," both in *Parliamentary versus Presidential Government*, ed. Arend Lijphart (New York: Oxford University Press, 1992).

10. This argument is made in Przeworski, *Democracy and the Market*. This argument rests, more generally, on John Rawls, *A Theory of Justice* (Cambridge: Harvard University Press, 1971).

11. This is not to argue, however, that those countries with completely new constitutions are without such problems. In the Bulgarian and Romanian cases, for instance, where there are new constitutions, there is nonetheless a great deal of confusion about the powers of the president, especially in foreign affairs.

12. Judith Pataki and John W. Schiemann, "Constitutional Court Limits Presidential Powers," *Report on Eastern Europe* 2 (Oct. 18, 1991): 5–9. Differences in the laws and the degree to which they allow individuals, not laws, to shape institutions was a big theme in interviews conducted by Maria Csanadi of the new Hungarian political elite. See Valerie Bunce and Maria Csanadi, "Uncertainty and the Transition: Post-Communism in Hungary," *Eastern European Politics and Societies* 9 (1993): 240–75.

13. See, for instance, the special issue entitled "The Media," *RFE/RL Research Report* 39 (Oct. 2, 1991). What is crucial to understand here is that one of the greatest powers of state socialist regimes was their control over the print and broadcast media. The experience thus far in Eastern Europe has been that breaking up this monopoly has proven difficult (especially in the broadcast area). This has been particularly the case, of course, where communists (now self-proclaimed ex-communists) have maintained significant political power. Moreover, new elites (communist, anticommunist, and ex-communist) have sometimes tried to exert their control over the media, which has produced a lot of political conflict, most notably in Hungary, Lithuania, and Croatia.

14. See, for instance, Peter McDonough, "Democratization and the Culture of Mass Politics: Comparing Spain and Eastern Europe," *Political Culture, Political and Economic Orientations in Eastern Europe during the Transition to Democracy,* vol. 2, ed. unpublished paper Arizona State University, 1994. Janos Simon, "A demokracia 'masnapja' Magyarorszagon—avagy hogyan is demokratizalodtunk 1991–ben?," in *Magyarorszag politikai evkonyve* (Budapest: Academy of Sciences, 1992).

15. See, especially, Jiri Pehe, "Building a State Based on the Rule of Law," *Report on Eastern Europe* 2 (Mar. 1, 1991): 7–11. Also see Iu. Feofanov, "Demokratiia i pravoi," *Izvestiia,* July 10, 1988.

16. David McQuaid, "The 'War' over the Election Law," *RFE/RL Research Report* 36 (Aug. 2, 1991): 11–14.

17. Not all postcommunist states look to liberal orders for ideas, particularly central Asian states. In Kazakhstan, for example, considerable interest has been expressed in the Chinese model; that is, in a model combining authoritarian politics and liberalized economics.

18. The American model has been influential insofar as construction of legal system is concerned. Moreover, there has been some (albeit quite selective) borrowing from the American presidential model.

19. See Saulius Gernius, "Lithuania: Former Communists Return to Power," *RFE/RL Research Report* 2 (Jan. 1, 1993): 99–101.

20. See, for instance, Julia Wishnevsky, "Antidemocratic Tendencies in Russian Policy-Making," *RFE/RL Research Report* 37 (Nov. 13, 1992): 21–25; Louisa Vinton, "Poland's 'Little Constitution' Clarifies Walesa's Powers," *RFE/RL Research Report* 35 (Sept. 4, 1992): 19–26; Michael E. Urban, "Boris El'tsin, Democratic Russia, and the Campaign for the Russian Presidency," *Soviet Studies* 44 (1992): 187–207. I am addressing formal powers here; whether those powers can be realized is another question (and one I address later in this chapter).

21. See Ivo Bicanic and Iva Dominis, "Tudjman Remains Dominant after Croatian Elections," *RFE/RL Research Report* 37 (Sept. 18, 1992): 20–26. On presidential power in the Macedonian system, see "The Challenge to Economic Recovery and Social Harmony in the Former Yugoslav Republic of

Macedonia," unpublished paper, World Bank, Central Europe Department, Washington, D.C., August 1992.

22. See, for instance, Vinton, "Poland's 'Little' Constitution"; Michael Shafir, "Romania's New Institutions: The Draft Constitution," *Report on Eastern Europe* 38 (Sept. 20, 1991): 22–28; Ustina Markus, "Ukraine: Stability Amid Political Turnover," *Transition: The Year in Review, 1994*, pt. 2 (Feb. 15, 1995): 66–70; Elizabeth Fuller, "Armenia's Constitutional Debate," *RFE/RL Research Report* 21 (May 27, 1994): 6–9. The distinctions among moderately strong and weak presidents are in fact quite hard to make, given the shifting reality of Eastern Europe. See below.

23. For an example of how system-type choices can be analyzed, see Philippe Schmitter and Terry Karl, "What Kinds of Democracy Are Emerging in Southern and Eastern Europe, South and Central America?" unpublished manuscript, Stanford University, Jan. 1992.

24. Poland was the first former Soviet-bloc country to break with communism, and this had enormous impact on the bargaining process. In practice, Solidarity, while commanding enormous public support during the Roundtable (albeit not as much support as in 1980–81), was nonetheless weakened in its capacity to extract concessions, given the absence of any precedent for a state exiting from communism and given the unpredictability of the Soviet position.

25. I would like to thank Jerzy Wiatr and Edmund Wnuk-Lipinski for their insights on the Polish Roundtable.

26. See, especially, Urban, "Boris El'tsin, Democratic Russia."

27. The decision to use proportional representation reflects the strong desire to have genuinely representative government and to avoid disenfranchising minorities. A question that must be addressed in debates on electoral system type is: What happens to societal conflict when a winner-take- all system is implemented?

28. See Ustina Markus, "Belarus Elects Its First President," *RFE/RL Research Report* 30 (July 29, 1994): 1–7.

29. See, for instance, Mainwaring, "Presidentialism in Latin America"; Mainwaring, "Presidentialism, Multiparty Systems, and Democracy"; Linz, "Perils of Presidentialism."

30. The arguments that follow are drawn from the following sources: Linz, "Perils of Presidentialism"; Juan Linz, "The Virtues of Parliamentarism," in Lijphart, *Parliamentary versus Presidential Government;* Mainwaring, "Presidentialism in Latin America," in ibid.; Lijphart, "Constitutional Choices for New Democracies"; Mainwaring, "Presidentialism, Multiparty Systems, and Democracy."

31. This was the argument, for example, of the opposition in the debates about presidentialism in Belarus. See Markus, "Belarus Elects."

32. In postcommunist Eastern Europe, there were few alternatives to a system of proportional representation. With such considerable regional,

ethnic, and religious diversity, these countries could not risk a winner-take-all system, which would violate the democratic norms of representation and, at the same time, risk alienating minorities, conflict between minorities and the state, and even conflict between the state and neighboring states. Thus, the question was not whether there should be proportional representation, but, rather, how the most destabilizing consequences of that system could be avoided. This meant, in practice, adding presidents to the equation, providing a threshold that parties had to meet to win seats, and making dissolution of government very difficult.

33. This is reminiscent of the interwar period. In the Bulgarian elections of 1927, thirty thousand candidates ran for 240 seats.

34. I do not have the space here to explain why there is so much diversity in Eastern Europe or why that diversity has so much impact on politics. But I would like to emphasize that ethnic and religious conflict today in Eastern Europe should not be understood as a consequence of removing the "lid" on ethnic, religious, and regional strife—that is, on removing state socialism from the region. State socialism, in fact, significantly contributed to the development of ethnic, religious, and regional conflict in Eastern Europe.

35. See, for instance, Bohdan Szklarski, "A Party 'Non-System'—The Relationship between Polish Parties and the Electorate in the Condition of Systemic Change," unpublished manuscript, Institute of Political Studies, Warsaw, June 12, 1992; Zoltan D. Barany and Louisa Vinton, "Breakthrough to Democracy: Elections in Poland and Hungary," *Studies in Comparative Communism* 23 (1990): 191–212; Rudolf Tokes, *From Post-Communism to Democracy: Politics, Parties, and the 1990 Elections in Hungary* (Bonn: Konrad Adenauer Stiftung, 1990); Herbert Kitschelt, "The Formation of Party Systems in East Central Europe," *Politics and Society* 20 (1992): 7–50; Jack Bielasiak, "Regime Transition, Founding Elections, and Political Fields in Post-Communist States," unpublished manuscript, Indiana University, Jan. 1991; M. Grabowska, "Lepsze wybory bez partii niz Partia bez wyborow?" *Politicus* 1 (1991): 15–24.

36. See, especially, Linz, "Perils of Presidentialism."

37. See, for example, William Smirnov, "Presidentialism vs. Parliamentarianism: The Russian Case," paper prepared for the Second International COVICO Conference, Albany, New York, Mar. 17–20, 1994.

38. Although it could be argued that such a mandate and such powers define a dictatorship, dictatorship requires more: a person who can implement policy and who can rouse a demobilized public. While the latter seems to fit Yeltsin, the former does not.

39. Here is yet another area of study in the discipline of political science that has suffered because of the artificial division between domestic and foreign politics. In much of the literature on presidents and the transition, and indeed, in much of the literature on democratic transitions in general, foreign policy and the international system are given little attention. A happy exception is Geofffrey Pridham, ed., *Encouraging Democracy: The In-*

ternational Context of Regime Transition in Southern Europe (New York: St. Martin's, 1991).

40. Dictatorial government may not be all that bad for the transition to democracy. It could be argued, for instance, that Russian President Boris Yeltsin's emergency powers were viewed by many as a force for the democratization of Russia, since the alternative—more power sharing with the Congress of People's Deputies—was viewed as inimical to democracy, given the political complexion of the Congress. Whether this is a good argument for Russian politics following the Dec. 1993 parliamentary elections is another question.

41. Przeworski, *Democracy and the Market.*

42. See Bunce and Csanadi, "Uncertainty and the Transition."

43. See, especially, Guillermo O'Donnell and Philippe C. Schmitter, eds., *Transitions from Authoritarian Rule: Tentative Conclusions about Uncertain Democracies* (Baltimore: Johns Hopkins University Press, 1986).

44. See, especially, Alfred Stepan, "Paths towards Redemocratization," in *Transitions from Authoritarian Rule: Comparative Perspectives*, ed. Guillermo O'Donnell, Philippe Schmitter, and Laurence Whitehead (Baltimore: John Hopkins University Press, 1986), 64–84. Some might counter (with some merit, in my view) that the so-called democracies of the past were significantly less than that.

45. Robert Fishman, "Rethinking State and Regime: Southern Europe's Transition to Democracy," *World Politics* 42 (1990): 422–40.

46. See, especially, Valerie Bunce, "Stalinism and the Management of Uncertainty," in *The Transition to Democracy in Hungary*, ed. Gyorgy Szobaszlai (Budapest: Hungarian Institute of Political Science, 1991).

Chapter 8
Bernhard, Semipresidentialism, Charisma, and Democratic Institutions in Poland

The author wishes to thank Kurt von Mettenheim, Krzysztof Jasiewicz, Suzie DeBoef, David Margolin, and Paula Golombek for their help on this chapter.

1. This chapter considers institutional development in Poland through the legislative elections of Sept. 19, 1993. Although the governing coalition of the Polish Peasant Party (PSL) and the Alliance of the Democratic Left (SLD), on which the last two governments (of Prime Ministers Pawlak and Oleksy) have been based, has enough strength in parliament to push through significant constitutional reform, it has not made substantial progress to date.

2. Maurice Duverger, "A New Political System Model: Semipresidential Government," in *Parliamentary versus Presidential Government*, ed. Arend Lijphart (New York: Oxford University Press, 1992).

3. Despite attempts to demarcate the scope of powers between the two

offices by the Little Constitution of October 17, 1992, a great deal of ambiguity exists in the areas of defense of foreign policy (see Articles 32–36 regarding presidential powers and Articles 52 and 61 regarding the powers and responsibilities of the prime minister and the government, in Prezydent Rzeczypospolitej Polskiej (President of the Polish Republic), "Ustawa konstytucyjna z dnia 17 października 1992 r. o wzajemnych stosunkach między władzą ustawodawczą i wykonawczą Rzeczypospolitej Polskiej oraz o samorządzie terytorialnym" (Constitutional Statute of October 17, 1992, on the Reciprocal Relations between Legislative and Executive Authority of the Polish Republic as Well as on Teritorial Self-government), *Życia Warszawy,* Dodatek specjalny (special insert), Nov. 19, 1992. Conflict over powers in the defense area was one of the issues that led to sharp conflict between the Olszewski government and President Wałęsa, contributing to the fall of the government. Continued controversy over the Ministries of Defense, Internal Affairs, and Foreign Affairs contributed to the replacement of the government of Prime Minister Pawlak of the PSL with Prime Minister Oleksy of the SLD.

4. All provinces have two senators with the exceptions of Katowice and Warsaw (city), which have three because of their large populations.

5. In order to override Senat rejection or amendment of a bill, the Sejm needs a majority of better than 50 percent of its members (bezwzględna większość). While the Senat has the right to initiate legislation, it does not have the right to move it on its own; legislation must first be ratified by the Sejm. For other details on the relationship between the two, see chapter 2 of the Little Constitution (Prezydent Rzeczypospolitej Polskiej, 1992).

6. Krzysztof Jasiweicz, "Poland," *European Journal of Political Research* 22 (1992): 489–502.

7. Krzysztof Jasiewicz, "Polish Politics on the Eve of the 1993 Elections: Toward Fragmentation or Pluralism?" *Communist and Post-Communist Studies* 26 (1993): 387–411.

8. Fred Riggs, "The Survival of Presidentialism in America: Paraconstitutional Practices," *International Political Science Review* 9 (1988): 247–78.

9. Fred Riggs, "Fragility of the Third World's Regimes," *International Social Science Journal* 45 (1993): 199–243.

10. Ibid., 220–21.

11. One potential criticism of Riggs's data is that they do not sufficiently differentiate between authoritarian and democratic presidential constitutions. He describes all of his cases as "open polities" (ibid., 219), yet they include a number of regimes that never approached institutionalized democracy or whose "democratic" constitutions never acquired any real force (220). Another potential criticism is that his list of surviving parliamentary regimes is primarily (two-thirds) composed of insular microstates. It also includes some very questionable democracies, such as Singapore and Lebanon (224).

12. Juan J. Linz and Arturo Valenzuela, eds., *The Failure of Presidential Democracy in Latin America* (Baltimore: Johns Hopkins University Press, 1994), 5.

13. Juan J. Linz, "The Perils of Presidentialism, *Journal of Democracy* 1 (1990): 51–69; Linz, "The Virtues of Parliamentarism," *Journal of Democracy* 1 (1990): 84–91; Linz, "Presidential or Parliamentary Democracy: Does It Make a Difference?" in Linz and Valenzuela, *Failure of Presidential Democracy.*

14. Linz, "Perils of Presidentialism," 53–56.

15. Donald L. Horowitz, "Comparing Democratic Systems," *Journal of Democracy* 1 (1990): 73–79; esp. 75.

16. Ibid, 76.

17. Scott Mainwaring, "Presidentialism in Latin America," *Latin American Research Review* 25 (1990): 157–79; Arturo Valenzuela, "Latin America: Presidentialism in Crisis," *Journal of Democracy* 4 (1993): 3–16.

18. For a balanced and comprehensive discussion of the relative merits and disadvantages of presidential, parliamentary, and semipresidential democracy, see Lijphart, introduction to Lijphart, *Parliamentary versus Presidential Government.*

19. Guiseppe Di Palma, *To Craft Democracies: An Essay on Democratic Transitions* (Berkeley: University of California Press, 1990.

20. David Stark, "Path Dependence and Privatization Strategies in East Central Europe," *East European Politics and Societies* 6 (1992): 19–70; esp. 17–18.

21. For instance, in Lijphart's account of constitutional choice in Poland, Hungary, and Czechoslovakia, his starting point is a modification of Rokkan's hypothesis. He argues that the logic of democratization in the three countries led in the direction of proportional representation and presidentialism. At the time of his writing, only three of the six institutional choices that this approach predicted were obtained, and Poland was the only country that conformed to the hypothesis. When the new rules for the Polish elections of 1993 went into effect, this fell to two out of six, with no country choosing as expected under the hypothesis. While Lijpart's article is a bold attempt at developing a simple and parsimonious explanation, the choices it predicts did not occur. See Arend Lijphart, "Democratization and Constitutional Choices in Czecho-Slovakia, Hungary, and Poland, 1989–1991," *Journal of Theoretical Politics* 4 (1992): 207–23; Stein Rokkan, *Citizens, Elections, Parties: Approaches to the Comparative Study of the Processes of Development* (Oslo: Oslo Universitetsforlaget, 1970).

22. Stark, "Path Dependence and Privatization Strategies," 17–54; Terry Lynn Karl, "Dilemmas of Democratization in Latin America," *Comparative Politics* 23 (1990): 1–22.

23. My stress on the importance of the terms of the extrication pact in Poland is strongly at odds with Przeworski's understanding of its relevance.

Adam Przeworski, *Democracy and the Market: Political and Economic Reforms in Eastern Europe and Latin America* (Cambridge: Cambridge University Press, 1991), 79.

24. The Roundtable negotiations convened in Warsaw on February 6, 1989, and ended in the signing of the agreement on April 5, 1989. I limit my discussion to the relevant political changes that the agreement inaugurated. The agreement included other provisions, including a far-reaching socioeconomic pact, which was quickly discarded. For a full text of the agreement, see "Umowa 'okrągłego stołu'" (Rountable Agreement), *Trybuna Ludu*, Apr. 7, 1989.

25. An earlier upper chamber, also called the Senat, was abolished in 1946 in a controversial referendum that played a role in the communist consolidation of power in postwar Poland.

26. One of the candidates elected from the National List was Mikołaj Kozakiewicz of the Peasant Party, an outspoken critic of the government in the previous Sejm. The other, Adam Zieliński, was alphabetically last on the list. Some speculated that he was elected because large X's drawn across the ballot missed his name or that voters' hands began to cramp at the end of the page.

27. Prezydent Rzeczypospolitej Polskiej, "Ustawa konstytucyjna."

28. Anna Bojarska, "Wokoł Niewiadomskiego (On Niewiadomski)," *Krytyka* 25 (1987): 63–72.

29. Jasiewicz (1991) reminds us that this support was not overwhelming. Solidarity has never been able to mobilize more than 40 percent of registered voters in any national electoral contest. Krzysztof Jasiewicz, "Polski wyborca—w dziesiec lat po Sierpniu" (The Polish Voter—Ten Years after August), *Krytyka* 36 (1991): 23–47.

30. The Solidarity campaign for the elections of June 1989 featured posters in which Wałęsa posed individually with each Solidarity candidate for the Sejm and the Senat (there was one exception, the Solidarity candidate who lost a Senat seat to Henryk Stoklosa). In the presidential campaign of 1990, a satirical poster put out by the Polish Students' Association (Zrzeszenie Studentów Polskich) showed Wałęsa in a sportjacket and tie, with his arms around a second Lech Wałęsa in shirtsleeves. Anna Uhlig, "Wizerunki kandydatów na prezydenta RP propagowane w toku kampanii wyborczej 1990 r." (Images of the Candidates for President of the Polish Republic Propagated during the Electoral Campaign of 1990), in Stanisław Gebethner and Krzysztof Jasiewicz, eds., *Dlaczego tak glosowano, Wyborg prezydenekie '90* (Why did They Vote That Way? The Presidential Elections of 1990), (Warsaw: Instytut Studiów Politycznych PAN, Instytut Nauk Politycznych UW, 1993), 136–37.

31. See, for example, the description of Wałęsa's antics during Havel's visit to Poland in early 1990 (Jaroslaw Kurski, *Lech Walesa: Democrat or Dictator?* trans. Peter Obst (Boulder: Westview, 1993); original: *Wódz* (The leader) (Warsaw: PoMOST, 1991).

32. Witold Pawłowski, "Skóra na niedźwiedziu" (Gains Not Yet Realized), *Polityka*, Mar. 3, 1990. Prior to Wałęsa's presidential bid, a number of small but vocal demonstrations that called for Jaruelski's resignation were organized by the Confederation for Independent Poland, a party of the nationalist Right Centered on its leader, Leszek Moczulski.

33. A typical example is the "appeal" that the Center Alliance issued on Aug. 28, 1990, calling for Jaruzelski's resignation. The appeal strongly linked Jaruzelski's ouster to the expansion of democratic reform. The version published in *Tygodnik Solidarność* was placed alongside a group portrait from before 1989 in which Jaruzelski posed with Gustav Husak, Erich Honecker, Mikhail Gorbachev, Nicolae Ceausescu, Todor Zhivkov, and Janos Kadar. Porozumenie Centrum (Center Alliance), "Appeal (August 28, 1990," *Tygodnik Solidarnosc* Sept. 7, 1990.

34. According to Stanisław Gebethner, Jaruzelski had been ready to resign in January 1990, but intervention by church circles dissuaded him. See Gebethner, "Geneza i tło polityczno-ustrojowe wyborów prezydenckich 1990 r." (The Genesis and Politico-systemic Background of the Presidenetial Elections of 1990), in Gebethner and Jasiewicz, *Dlaczego tak głosowano*, 15 n5.

35. The logic of the Center Alliance seems quite correct. In a head-to-head contest with Mazowiecki, Wałęsa would probably would have won with a coalition of the more conservative and nationalist Solidarity deputies and senators, the peasant deputies (who had begun to strongly oppose Balcerowicz's economic policies because of the effects they were having in the countryside), at least one postcommunist splinter group (PUS), and other small groups from the former ruling coalition (SD, PAX, etc.).

36. The logic here is straightforward. As discussed in the note above, Wałęsa probably would have won in the parliament, but even if Mazowiecki could have mustered a parliamentary majority it would have been a political disaster. This is because most of the SdRP's deputies would have sided with Mazowiecki because they found his talk of putting the past behind them more attractive than Wałęsa's confrontational rhetoric. Thus, direct election was the only viable option for Mazowiecki and his supporters, because a parliamentary victory would have been colored by postcommunist support.

37. Wałęsa seems to have exercised prudent political judgment on this score. It would have been politically awkward, if not damaging, to have been elected president by the contract parliament, particularly since Wałęsa had made his run for office by painting the Roundtable Agreement, which had selected that parliament, as outmoded and undemocratic. Further, it is unlikely that the contract parliament would have voted for early elections prior to a resolution of the controversy surrounding the presidency.

38. Stanislaw Gebethner, "Geneza i tło polityczon-ustrojowe wyborów prezydenckich 1990 r." (The Genesis and Politico-Systemic Background of the Presidential Elections of 1990), in Gebethner and Jasiewicz, *Dlaczego tak glosowano*, 20–21.

39. Public opinion polls from as late as October 24, 1990, put Prime Minister Mazowiecki in the lead over all other candidates. After this date, polling shows Wałęsa taking the lead. While Tyminski began to gain rapidly on the fading prime minister sometime in early November, his second-place showing still came as a surprise, as neither of the major Polish public opinion centers showed him passing Mazowiecki in polls taken just days before the first round. See Jerzy Bralczyk and Mrozowski Maciej, "Prezydencka kampania wyborcza w telewizji" (The Presidential Campaign on Television), in Gebethner and Jasiewicz *Dlaczego tak glosowano*, 149.

40. For a highly detailed account of the respective constituencies of the candidates and an explanation of the final outcome of the presidential election, see Jasiewicz, "Polski wyborca."

41. Solidarity won just over 40 percent of the seats on local councils but did much better in large cities, compared to rural areas. The PSL, which came in second, took just under 6 percent of the seats, predominantly in the countryside. Independents, who won just under 40 percent, probably included large numbers of candidates who were associated with the old regime but who felt that their chances for election over better if they identified with no political party.

42. Early drafts of the electoral statute, influenced by Professor Geremek of UD and the president, included proposals for between 115 and 230 Sejm deputies (25–50%) to be elected from single-member districts, in combination with proportional elements like the national list and electoral districts like those created by the statute that was finally adopted.

43. Under Hare-Niemeyer, seats are apportioned to parties on the basis of the following formula: number of valid votes cast for a party's list ÷ total number of valid votes cast = number of seats. In Poland, this was calculated individually for each electoral district. The number of votes for an individual candidate on the preferred party list served to rank him or her on the list of number of seats won. Thus, if a party won three seats in a district, its top three vote getters received the seats.

44. There were exceptions to this rule in the case of national minorities, which explains why the German minority won seats in the Sejm.

45. For details on the d'Hondt method, see Rein Taagepera and Matthew Soberg Shugart, *Seats and Votes* (New Haven: Yale University Press, 1989), 32–33. See also Ordynacja wyborcza, Ustawa z dnia 28 maja 1993 r., "Ordynacja wyborcza do Sejmu Rzeczypospolitej Polskiej" (Statute from May 28, 1993, the Electoral Law of the Sejm of the Polish Republic), *Dziennik ustaw Rzeczypospolitej Polskiej*, June 2, 1993, 841–64; Agata Nowakowska, "Silny będzie silniejszy" (The Strong Will Be Stronger), *Gazeta wyborcza*, Sept. 17, 1993.

46. See Przeworski, *Democracy and the Market*.

Chapter 9
Harris, President and Parliament in the Russian Federation

1. The text is published in *Argumenty i Fakty*, no. 17 (1990): 4. Despite the conflicts over the powers of the president and parliament, the authors of this draft agreed that the Congress of People's Deputies should be abolished and that the Supreme Soviet remain the country's only legislative body.

2. Ibid., 5.

3. A full text of the amended constitution has yet to be published. The amendments adopted in May 1991 were published in *Vedomosti S'ezda narodnykh deputatov rossiiskoi federatsii i verkhovnovo soveta rossiiskoi federatsii*, no. 22 (1991): 872–80.

4. For an excellent discussion of this campaign, see Michael E. Urban, "Boris Yeltsin, Democratic Russia, and the Campaign for the Russian Presidency," *Soviet Studies* 44 (1992): 187 207.

5. Ibid.

6. Interview published in *Sel'skaia Zhizn*, June 6, 1991, 1–3.

7. Yeltsin declared that "progressive people with their eyes on the future who want to make Russia prosperous and rich form a considerable majority of the CPSU," ibid., 2.

8. Rutskoi had been a popular figure in the orthodox CP/RSFSR. In April 1991, the party launched a major assault against Yelstin in the parliament, and some observers concluded that the CP/RSFSR leaders actually sought to oust Yeltsin. Whatever their objectives, Rutskoi broke dramatically with the orthodox leadership and created his own parliamentary fraction of reform communists, who backed Yeltsin.

9. He declared that, "for the first time in the one-thousand-year history of Russia, a president was taking an oath to his own citizens" and further, that state power was responsible to the "people who had chosen it" and that the people were responsible to the state it had "placed upon itself." *Izvestiia*, July 10, 1991, 1.

10. For the text of this decree, see Vedomosti, *S'ezda narodnykh deputatov rossiiskoi federatsii*, no. 31 (1991): 1318–22.

11. For an excellent discussion of the political reaction to Yeltsin's decree, see Elizabeth Teague and Julia Wishnevsky, "Eltsin Bans Organized Political Activity in State Sector," *Report on the USSR*, Aug. 16, 1991, 21–26.

12. *Megapolis-Express*, Aug. 19, 1991, as translated in *Current Digest of the Soviet Press* (*CDSP*) 43 (1991): 6–7.

13. *Rossiiskaia Gazeta*, Aug. 27, 1991, 3; ibid., Aug. 30, 1991, 2.

14. *Izvestiia*, Aug. 23, 1991, 1.

15. Ibid., Aug. 26, 1991, 3.

16. *Vedomosti*, no. 34 (1991): 1403–04.

17. *Izvestiia*, Sept. 20, 1991; ibid., Sept. 21, 1991.

18. Ibid., Oct. 16, 1991, 1; *Rossiiskaia Gazeta*, Oct. 18, 1991, 1.

19. *Izvestiia*, Oct. 29, 1991, 1.

20. Ibid., Oct. 30, 1991, 1; ibid., Nov. 2, 1991, 1.

21. *Rossiiskaia Gazeta*, Nov. 9, 1991, 2.

22. *Izvestiia*, Nov. 18, 1991, 1.

23. Ibid., Nov. 25, 1991, 1.

24. Ibid., Dec. 2, 1991, 1; ibid., Dec. 5, 1991, 1–2.

25. *Rossiiskaia Gazeta*, Dec. 25, 1991, 1.

26. *Pravda*, Jan. 15, 1992, 1; ibid., Jan. 18, 1992, 1–2.

27. I presume that the Commonwealth of Independent States has no real authority over the government of the Russian Republic.

28. Khasbulatov made these comments in an "unofficial" interview with Italian legislators. *Izvestiia*, Jan. 15, 1992, 1.

29. Russian TV/First Program, Jan. 15, 1992; trans. in *Foreign Broadcast Information Service* (*FBIS*), SOB 90-010, Jan. 15, 1992, 51.

30. *Izvestiia*, Jan. 17, 1992, 1.

31. *Pravda*, Jan. 11, 1992, 2; ibid., 18, 1992, 2.

32. Ibid., Jan. 30. 1992, 1, 3; ibid., Feb. 8, 1992.

33. Ibid., Feb. 8, 1992.

34. *Izvestiia*, Mar. 28, 1992, 1.

35. See the text in *Argumenty i Faktv*, no. 12 (1992): 3–5.

36. *Rossiiskaia Gazeta*, Apr. 3, 1992, 1–2.

37. *Post Factum*, Apr. 6, 1992, trans. in *FBIS*, SOV-92-0685, Apr. 8, 1992.

38. *Rossiiskaia Gazeta*, Apr. 8, 1992, 1, 3–4.

39. Ibid., Apr. 12, 1992, 1–3.

40. Ibid., Apr. 14, 1992, 4–5.

41. Ibid., Apr. 23, 1992, 3.

42. *Izvestiia*, May 6, 1992, 2.

43. Ibid., June 12, 1992, 1.

44. Some of President Yeltsin's actions at the time suggest that he feared that his resignation as prime minister might undermine his authority. A few days before his resignation, the president created a new presidential security council with an extraordinarily broad mandate to deal with security issues. *Rossiiskaia Gazeta*, June 11, 1992, 3. His associates implied that the new body was designed to forestall any attempted coup by "fascist type national patriotic organizations." Ibid., 5.

45. *Izvestiia*, July 10, 1992, 1; ibid., July 14, 1992, 2; ibid., July 17, 1992, 1.

46. Ibid., Aug. 8, 1992, 1–2.

47. *Sovetskaia Rossiia*, Sept. 22, 1992; trans in *Current Digest of the Post-Soviet Press* (*CDPSP*) no. 38 (1992): 5–6.

48. *Rossiiskaia Gazeta*, Oct. 7, 1992, 1–2.

49. *Izvestiia*, Sept. 22, 1992, 2. Khasbulatov had cut off a number of votes of no confidence at the Supreme Soviet to ensure that a confrontation would develop in the Congress. Ibid., Sept. 24, 1992, 2.

50. In late October, President Yeltsin sought to ban the activities of the National Salvation Front, which sought to establish local committees throughout the country to organize opposition to the president. See *Rossi-*

iskaia Gazeta, Oct. 30, 1992, 2. Also see *Nezavisimaia Gazeta,* Nov. 5, 1992, 2, trans. in *CDPSP* no. 45 (1992): 1.

51. *Rossiiskaia Gazeta,* Dec. 2, 1992, 3–4.

52. Ibid., 3.

53. Ibid., Dec. 19, 1992.

54. *Izvestiia,* Dec. 10, 1992, 1.

55. *Nezavisimaia Gazeta,* Dec. 11, 1992; trans. in *CDPSP* no. 50 (1992): 4. While the Congress assailed the referendum proposed by the president as an effort to destroy the constitution, Yeltsin told a rally of his supporters that the majority of the deputies had been put there by the party apparatus. *Izvestiia,* Dec. 11, 1992.

56. *Rossiiskaia Gazeta,* Dec. 15, 1992.

57. Ibid., Dec. 18, 1992.

58. *Izvestiia,* Jan. 15, 1993.

59. *Komsomolskaia Pravda,* Jan. 30, 1993; trans. in *CDPSP* no. 5 (1993): 17; *Izvestiia,* Feb. 10, 1993.

60. To help to achieve this objective, the president created a new consultative council of chief administrators from the various regions. *Izvestiia,* Feb. 26, 1993, 2.

61. *Rossiiskiye Vesti,* Mar. 12, 1993, 2. Yeltsin rather belatedly made public the questions he wanted on the referendum. They included loaded questions on the desirability of a presidential republic, a bicameral legislature, a constitutional assembly, and private ownership of land. *Izvestiia,* Mar. 10, 1993, 1.

62. The most significant amendment granted the Supreme Soviet power to abrogate presidential decrees deemed unconstitutional by the Constitutional Court; *Rossiiskaia Gazeta,* Mar. 13, 1993, 1.

63. *Rossiiskiye Vesti,* Mar. 23, 1993, 1–2.

64. *Izvestiia,* Mar. 23, 1993, 1.

65. *Rossiiskaia Gazeta,* Mar. 23, 1993, 2.

66. Ibid., Mar. 24, 1993, 3. A minority of the Constitutional Court declared that the address had merely discussed intent rather than actions. *Izvestiia,* Mar. 24, 1993, 3. In fact, Yeltsin never issued the decree he discussed in his address.

67. *Rossiiskaia Gazeta,* Mar. 27, 1993, 1–2.

68. Ibid., Apr. 1, 1993, 8.

69. *Nezavisimaia Gazeta,* Mar. 30, 1993; trans. in *CDPSP* no. 13 (1993): 6–7.

70. The Congress abolished the president's personally appointed representatives in the regions (who ostensibly served as presidential watchdogs, although their authority was extremely limited), suspended a number of his decrees pending their constitutional review, and shifted some official agencies from the president's office to the Council of Ministers. *Rossiiskaia Gazeta,* Apr. 1, 1993, 1.

71. Personal copy of the referendum ballot. The Congress initially stipu-

lated that 50 percent of all registered voters (as opposed to 50% of the participating voters) were needed to make decisions valid. The Constitutional Court later decided that only the last two questions had to meet that test.

72. *Izvestiia* (Apr. 28, 1993, 2) reported that 64.6 percent of the voters took part in the referendum; 58.05 percent declared their trust in the president, 52.88 percent endorsed his social-economic policies; 32.64 percent called for new elections for president; 41.4 percent called for new elections for the Congress.

73. Ibid., Apr. 30, 1993, 2.

74. While Khasbulatov sought to discourage participation in the assembly, Chairman Zorkin challenged its constitutional legitimacy. *Nezavisimaia Gazeta*, May 13, 1993; trans. in *CDPSP* no. 19 (1993): 1–2. Yeltsin's most vehement opponents organized an alternative constitutional conference, which denounced his initial draft as an effort to "legalize the dictatorship of the comprador bourgeoisie." *Sovetskaia Rossiia*, June 5, 1993; trans. in *CDPSP* no. 22 (1993): 8–9.

75. *Izvestiia*, June 6, 1993, 3.

76. Although the president was described as "head of state" rather than "chief executive," he was described as the "guarantor of the constitution of the Russian Federation and the rights of citizens" and as responsible for defining the "basic directions of foreign and domestic policy." The president nominated the chairman of the Council of Ministers with the approval of the State Duma, the lower house of the new bicameral legislature, and could dissolve the Duma if it refused his nomination three times in a row or repeatedly voiced no confidence in the government. The president could dismiss the government, could appoint and dismiss its members with the advice of the chairman, and had vast appointive powers. In addition, he could resolve conflicts between lower bodies and suspend their decisions if they were found unconstitutional. While he could be impeached, the process was far more complex than existing practice. *Izvestiia*, July 16, 1993, 3–4.

77. For example, the Supreme Soviet called for the dismissal of key ministers on the grounds that they had been found guilty of corrupt practices. Khasbulatov insisted that the Supreme Soviet would not participate in the assembly's deliberations while the ministers retained their posts. *Nezavisimaia Gazeta*, June 25, 1993; trans. in *CDPSP* no. 25 (1993): 25.

78. Yeltsin's opponents were correct. The constitutional amendments establishing the presidency in the spring of 1991 prohibited such dissolution. For the various decrees of the president and the Congress, see *Rossiiskaia Gazeta*, Sept. 23, 1993, 1–2.

79. Yeltsin may also have been influenced by public opinion polls that indicated that a significant minority blamed both the president and the parliament for the use of violence in October 1993. *Argumenty i Fakty*, No. 41 (1993): 1.

80. Russian observers' estimates of the exact size of the various factions

vary considerably; see Y. Grishin, "Who's Who in the Russian Parliament," *Russian Life* (Jan.–Mar. 1994): 6–8; V. Pribylovski and Gr. Tochkin, *Politicheskii sostav federal'nogo sobraniia* (Moscow: Panorama, 1994).

81. Ibid.

82. *Rossiiskaia Gazeta*, Feb. 24, 1994, 2.

83. Yeltsin called the new constitution a "real basis for the establishment of cooperation in Russian society, first of all between the branches of federal power." Ibid., Feb. 25, 1994, 1.

84. Ibid., 3.

85. Ibid., 5.

Conclusion
von Mettenheim and Rockman, Presidential Institutions, Democracy, and Comparative Politics

1. In addition to Juan Linz's original criticism. "The Perils of Presidentialism," *Journal of Democracy* 1 (1990): 51–69, see Alfred Stepan and Cindy Skatch, "Constitutional Frameworks and Democratic Consolidation: Parliamentarism versus Presidentialism," *World Politics* 46. (1993): 1–22; Juan Linz and Arturo Valenzuela, eds., *The Failure of Presidential Democracy in Latin America* (Baltimore: Johns Hopkins University Press 1994); and the selections in Arend Lijphart, *Parliamentary versus Presidential Government* (New York: Oxford University Press, 1992).

2. For a general discussion of the causal role of institutions, see R. Kent Weaver and Bert A. Rockman, eds., *Do Institutions Matter? Government Capabilities in the United States and Abroad* (Washington, D.C.: Brookings, 1993).

3. Aside from Jones's chapter in this volume, see David R. Mayhew, *Divided We Govern: Party Control, Lawmaking, and Investigations, 1946–1990* (New Haven: Yale University Press, 1991).

4. John Keeler and Martin Schain (chap. 4) refer to Duverger's analysis: Maurice Duverger, "A New Political System Model: Semipresidential Government," in Lijphart, *Parliamentary versus Presidential Government.*

5. See Linz and Valenzuela, *Failure of Presidential Democracy.* See also Scott Mainwaring and Matthew Shugart, eds., *Presidentialism and Democracy in Latin America.* (Cambridge: Cambridge University Press, forthcoming).

6. Richard Rose, "Government against Subgovernments: A European Perspective on Washington," in *Presidents and Prime Ministers,* ed. Richard Rose and Ezra N. Suleiman (Washington, D.C.: American Enterprise Institute, 1980).

7. On electoral realignment, see: David Brady, *Critical Elections and Congressional Policy Making,* Stanford, CA: Stanford University Press, 1988 and Bryan E. Shafer, ed. *The End of Realignment? Interpreting American Electoral Eras.* Madison, WI: University of Wisconsin Press, 1991. On the im-

portance of analyzing sudden institutional change in historical perspective, see: Sven Steinmo, Kathleen Thelen, and Frank Longstreth, eds., *Structuring Politics: Historical Institutionalism in Comparative Analysis* (Cambridge: Cambridge University Press, 1992); and Stephen Skowronek, *The Politics Presidents Make: Leadership from John Adams to George Bush* (Cambridge, MA: Belknap Press, 1993).

Contributors

Michael Bernhard is an associate professor of political science at Pennsylvania State University. He is author of *The Origins of Democratization in Poland* (Columbia University Press, 1993). He is editor (with Henryk Szlajfer) of *From the Polish Underground: Selections from Krytyka, 1978–1993* (Pennsylvania State University Press, 1995) and translator (with John Micgiel) of Krystyna Kersten's *The Establishment of Communist Rule in Poland, 1943–1948* (University of California Press, 1991). His current research concerns democratization in Poland and Germany in the twentieth century.

Valerie Bunce is professor of government and director of the Slavic and Eastern European studies program at Cornell University. She is completing a book comparing the end of the Soviet, Yugoslav, and Czechoslovak states.

Eduardo A. Gamarra is associate professor in the Department of Political Science, Florida International University. Recent publications include *Dictators, Democrats, and Drugs: A Brief History of U.S-Bolivia Counternarcotics Policy; Democracy, Markets, and Structural Reform in Latin America: Argentina Bolivia, Brazil, Chile, and Mexico* (co-editor); *Latin American Political Economy in the Age of Neoliberal Reform: Theoretical and Comparative Perspectives for the 1990s* (co-editor); and *Revolution and Reaction: Bolivia 1964–1985*. Professor Gamarra is editor of both *Hemisphere* magazine and the annual *Latin American and Caribbean Contemporary Record*, and has testified before the United States Congress on Andean counternarcotics policy.

Jonathan Harris is associate professor of political science at the University of Pittsburgh and editor of the Russian and Eastern European monograph series for the University of Pittsburgh Press. Professor Harris specializes in internal political developments in the Russian Federation; his articles and reviews have appeared in *Soviet Union*, The *Slavic Review*, The *Russian Review*, and *Survey*. His most recent publications include monographs on General Secretary Gorbachev's major lieutenants, published in *The Carl Beck Papers in Russian and East European Studies*. Articles on Ruslan Khasbulatov (former chairman of the Supreme Soviet of the Russian Federation) and on the system of self-government in the city of Novosibirsk are forthcoming.

Charles O. Jones is Hawkins Professor of Political Science, University of Wisconsin—Madison, and a nonresident senior fellow of the Brookings Institution. He is a former editor of the *American Political Science Review* and a former president of the American Political Science Association. His most recent publications on the presidency are *The Presidency in a Separated System* (Brookings, 1994) and *Separate but Equal Branches: Congress and the Presidency* (Chatham House, 1995).

John T. S. Keeler is professor of political science and director of the Center for Western European Studies at the University of Washington. He is the author of *Réformer: Les Conditions du Changement Politique* (1994) and *The Politics of Neocorporatism in France* (1987) as well as numerous articles in journals such as *Comparative Politics, Comparative Political Studies, Western European Politics,* and *French Politics and Society.* He has also co-edited *Chirac's Challenge: Liberalization, Europeanization, and Malaise in France* (1996) and edited a special issue of *Comparative Political Studies,* "The Politics of Reform in Comparative Perspective" (1993). He recently served as a USAID consultant to the Supreme Rada of Ukraine on issues of constitutional development.

B. Guy Peters is Maurice Falk Professor of American Government and chair of the Department of Political Science at the University of Pittsburgh. He previously taught at Emory University, Tulane University, and the University of Delaware. He has had Fulbright fellowships at the University of Strathclyde (Scotland) and at the Hochschule St. Gallen (Switzerland), has had a Hallsworth Fellowship at the University of Manchester, and has been a fellow at the Canadian Centre for Management Development. He has also held visiting positions in Norway, Sweden, Mexico, and the Netherlands. Professor Peters has published a number of books, including *The Politics of Bureaucracy, the Politics of Taxation: A Comparative Perspective, Comparing Public Bureaucracies, American Public Policy, Rethinking European Politics, Policy Dynamics* (with Brian W. Hogwood); *The Pathology of Public Policy* (with Brian W. Hogwood); and *Can Government Go Bankrupt?* (with Richard Rose). He has also edited *Organizing Governance, Government Organizations* (with Colin Campbell) and *Advising Western European Governments* (with Anthony Barker). He is past editor of *Governance* and current editor of the *International Library of Comparative Public Policy.*

Bert A. Rockman is professor of political science and research professor in the University Center for International Studies at the University of Pittsburgh, where he also holds an appointment in the Graduate School of Public and International Affairs. He has most recently published *The Clinton Presidency: Early Appraisals,* with Colin Campbell; and *Agenda for Excellence 2: Administering the State,* with B. Guy Peters. He is currently working on *The Changing Federal Executive,* with Joel D. Aberbach.

Martin A. Schain is professor of politics, and chair of the Center for European Studies, New York University. He is co-editor of *Chirac's Challenge:*

Liberalization, Europeanization, and Malaise in France; The Politics of Immigration in Western Europe; The State, Socialism and Public Policy in France; French Politics and Public Policy. He is co-author of *European Society and Politics;* and *Politics in France.* He is author of *French Communism and Local Power.* He has also published numerous scholarly articles and book chapters on politics and immigration in France, Europe, and the United States, on the politics of the extreme Right in France and political parties in France, and of trade unions in France and Britain. He has taught in both France and England and has lectured throughout Europe.

Kurt von Mettenheim is assistant professor in the Department of Political Science, University of Pittsburgh. He has conducted extended field research in São Paulo on an Inter-American Foundation dissertation fellowship and in Berlin on a German Marshall Fund fellowship for younger U.S. scholars. His publications include *The Brazilian Voter: Mass Politics in Democratic Transition, 1974–1986; Deepening Democracy in Latin America* with James Malloy (forthcoming); and "The Protestant Ethic and the Spirit of Democracy: Paths in Democratic Theory from Weber to Hegel" (forthcoming).

Index

Library of Congress Cataloging-in-Publication Data

Presidential institutions and democratic politics : comparing regional and
national contexts / edited by Kurt von Mettenheim.
    p.   cm.
   Includes bibliographical references and index.
   ISBN 0-8018-5313-3 (hardcover : alk. paper).—ISBN 0-8018-5314-1 (pbk. :
alk. paper)
   1. Presidents.   2. Democracy.   3. Separation of powers.   4. Comparative
government.   I. Mettenheim, Kurt von, 1957– .
JF255.P73   1997
324.6'3'0973—dc20   96-21694
                                                CIP